THE WAY WE DIE

The Way We Die

An Investigation of Death and Dying in America Today

DAVID DEMPSEY

McGRAW-HILL BOOK COMPANY

NEW YORK · ST. LOUIS · SAN FRANCISCO · BOGOTA
DÜSSELDORF · MADRID · MEXICO · MONTREAL
PANAMA · PARIS · SÃO PAULO · TOKYO · TORONTO

First McGraw-Hill Paperback Edition, 1977

2 3 4 5 6 7 8 9 MU MU 7 9 8 7

Reprinted by arrangement with Macmillan
Publishing Co., Inc.

Library of Congress Cataloging in Publication Data
Dempsey, David K
    The way we die.
    Reprint of the ed. published by Macmillan, New
York.
    Includes bibliographical references and index.
    1. Death. I. Title.
[BD444.D46 1977]   128'.5   76-51356
ISBN 0-07-016340-5

This book
is for my wife Evangeline
and my children Karen,
Kevin, and Ian.

Contents

ACKNOWLEDGMENTS

Parts of this book, in somewhat different form, were originally published in *The New York Times Magazine*. Many people were helpful in its preparation but three in particular deserve special thanks. Dr. Austin H. Kutscher and his wife Lillian went beyond the call of duty in making available their extensive files of thanatological material, as well as offering valuable suggestions. And Miss Lillian Wahrow's assistance in opening the medical library of New York Hospital, Westchester Division, to a nonprofessional is likewise deeply appreciated.

CHAPTER I

The God from the Machine

MY FATHER'S AUNT ANNIE was the tough one in our family. She never seemed to get sick. Widowed at sixty-five, she moved to California, bought a house and lived alone for another twenty-eight years. Annie viewed her old age as a moral triumph for which the doctors deserved no credit at all. At ninety-three, she fell off a ladder while repairing a drainpipe, was seriously injured and died a few days later. My father used to say that Annie's life had been "cut short."

My mother's mother died a lingering death at seventy-eight, in an upstairs bedroom of my uncle's house, in a small midwestern city half a mile from where we lived. Grandma had always been a tiny woman, scarcely five feet tall and weighing not much more than a hundred pounds. As her illness progressed, she all but withered away, dying a step at a time as if to make this final departure unobtrusive. The doctor came once a day to chat with her and prescribe the few drugs that were necessary. Although my grandmother had given birth to seven children she had never been in a hospital and it did not seem to anyone that this was the time to begin. The diagnosis was cancer. Actually, she died of pneumonia, although it was commonly assumed that the real culprit was old age.

What impresses me most in recollection is that we grand-children were not sheltered from the events of those final weeks, and, more to the point, she was not sheltered from us. Coming home from school during that spring, my cousins and I would stop at the vacant lot next door to shoot baskets. An old galvanized iron bucket with its bottom rusted out was fastened to a tree, and from her window my grandmother watched us toss the ball at our makeshift basket. We discovered that she did not understand what was really taking place. One day, when we went inside to get warm, she said, "You boys try so hard to throw that ball into the bucket, but I've never seen you get it in."

Here was a dilemma for us: Should we tell her the truth? I think we realized that to do so would be unkind. She wanted to see the day when one of us made the ball stay in. Psychologists would say that this experience had some kind of life meaning for her. In any case, I like to think that she died with some of the illusions, as well as the frustrations and defeats, with which she lived.

Certainly, one illusion she did not have was that mortal life could be prolonged, even for a short while, against all the odds of nature. Hers was a dignified death, a fitting end to a hard-working, simple existence, a rounding off that seemed appropriate not just to her own passing but to the very idea of dying.

The visitation took place in the big downstairs living room where the funeral was to be held a few days later. At that time, almost fifty years ago, undertakers had not generally begun calling themselves funeral directors; funeral homes were not yet parlors, lights had not been planted in the shrubbery, and it was only beginning to be customary for the embalmer—before he became a mortician—to make the deceased look as lifelike as possible. Although my grandmother had never used lipstick or rouge, he fixed her up like an aging flapper. Cotton was stuffed into her sunken cheeks, and she was dressed in her finest. I thought this quite proper; clearly she was about to go on some kind of journey and had to look her best.

One thing didn't happen: we grandchildren were not allowed to have our pictures taken standing at the side of the coffin. The Pepper kids had it on us there. When Grandpa Pepper died, they had posed, one at a time, beside the old man's casket. These photographs had been circulated in school, and for a time the Peppers were the envy of the neighborhood. But our parents drew the line; they weren't the kind to wallow in sentiment or, for that matter, grief. Enough was enough. Still, it was a nice funeral.

Not long ago an acquaintance of mine died of cancer. I knew him as a vigorous, practical-minded man who, until the last few months of his life, rarely knew defeat. Hopelessly ill, he had been moved into an intensive care unit where all the miracles of modern science were turned loose on his ravaged body. Fed by tubes, punctured like a dart board from numerous injections, he lay unconscious, and his wife protested that it was time to stop. Near the end, it was decided to attempt a blood transfusion. Because the arteries had collapsed this seemed impossible, but then a vein that could take a needle was discovered in one foot. New blood was pumped in, to no avail. And this is how he died.

When I told this story to a doctor at a large New York City medical center, he shrugged. "Your friend was lucky," he said. "To begin with, he was not in pain. And then, you know, they might have kept him going much longer."

He then asked if I would care to see an "interesting case." Accompanying him to the intensive care unit upstairs, I saw a young girl, seventeen or eighteen years old. Her color was good, but she was obviously unconscious. Intravenous tubes were attached to her arm and a heart-lung machine regulated her breathing. "She has been dead for four days," the doctor told me. "She had a brain injury. There is no EEG [electroencephalogram] reading whatever. We are waiting for a request for a kidney." A few days later, such a request was received from an upstate hospital. The kidney was removed, the machine that had kept the girl breathing turned off. And this is how she "died."

Myrtle L. was a college student who had Hodgkin's disease. When I saw her she had advanced to stage IV, the terminal period. This is often characterized by internal bleeding, and Myrtle was receiving transfusions at the same time that suction tubes were draining blood from her mouth. A tracheotomy had been performed to facilitate her breathing. She was conscious and able to talk to her family, but, although she was in no great physical pain, it was obvious that she suffered greatly—not from her illness, but from what was being done for her.

Myrtle, of course, wanted to live—who of us does not?—but she had fallen victim to a curiously punishing kind of technology and, perhaps worse, a social attitude that regards death as unnecessary and obscene. Medicine today has more tools at its command than it had in my grandmother's time. If it can conquer illness, why not death? At the very least it can keep the body's machinery going long after it might ordinarily have stopped, a tribute not to the healing arts but to the technician.

The public utility that serves our community recently sent a notice to its customers drawing their attention to the vast array of life-sustaining equipment that runs on electric power. Iron lungs, respirators, kidney machines, ultrasonic nebulizers, suction pumps and rocking beds head the list. "The number of these machines is growing, and so is the number of people who rely on them," the company declared, adding that it was their desire "to give you the best service possible." The implications of this little notice are frightening. For those who have not made emergency preparations, a power blackout—not uncommon as peak demands overload the system—could conceivably (and suddenly) end the lives of hundreds, if not thousands, of people. (An even more sinister reading: Pay your bill or we'll turn off your iron lung!)

But perhaps the real significance to be gleaned from the rapid expansion of life-support equipment is more profound. Whereas the human body once drew strength from its own resources—its ability, with medication, to resist the ravages of disease and old age—it has become today increasingly dependent on exterior sources of power. We are literally plugged in to an outside mechanism and wholly dependent on its uninterrupted functioning. And, no doubt, we are a little less firmly "plugged in" to a cosmological system that might include God, or at least nature's own self-contained and self-limiting theorems, as the source of life. For more and more people, reaching the magic three-score-and-ten is no longer a good reason to start winding down life; it is a signal to start up the machinery.

Nonetheless, machines occupy a relatively modest place in this new armamentarium. We are also becoming a nation of borrowers, taking organs from the living and the dead alike. We graft skin, bypass clogged heart valves with arteries from the leg, install real hair on bald heads and implant sections of bone in human limbs. We borrow blood almost routinely and pay it back. Eye banks store corneas for grafting onto suitable recipients, and there are predictions that the ear will be transplantable by the end of the century. The heart transplant is certainly the most heroic attempt to live out life on someone else's vital organ; kidneys are now transplanted with good outcome, and efforts are being made to do the same for livers and spleens. From both the living and the dead, medicine seeks to fashion a composite man.

Finally, we have learned that it is possible to do without some organs at all. When the surgeon is not adding new or used parts to the human body, or overhauling the existing mechanism, he is likely to be taking out diseased or obsolete organs. A lung is removed and we go on breathing; mastectomies leave us with one breast and ileostomies dispense with most of our lower bowel. Except for childbearing, the uterus serves no useful purpose, and many women find that they are healthier without it. All this is a stunning tribute to medical progress, but it has also created a success syndrome that threatens to make progress self-defeating. In brief, medicine doesn't always know when it's time to stop, and maintaining life at all costs has become an end in itself. When applied to those for whom life is truly coming to an end, plugging the body into one more machine, or replacing an organ, can be as fanatical—and ultimately as futile—as ancient man's worship of totems in the hope of curing sickness and prolonging earthly existence.

This scientific capability has given doctors a new role, making them, in effect, the arbiters of life and death. The psychologist Richard Kalish has noted that modern man has come to believe in medicine as his ancestors once believed in religion. This has detached us from the sense of nature's inevitable finitude, dangling before us new and illusory notions of immortality—the life everlasting of the human body. Having lost a holistic view of itself through intensive specialization, medicine has also lost a holistic view of the organism that is man. It treats the parts, not the whole, and some of the parts can be made to function long after the whole man has died.

Ironically, the whole man often dies an agonizing death that may be quite unrelated to the nature of his illness. In concentrating its skill and energy on biological man, medicine has all but abandoned social and psychological man, has shunted him into intensive care units or hooked him up to equipment that, no matter how miraculous, all too often becomes indifferent to the person being treated. Dr. Herman Feifel, a psychologist with the Veterans Administration in Los Angeles, has written, ". . . we die in the 'big' hospital with its impersonal intravenous tubes and oxygen tents. It is as though death's reality were being observed by making it a public event, something that befalls everyone, yet no one in particular."

"Patients in hospitals no longer die," writes Patricia M. Grosso, a psychiatric nurse in New Jersey—

> They go to intensive-care units. There, beneath the tubes and tents, they are made dead. When your lungs give out, a shiny new MA-1 respirator will be wheeled in to pump air into your

lungs and suck it back out again. If your heart refuses to beat, electric pacemakers will circulate your blood and if you cannot digest food an ingenious process called hyperalimentation can inject nutrients directly into your bloodstream and maintain nutrition for years.

Many physicians find themselves as enslaved by the machines as are their patients. In effect, they are accountable to a legal code that was drafted long before the awesome power of life or death became so easily manipulated by technology. Under the dual demands of the law and of his own profession, the doctor has little choice but to prolong lives which have ceased to have meaning. No wonder the human touch is so often missing.

It is not surprising that medicine seeks a way out of this dilemma. "Pulling the plug" is not uncommon, and, for that matter, not illegal. Passive euthanasia of that sort is well within the limits of medical discretion. But there are not always plugs to pull, and if the physician actively intervenes to shorten life he is committing murder. Early in 1974, Dr. Vincent Montemarano of Mineola, Long Island, described as "a mild mannered physician who is highly regarded both professionally and personally," injected an overdose of potassium chloride into a cancer patient who was expected to die within forty-eight hours. Death came within five minutes, and the physician was accused of willful murder. A jury did not agree, and Dr. Montemarano was acquitted. Indeed, in the several such trials that have been conducted in England and the United States, no doctor accused of mercy killing has ever gone to jail.

Such incidents achieve notoriety because they come to the attention of the courts. Yet, according to a surgeon with the United States Public Health Service, thousands of hopeless patients are hastened into death, although somewhat less promptly, by means of drugs. "It is morphine, not cancer, that finally kills them," he says, adding that it is common practice to "snow" such people with massive doses when it becomes apparent that there is no hope of recovery. Ironically, it is medicine's ability to extend the lives of the terminally ill that makes such subterfuges necessary.

The decision to continue or end human life is increasingly in the hands of a single group—the doctors. Although their power is limited in the case of the very old and the fatally ill, its exercise can be dramatically seen in cases where life is simply marginal: the unconscious stroke victim who may live for years with intravenous feeding; the individual surviving in an iron lung or on a kidney machine. And because there are not enough of these life-support resources to go around, the physician assumes the godlike role of deciding who shall live and who shall die. Medicine has, indeed, showed us that it is possible to live on borrowed time.

This prospect is highlighted as more and more people live to an age when life becomes marginal. In 1900, an American could expect to die, on the average, at forty-seven. By 1974, he could look forward to a life-span of some seventy years. Are people living longer? Not really. They are simply not dying prematurely of infectious and formerly incurable diseases. We not only get old; we *live* old. And this fact raises an agonizing problem for the children of the elderly: what to do with the "vegetables?"

Today I went to visit Bill, a former colleague who is chronically afflicted with a strange, disabling neurological disease. He is not dying, the doctors assure him, but neither will he recover. Because he has no family, he lives in a nursing home.

There are 23,000 of these homes in the United States, many of them supported by Medicare and Medicaid payments. Most of them are dreary places, although they bear such names as Pleasant View and Restful Haven. The home I visited is called Gotham Health Institute.* It is expensive and well managed,

* pseudonym

and, although Bill is not dying, it is quite obvious that most of the patients are. Every room is private. Signs in the reception room announce, "We Care." Why, then, did the old woman rolling down the hallway in a wheelchair call out, "Help me! Help me!"? I had no idea what she wanted but I got an attendant who told me, "Pay no attention to her; she's just confused." Still, I was bothered. Why was the woman wheeling around so furiously?

The well-stocked library is impressive—to visitors, at least—but it seemed to be unused most of the time. The odor of incontinence is troubling, but I took it to be unavoidable. Most doors are open and one can see the old people propped on beds or hunched down in their overstuffed chairs. A few watch television. At Halloween, I am told, every resident has a cutout paper pumpkin pinned on his door. For those who can make it, there is an apple cider party.

Gotham is probably no worse than most such places, and it may be better than many, but at its best it is a cheerless storage bin for those who seem to be living too long. A majority of the patients are not terminal in any true sense; they are simply waiting to become terminal. Aside from ministering to their bodily needs, nobody pays much attention to them. Their isolation and loneliness appear to overshadow their feebleness, their aches and pains. "Old people," a nurse told me, "are very difficult to please." (It seems not to have occurred to her to try.) If they "take a turn for the worse," she added, they are rushed to a hospital two miles away. One very elderly man suffering chest pains was transferred just in time to undergo electric resuscitation for cardiac arrest. He is now back at the home, waiting for the next attack.

In 1967, at London's Neasden Hospital, the medical superintendent posted on the bulletin board a notice that read in part: "The following patients are not to be resuscitated: very elderly, over 65; malignant disease. Chronic chest disease. Chronic renal disease. Top of treatment card to be marked

NTBR [Not to Be Resuscitated]." So great was the outcry in the press against this "cold-blooded" edict that a board of inquiry appointed by the British minister of health all but forbade the policy. No person, it suggested, should, by reason of age alone, be excluded from resuscitation. A London newspaper, the *Evening Standard*, ran a cartoon showing one elderly patient asking another, "Is this one of those hospitals where one daren't stop breathing?"

A Swedish magazine, in a survey of persons prominent in the arts and entertainment world, found that two-thirds of the men and one-third of the women, wanted to die "suddenly and unexpectedly." The interesting aspect of these findings is that the age of the respondent made little difference; old and young shared this desire in about the same proportion as the middle-aged.

Gunnar Biörck, writing in the *Archives of Internal Medicine*, raises the question, "If there is a tendency in modern Western society to wish for a sudden, unexpected death—why then make great effort to deprive people of this privilege?" Why, indeed? The prospect of living to a ripe old age, with its attendant discomforts, isolation and, very likely, institutionalization, may be one reason why most of us dread growing old; why we think we would welcome that fatal heart attack. We do not fear death so much as we fear the efforts that may be made to keep us alive. Geriatrics is the fastest growing branch of medicine, and, whether we like it or not, those of us past sixty-five can look forward to joining what has been called the bedridden generation. It is a way of life over which we have increasingly less control. At worst, hostage to a machine, at best, to the judgment of the doctor, we have quite literally surrendered our own freedom to live or die.

Dr. Andie L. Knutson, a physician active in public health work, thinks these life-or-death decisions will ultimately "involve choices about the relative worth of people. They are decisions directly concerning the nature of the compositions of our future population." Yet only 11 percent of the public health professionals he queried in a survey believed that physicians alone should have the right to decide whether to continue or to end a mature human life. A majority (49 percent) assigned this right to the individual himself, but even the wishes of the spouse or other responsible survivor was preferred (19 percent) to those of the doctor.

When it comes to judging the relative value of one human life against another, Knutson found that "almost three-fourths of the respondents consider service to mankind or service to society as the significant criterion. Of lesser significance was service to one's family or intimate group (33 percent), service to God (20 percent) and the personal achievements of the individual (19 percent)."

This is the doctor's dilemma: To what extent shall social as well as medical considerations dictate who among us will have his life extended? It is estimated that 58,000 Americans die each year of kidney disease because there is a shortage of hemodialysis machines and available organs for transplant. A medical team decides who shall be saved. The patient's condition—his chances of survival—may be the prime consideration. Age is a factor; the young are usually given preference (understandably so) over the old. One's social or economic importance is also taken into account, although this is not generally acknowledged. A vagrant, dying of renal failure, will not likely be put on a kidney machine, at a weekly cost of $500; the governor of a state almost certainly will.

With an accelerating trend toward an old-age society, economic considerations arise. What is the cost of maintaining life in too large a group of helpless older citizens? How long will we continue to support those who are clearly a burden to society, even though medicine's ability to do so is at hand? Marya Mannes, in her novel *They*, pictures a future in which the elderly are simply banished to an island to fend for themselves. Such a solution is not likely, yet the question remains.

Nature's weeding out of the vulnerable and infirm is being tampered with. Everyone is a candidate for longevity, or at least a final ride on the life-support machines. As a result, dying has become expensive. Even for the terminal patient, doctors don't like to make house calls. (A cartoon in the *New Yorker* shows a bedridden man, his wife next to him talking on the telephone. "We understand perfectly, Doctor. Just send the death certificate over and we'll sign it ourselves.") With hospital rates ranging upward of $100 a day, the terminal period can be seen as a poor investment. Patient and family are likely to feel guilty about the high cost of dying—and they are right. They may also go bankrupt.

"There is also the anguish of the relatives, the visiting—all spelling time and money away from children, from leisure much needed for the hard-working," a woman in Massachusetts writes me. "There is often resentment to a sad and a bad ending to a life-long attachment. . . . A man I know well shot himself. His own father had been kept alive three years. The family was completely drained of resources. When the time came, knowing he had a fatal disease, hearing the words, 'Tom, you'll be better off in the hospital,' he had no hesitation. He did this because he truly loved his family."

Expensive care is compounded by the secretiveness that surrounds most deaths. Few people, least of all the physicians, are willing to sit down with the patient and discuss his illness. Said one elderly man, "It's hard to carry on a conversation with Dr. ———— when he comes in the room with a stethoscope in his ears and puts a thermometer in my mouth." Even fewer physicians are willing to tell a person that he is dying (and not everyone wants to be told), yet the screen of silence that descends around the bedside conveys its own chilling message.

The dying person instinctively yearns to unburden himself; he wants someone close to him who can share his sadness and grief. Instead, he is surrounded by hospital busy work, goes through another battery of tests, and near the end is sent to "death valley" (intensive care). It is isolation and neglect, not the fact of dying, that people fear most, according to Dr. Avery Weisman, a Boston psychiatrist who has worked with hundreds of terminally ill persons. Dr. Richard Kalish echoes this view. People are abandoned socially, he says, long before they die physically.

Within the past decade, problems such as these have occupied the attention of an increasing number of people whose professions bring them into close contact with the aged, the terminally ill and their families. Physicians are only beginning to understand the implications of the nonmedical aspects of dying; psychiatrists, social workers and ministers have been quicker to see the problem in its larger perspective. And the public at large is wondering if the new emphasis on death with dignity is not something that should concern them, the ultimate consumers. As a result, a new discipline, thanatology (from the Greek *thanatos*-death) has come into existence. The word means simply the study, or science, of death.

This book attempts to explore the subject in its various ramifications. Is there a better way of dying, an approach that does not surrender the achievements of science, yet is no longer in bondage to its dehumanizing excesses? Can the patient himself be restored to the center of the stage in the final drama? It also explores the issues of the bereavement of survivors, the rituals with which we commemorate and bury the dead, and, above all, the social and financial price that is paid to die in America.

Although relatively new, the field of thanatology is by no means unexplored. Once taboo, death has become "fashionable" enough to take its place among the television specials and in the college curricula. Researchers are investigating the experience of dying while philosophers brood on its meaning. The new concern threatens to become an obsession just as unhealthy as the old taboo. What we seek is a proper balance between the complete denial of death—the "better-not-to-talk-about-it" attitude—and the belief that the accumulation of data somehow explains the age-old mystery of man's ultimate destiny and removes its sting.

No discussion of thanatology can begin without reference to Dr. Elisabeth Kübler-Ross, a Swiss-born psychiatrist who lives and works in Chicago. Before Dr. Ross took up the cause of dying, psychological insights on death remained buried in professional journals. Books were written about the philosophical implications of death and ministers became aware that there was more to the subject than saving souls. To adapt Mark Twain's observation, many people talked about dying but nobody did anything about it.

Elisabeth Kübler-Ross did something, and she did it with the zeal of a missionary bent on lifting prevailing attitudes about dying out of the dark ages. Her book, *On Death and Dying*, has been a hidden bestseller for years and she herself has become the guru of a movement whose adherents include many of the health-care professionals of the nation.

Her most important achievement is teaching others how to listen to the dying and what to listen for. At least seventy-five universities, teaching hospitals, nursing schools and theological seminaries now offer courses on death and dying based on Dr. Kübler-Ross's approach. She also lectures widely and, from her home just outside Chicago—a seventy-year-old restored Louis Sullivan house that resembles a Swiss chalet—corresponds with dying people who write to her for help.

Elisabeth Kübler-Ross is a complex, intense person. Some who find her too obsessed with her calling describe her as a minister of death. Yet no other single person has so dramatically turned around a whole generation of opinion-makers on a single subject. To those who know her well, she has her lighter moments. Amidst the Swiss bric-a-brac, the wall hangings and the huge bellows that serves as a coffee table in her house stands a regulation pool table; visitors may be challenged to a game of snooker. And although Elisabeth Kübler-Ross has lived in this country for fourteen years, she still yodels. "When I was a little girl in Switzerland," she says, "we had a big wine cellar. When we had guests our father would send us down there to get a bottle of wine. I remember very vividly the darker it was, the louder we yodeled." Death, she thinks, can be compared to a dark wine cellar. We yodel to reassure ourselves.

Figuratively speaking, death remains hidden in the wine cellar—call it the subconscious—of Western society. Why is this so? The social historian Philip Aries writes that our society has interdicted death because it violates the rule that life must at all times be happy. A Michigan doctor reports that in the 1940s Detroit police put up skull-and-crossbones signs at dangerous intersections. But after a few weeks the warnings had to be removed. They made drivers nervous, this physician believes, and uncovered a death anxiety that people prefer to suppress.

It is hardly necessary to point out the widespread use of such euphemisms as "passed away," "departed" and "taken from us." The physician himself is not trained to deal with dying as a medical phenomenon, and I have been told by one doctor that the word *death* is not even to be found in the indexes of most medical and surgical textbooks.

It seems that we prefer the word *killed* to the word *die*. Newspaper and magazines describe cancer in much the same vein that they report automobile deaths. Even medical journals speak of heart disease as "the number one killer" rather than as a physiological process. Death is something that happens to us as a result of outside intervention.

We shield ourselves from the dying by shifting them to nursing homes or the isolation wards of hospitals. Once dead, they are spirited down the freight elevator, possibly to be cremated, their last physical link with the world of the living destroyed as quickly as possible. We even freeze the dead in the hope that someday, when a cure for what killed them is found, the corpse can be revived and sent on its way. Funerals give way to memorial services and the custom of viewing the body is rapidly declining as more and more people look upon this practice as uncivilized.

Quite obviously, then, we want little to do with death. This is a paradox, since at no time in history has its presence been so much a part of our lives. Not only are the holocausts of recent wars fresh in our memory, but the threat of man's annihilation by the bomb—megadeath—hangs over the future. We read almost daily of some act of terrorism committed against the innocent; letter bombs, airport massacres and assassinations have become commonplace. And if this were not enough, our movie and television screens are replete with mayhem unequalled in past times. We have made killing a form of entertainment, but it does not apply to us! Why do we deny it in our lives? There are a number of reasons, most of them unique to our age.

To begin with, the murder that is seen on television is obviously staged; we are not meant to believe it. The very ubiquity of this kind of entertainment weakens its impact. When slaughter is seen as unreal, a diverting fiction, death becomes less threatening. One might even argue, as some do, that this kind of violence has a purgative effect similar to that experienced by the Greeks and Elizabethans when they watched the bloody dramas of Aeschylus and Shakespeare. Man learns to control his murderous impulses by seeing them acted out in a make-believe setting.

Another reason for our denial of death is the sheer pervasiveness of real violence. Psychologically, we turn off. This is one way man defends himself against unacceptable hazards, and in doing so, he ignores danger. The fact that 53,000 Americans are killed in highway accidents each year does not keep us from driving cars. We are almost certain that it won't be us. Exactly the same psychology is at work on the battlefield: the soldier assumes, however blindly, that others may die, but not he. Without this blind faith, he could not fight.

Man no longer has a fatalistic attitude toward his death. When plagues swept Europe and North America men felt that there was very little that could be done about it. Natural catastrophes such as floods, storms, and earthquakes were looked upon as acts of God. Although they still wreak havoc, we have learned how to minimize their destructiveness. And whatever the reality of war, terrorism and genocide, we perceive these horrors as somehow controllable, problems that can be solved. *Society is working on them.*

It may seem irrelevant to blame the social welfare state for our inability to come to grips with the idea of death, but it is clearly implicated. Our society has secularized life. In so doing it has removed death from its traditional religious context, the belief that it is part of the natural order of things. The historian Arnold Toynbee has written, "Death becomes an infringement on our right to life, liberty and the pursuit of happiness." It is an affront to individual rights which we resist as we might the effort to do away with the right of free speech. This has not always been the case. When death was viewed more theologically, when suffering itself was thought of as spiritually purifying, when men believed in some kind of afterlife that justified suffering, death was more acceptable.

Much of this can be traced to an almost euphoric optimism about the wonders of science and the notion of progress. No doubt about it, in many ways life *is* better. Medicine's conquest of innumerable diseases, our chances of living out a full lifespan, has given us a new faith in the science of healing. People are literally pulled back from the grave at the last moment. Our hospitals are vast laboratories of positive thinking; science tempts us with the means to defeat death and our humanitarian tradition tells us that we must make every effort to do so. Modern man no longer accepts the inevitable march toward old age and death, but struggles to rejuvenate himself through faddish diets, organ transplants and electric wheelchairs. Because he is less inclined to believe in a transcendant immortality, he turns to science. All this has made it difficult for him to come to terms with death.

The device employed by the Greek dramatists to rescue their

heroes from mortal destruction, the *deus ex machina*, has acquired a strangely contemporary meaning. Today's gods do spring from technology. In the succeeding chapter, we will see what this machine is like. One of its most immediate achievements is to make the moment of death debatable by using brain waves rather than heartbeat as the criterion—in a sense, to make it harder to die.

CHAPTER II

Violent Death — and the Gift of Life

EVER SINCE APRIL, 1974, Tim Curtin,* a forty-four year-old assistant general sales manager for the Titanium Metals Corporation of America, has been living without kidneys, the result of an operation to save his life. Three times a week this tall, once energetic man travels from his New York apartment on East End Avenue to Columbia-Presbyterian Hospital's hemodialysis center on the West Side. There, for six hours, he stretches out in a reclining chair while blood is drawn from his veins and circulated through the filtering mechanism that does the work of the human kidney. Curtin submits to this uncomfortable treatment between midnight and six A.M. (the only time a machine is available to him). He is one of twelve patients being dialyzed simultaneously at the center.

As Curtin dozes during the long, silent hours in this twilight world, he often indulges in fantasy. The most recurrent image— inspired sometimes by the wail of an ambulance siren outside— is that an accident or homicide victim will be brought to the hospital's emergency room and die soon afterwards; in his wallet will be found a donor card, the little pocket will declaring

* pseudonym

19

that the bearer agrees to give his organs for transplantation. As Curtin's fantasy continues, cross-matching between the donor's tissue and his own indicates compatibility, so that the kidney is not likely to be rejected. In the final act, Curtin is rushed to the operating room where a transplant team, with surgical derring-do that has become relatively common in the past few years, implants a kidney that will give him a normal life. The cost—$10,000 or more—is no problem; Medicare pays 80 percent of the operation and his insurance company will pick up the balance.

The major difficulty with this fantasy is that it is shared by at least two-thirds of the transplant candidates in this country— an estimated 8,000—who must wait for someone else to die if they are to have a second chance. (The luckier one-third look to a living donor, usually a member of the family.) Yet only about 30 percent will receive a graft; there are simply not enough accidents occurring in the right place at the right time. "Thousands of people," says Dr. Donald Kayhoe, who oversees tissue-typing research for the National Institutes of Health, "look forward to claiming the heart, liver or kidneys from the latest seventeen-year-old boy who is killed on a motorcycle." Such a person, Dr. Kayhoe notes, makes the best organ donor, although he is least likely to carry a donor card.

In the San Francisco Bay area, the state highway patrol notifies the University of California Medical Center whenever it investigates a serious accident; victims are taken directly to the center, where a transplant team is standing by in case injuries prove fatal. In a Swiftian article in *Medical Opinion and Review*, Dr. Warren J. Warwick, of the University of Minnesota Medical School, foresees the time when "mobile body-rescue teams . . . accident watching clubs . . . as well as television monitors" will be common along busy highways. Dr. Warwick's "modest proposal" also includes prohibition of seat belts and cancellation of speed limits to increase the number of accidental deaths.

Waiting for the Brain to Die

But was the young girl referred to in the previous chapter alive or dead during the four days she remained on the respirator while doctors waited for a kidney request to come in? A generation ago, the question would not have been asked. A person died when breathing stopped and no heartbeat could be detected. Rigor mortis, dilation of the pupils and a relaxation of the sphincter muscle were other clinical signs. Even though one's terminal illness might be protracted, the end was seen as sudden, often preceded by a death rattle in the throat.

We know now that dying is not that simple. Modern medicine has added a neurological definition of death. Where there are sparks—the brain waves that are measured by an electroencephalogram—there is life. A flat EEG reading indicates death, no matter how vital the other organs may seem under resuscitation. Thus the brain often becomes the final factor in determining when a person is dead.

Is such a criterion always reliable? In 1962, the brilliant Russian physicist, Lev Davidovitch Landau, was crushed in his car by a truck. Describing the heroic attempts that were made to save his life, Dr. Louis Lasagna writes, "Four days after the accident, Dr. Landau 'died': his pulse and blood pressure disappeared, and the EEG became flat." The scientist was deaf, blind, speechless and without reflexes. For two months he was in a state of coma, during which time more than one hundred physicians came to Moscow to treat him. ". . . they transfused blood into his radial artery, and gave intravenous adrenaline and digitalis. . . . Eleven months after the accident, he was able to sit up in bed and smilingly accepted his Nobel Prize." Although Landau never fully recovered, he lived another six years.

Lasagna makes the point that society would not likely undertake such heroic efforts for a vagrant. But an even more interesting implication emerges. The incident occurred before lack of brain functioning was widely accepted as a final criterion of death. Had the doctors used only this measure, they would have given up on Landau quite early in the game.

How long should the EEG reading remain flat? In 1968, the Harvard Medical School's Ad Hoc Committee to Examine the Definition of Brain Death recommended at least ten minutes and preferably twenty. The committee also emphasized lack of response, movements, reflexes and breathing. But even with these criteria there are hazards. An excessive intake of barbiturates can depress the functions of the central nervous system to a degree that simulates the brain-death syndrome. For this reason, a flat reading of at least four hours is preferred by many physicians when barbiturate usage is suspected, and some believe that even this is too brief a period. The late Sen. Robert F. Kennedy maintained breathing and heartbeat (under resuscitation) for seven hours, with a flat EEG, before the doctors gave up. Today, it is recommended that the test be repeated after twenty-four hours just to make sure.

Such a lengthy wait, however, might be too long if there is a heart recipient waiting in the wings. In a landmark case in 1968, a Virginia jury gave the green light to death by transplantation. Late on May 24 of that year, Bruce Tucker, a laborer, sustained a massive brain injury in a fall. Operated on at the Medical College of Virginia, he was placed on a respirator at 11:30 A.M. the next day. Although the EEG was flat, Tucker's other vital signs—body temperature, blood pressure and rate of respiration—remained normal. This was in the early days of transplants, and a heart recipient, Joseph Klepp, was waiting. Thanks to the surgeons at Virginia Medical College Hospital, he did not have to wait long. Four hours after the respirator was turned on—and with no attempt to locate Tucker's next of kin—it was turned off. Tucker's heart was removed about an hour later, and while they were at it surgeons also took out his kidneys, for possible future use. The unseemly haste with which all this was done, without permission of relatives, caused Tucker's brother to sue for $100,000 damages. The transplant team, he charged, was engaged in a "systematic and nefarious scheme to use Bruce Tucker's heart and hasten his death by shutting off the mechanical means of support." During the trial, a number of Harvard Medical School professors were imported to testify for the defense. A man whose brain has died, they said, cannot be resuscitated. Their view was shared by the jury, which refused damages. Yet it was pointed out that "the patient was pronounced dead less than two hours and 35 minutes after the electroencephalogram reading," far too short a time, if not to determine death, at least to look for relatives. Perhaps Tucker's death was, indeed, foredoomed. But its timing was clearly one of convenience. Joseph Klepp, incidentally, died a week later.

The problem of deciding when a person has actually died stems from medicine's ability to resuscitate. The heart can go without beating for as long as half an hour and then be revived by cardiac massage or electric stimulation, but the brain, which can do without blood circulation for only a few minutes, would be irreparably damaged. This suggests yet another definition of death: assuming the brain is alive, one dies *only when resuscitation is not possible.*

In Arkansas, a man and his wife were killed in a car crash. What mattered in this case was the order of death, which had to be established for inheritance purposes. Although witnesses agreed that the husband had died almost instantly, two of them testified that the wife exhibited signs of life for a short time— she had moved, gasped for breath and moaned. Despite this, the husband's heirs went to court, contending that technical advances in medicine had outmoded the coroner's definition of death. A proper definition, they argued, would not be based on the cessation of breathing and heartbeat, but on medicine's inability to resuscitate. Both the lower and an appeals court, however, disagreed, and the wife's heirs inherited the estate.

Had the couple reached a hospital in time for resuscitation, the outcome might have been different. Assuming that death was inevitable for both, when it took place might very well have depended upon the physician's decision to cut short the intervention. And this, in turn, would in all likelihood have been based not on breathing and circulation, but on the EEG reading given off by the brain.

An Oklahoma man, beaten unconscious in a fight, was operated on for massive brain injuries. During surgery, his breathing stopped and he was put on a respirator. When it was decided that he would not recover, doctors got his wife's permission for a kidney transplant. After the kidney was removed, the respirator was turned off. This straightforward medical decision presented the law with a ticklish question because the victim's life insurance lapsed on the day normal breathing stopped. At what moment did the man actually die? If it could be said he died when he stopped breathing, at which time the insurance was still in force, his widow would receive payment. If, on the other hand, he was declared alive until the respirator was turned off, she would not. The coroner in this case took the position that the man was, in fact, dead when he stopped breathing the first time, even though other vital functions continued. Quite the opposite conclusion was reached by a coroner in England, however, who ruled that a patient remained legally alive until the respirator was unplugged to remove the kidney.

At present, the law in this country is divided on this issue. Most states accept cessation of breathing and heartbeat as sufficient evidence of death. (This sometimes has bizarre results. In one case, the court held that a woman who had been decapitated in an accident outlived a companion because the blood gushing from her neck was evidence that her heart was still beating, even though her head was ten feet away!) Two states, Kansas and Maryland, have updated their definition of death by adding lack of neurological function to the traditional criteria. In Kansas, it is harder to die if there are respirators handy. The supreme court in that state, in a decision about the moment of death that involved estates of a husband and wife, declared that "death is complete cessation of all vital functions *without possibility of resuscitation.*" (Italics added.) But even in this situation the actual moment of death can be debatable. When organs are needed for transplantation, the doctor's decision may differ radically from that in cases where there is no potential recipient.

This was substantially the issue in a murder trial in Oakland, California. A. D. Lyons was accused of murdering his companion, Samuel M. Allen, Jr., during an argument. A bullet lodged in Allen's brain was removed by surgeons and the man was kept alive on a respirator. At about this time a request for a transplantable heart came from Stanford University hospital. Allen was declared neurologically dead, the respirator turned off, and his heart removed.

The assailant's defense was simple: the doctors, not he, had killed Allen, whose heart, in the words of the defense attorney, "was pumping merrily along." A jury did not agree, however, and Lyons was convicted. It is clear, nevertheless, that although physicians did not cause death, they did determine the time of death. Whether they would have been in quite such a hurry had a transplant team not been standing by is another question.

The Road to an Early Grave

In the time before today's refined criteria had been established, doctors could not always be sure just when a person had died. Medical literature is replete with instances of premature burial. Cataleptic fits, trances and ecstasy were often mistaken for death in the nineteenth century, and their victims rushed into an early grave. The psychologist Robert Kastenbaum comments that "a good swooner and a hasty undertaker make a bad combination." Kastenbaum uses the term *thanatomimesis*, or death-feigning, to explain certain aspects of this phenomenon. In some instances, he thinks, such behavior is adaptive or purposeful; the "playing 'possum" strategy, for example, might be employed by someone in mortal danger. Indeed, an experiment by three Los Angeles scientists demonstrated that oppossums threatened by danger in many cases simply freeze up to feign death. The scientists implanted electrodes in the skulls of fifteen oppossums, then used artificial dog jaws to clench and shake them, while recorded barks and growls were played in the background. Although biological life was at a standstill, EEG recordings showed an alert cortical state. The oppossums revived when the experiment ended.

Although premature burials were sometimes the result of death-feigning, many more can be traced to the inexactitude of death diagnosis during a severe illness. A heart that seems to have stopped beating may spontaneously recover. These cases of suspended animation often slipped past the doctors and, more especially, the coroners, many of whom had no medical background. (Even today, only two of the thirty-nine states using coroners require that he be a licensed physician.) The actual prevalence of premature burial is difficult to assess, but some indication that they were by no means rarities can be seen when old cemeteries are moved to a new location, and bodies dug up for reburial. T. M. Montgomery, reporting on the moving of the Fort Randall Cemetery in 1896, writes that "nearly 2 percent of those exhumed were no doubt victims of suspended animation." A soldier who had apparently been struck by lightning and declared dead had attempted to push his coffin lid open. Another was found with his hands clutching his clothing. Dr. Alexander Wilder writes of a thirty-five-year-old man "dead" of scarlet fever who was exhumed two months later. "The coffin was found to have the glass front shattered, the bottom kicked out and the sides sprung. The body lay face downwards, the arms were bent and in the clenched fists were handfuls of hair."

The extent to which some people feared finding themselves prematurely consigned to the grave—rightly or wrongly—is illustrated by the ingenious coffins sold in the United States in the last century. Various devices provided the occupant with contact with the outside world. One such was a chain, placed in the hand of the "corpse," that needed only to be tugged to ring a bell aboveground. It is now clear, on the basis of our current knowledge, that many of these unlucky persons were simply in a state of clinical death.

Even today, there is no certainty that physicians will always distinguish between real and clinical death. In May 1974, a British newspaper reported that "a woman was discharged from a hospital alive and well on Tuesday, two weeks after she was certified dead and taken to a mortuary." The victim of this mistaken diagnosis, an elderly mental patient, had been transferred from an asylum to a general hospital, pronounced dead and shipped to a mortuary. It was the undertaker who detected signs of life.

Until recently, very little attention was paid in medical schools to diagnosing death. Doctors John D. Arnold, Thomas F. Zimmerman, and David C. Martin sampled fifty textbooks going back several decades and found that only one discussed the problem. In a survey of hospital interns and residents from fifteen medical schools, not one doctor could remember receiving instructions concerning the requirements for accurately diagnosing death. One young intern replied that on his first real test he turned to the nurse for instructions. The authors remark that "the twentieth-century practices of embalming all persons pronounced dead has served to remove any mistakes from view."

Life with Borrowed Organs

The physician today not only defines the final moment, he may also determine it. Once he is satisfied that the brain has died, no matter how viable other organs may be, his incentive to prolong life is diminished. Thus what began as heroic medicine, in the gallant sense of the word, threatens to become a device to regulate the death of one person for the benefit of another. Dr. Henry K. Beecher, of the Harvard Medical School, warns against using brain death as the sole criterion to facilitate the transplant; Dr. Louis Lasagna remarks, "Since 'young' hearts will make better transplants than 'old' hearts, this may become one area where the present inclination of doctors to favor the young patient in prolonging life may be reversed."

Such trends raise serious questions of medical ethics. The criterion for death is shifted, however subtly, from whether the injured has a chance to survive to whether the transplant has a chance to succeed. Dr. Beecher thinks that the body snatcher of the nineteenth century may be replaced by the organ snatcher of today. Other physicians are beginning to describe intensive care units in some large hospitals as spare-parts wards and even see a possible black market in organs as transplantation becomes more feasible and widely employed. Death is declared when the needed organ finds a borrower—at the doctor's convenience.

Often overlooked in this scramble for spare parts is the right of the patient. He may not want heroic measures, yet, being unconscious, can say nothing about them. The emotional agony and cost to the family is frequently ignored. If society is paying the bill, could not the money spent on hopeless patients be better used for those who might recover? Such questions can only be weighed against society's need for the tissues and organs, and there is no doubt that the demand for these is mounting.

About 5,000 kidney transplants are performed annually in this country. Impressive as this figure is, it represents no more than a third of the number of people dying of renal disease each year who might survive with a borrowed organ. Fortunately, since the kidney comes in pairs, one can be provided by a live donor. Single organ transplants—the heart, spleen and liver—must be taken from the newly dead. Any rejection of neurological criteria for death, therefore, poses serious problems for transplant medicine.

A flat EEG reading may be too late for a transplant. Successful transplant surgery depends upon obtaining organs in as good condition as possible. If blood pressure falls while there is still brain life, the organ may be irreparably damaged. This raises the disturbing prospect, as Dr. Charles K. Hofling points out, that death may have to be defined as occurring before the determination of a flat EEG; the definition may have to focus on the brain's psychic rather than its purely functional state. How aware is the person of his surroundings? If comatose, what chance is there that he will regain consciousness? Medicine's temptation to write off these living dead may inadvertently hasten death.

Dr. Hofling suggests that the question of when a person is considered dead may have to be solved by setting up "death boards" with the power to "regulate legally the occurrence of elective deaths." Such boards have in fact come into existence and reflect a situation in which there are fewer potential donors than borrowers of organs. Who shall the lucky survivor be?

A few years ago, at Seattle's Swedish Hospital, a "life or death" committee, composed of anonymous local citizens, was appointed to select the most suitable candidates for dialysis and kidney grafts. Although representing a cross section of the community, it soon found itself wrestling with such criteria as the patient's marital status, his income and net worth, educational background, social and professional status, and his future potential. In some cases, the patient died while the committee deliberated. ". . . committee decisions reflected the middle class prejudices of its members and ruled out 'creative nonconformists' who rub the bourgeoisie the wrong way," observed two law professors at the University of California at Los Angeles. "The Pacific Northwest is no place for a Henry David Thoreau with bad kidneys." The committee has since disbanded.

Those seeking dialysis as a prelude to transplantation may also be screened for a variety of nonmedical attributes. In a 1969 survey of eighty-seven dialysis centers in this country, two investigators, A. Katz and D. Proctor, found that great emphasis was placed by the doctors on the patient's intelligence, since this factor presupposed ability to cooperate in the treatment. The individual's demonstrated social worth was often taken into account and in some cases it came down to how congenial and likable he seemed; such people might well be entitled to go on living.

Katz and Proctor also found that 91 percent of all dialysis patients were white. (This was before Medicare assumed the major expense in 1973.) Among this group, 45 percent had attended college for at least a year (compared with 18 percent of the general adult population), and "60 percent had incomes . . . at, or above, the U.S. median family income." As the shortage of kidneys grows, and as more people are referred for treatment under Medicare, eligibility requirements may also tighten. Within five years, says Dr. Benjamin Burton, head of the artificial kidney program at the National Institutes of Health, there will be 60,000 patients in a dialysis-transplant "holding pattern." Today, the average time on dialysis is eleven years. "It's a life-net, but life-nets are not comfortable to live in," Dr. Burton says. "Half of these people do not lead productive lives." Not long ago, a Detroit man, tired of waiting, placed an ad in a local newspaper offering $3,000 for a kidney and got 100 replies from people willing to sell. (The hospital, however, refused to accept a purchased organ.)

Irving Ladimer, of the National Transplant Information Center, believes that the shortage will continue as long as there is no money in "harvesting" organs. "Medicine is a free-market enterprise," he says, "and it is not economically feasible for hospitals to salvage them. It just adds to their deficit." (A proposal by Ladimer, by which hospitals in the New York area would be paid for sharing organs through a cooperative, regional arrangement, failed to catch on.)

The shortage of transplantable hearts is equally serious. After an uncertain and highly publicized beginning in the late 1960s, these grafts have also shown a dramatic increase in survival rate as more has been learned about the body's immunology— its genetic tendency to reject foreign bodies. Although only 49 out of 273 heart recipients during the last six years are still alive, 8 have survived at least five years and one has lived almost seven. But this does not tell the whole story. The quick rejections that characterized the early days of transplant surgery are declining markedly and the rate of survival is now higher than ever before.

At Stanford University, a team led by Dr. Norman Shumway has done seventy-three grafts, most of these in the last few years. One-third of all his patients are alive, 20 percent have survived at least four years and an astonishing 50 percent have lived at least a year. Because of the recentness of the operations, there is really no way of predicting how much longer these recipients will remain healthy. But Dr. Shumway believes that with better heart monitoring and immunosuppressive techniques people with transplanted organs will eventually be able to live relatively average life-spans.

One of Shumway's patients is Richard Cope, a methods engineer at the Grumman Aerospace Corporation on Long Island. Cope got his new heart in 1970. Now fifty, he is physically active, climbs and prunes trees, swims daily and, with the help of his son, has just added an extension to his house. His donor was the proverbial seventeen-year-old boy killed in a motorcycle accident. Although he takes sixty pills a day and has shrunk almost three inches as a result of bone calcium loss due to the drugs, he feels like a new man. His sex life, he says, has actually improved. "It's a seventeen-year-old heart with thirty years of experience."

Shumway has transplanted more hearts than any man in the world. Deliberately avoiding publicity, he stays off talk shows, limits most of his public statements to medical conventions and professional journals, and otherwise tries to keep a low profile. At Stanford, Shumway "wears an old pair of sneakers and an old green smock, and far be it from him to look like a famous heart surgeon," Cope told a reporter for *Medical World News.*

Shumway's improved success rate with hearts and the extraordinary survival rate now being shown by kidney grafts have intensified the demand for transplants of all kinds. Skin, bone, and cornea grafts have long been common. Thymus gland tissue has been implanted in babies who were born without a thymus. Experimental work has been done with parts of the small intestine, lymph glands, ovaries and testicles. The liver has been successfully grafted into the dying and, although the survival rate is low, one patient lived six years. In their euphoric moments, some surgeons envision a composite man consisting almost entirely of spare parts. And with artificial organs on the drawing board—the heart, in particular—there is no reason why, in theory, at least, a person should ever wear out.

Promising as it may be, this recycling of the human body has presented both medicine and society-at-large with a new range of problems. On the medical side of the ledger, transplants often substitute one disease for another. Kidney patients run a higher than normal risk of getting cancer, probably because of the drugs they need. People with heart grafts often develop premature sclerosis of the coronary arteries, and many die of strokes.

The cost of getting a transplant, moreover, is formidable. The average heart graft runs about $20,000 and with complications can go to $100,000. In one recent year, more than $650,000 was spent for such cardiac derring-do, most of it paid by the government and private philanthropic agencies. Although kidney transplants are somewhat cheaper and fall under Medicare for 80 percent of the cost, the sheer number of such grafts is presenting society with an ever-increasing bill. Dr. Benjamin Burton, of the N.I.H., estimates that by 1980 the government will be spending at least $1 billion for combined kidney dialysis-transplant procedures. Critics wonder if this money wouldn't be better spent on preventing disease among the many, rather than providing new organs for the few.

Psychologically, life with a stranger's organ can be difficult. Some recipients report of being haunted by the feeling that they are somebody else. Those who receive live-donor kidneys often feel excessively grateful, and guilty. Almost all transplant recipients live a life of nervous uncertainty. And people waiting for an organ, especially the dialysis patient, commonly get depressed and some become psychotic. One study of 127 dialysis centers showed that the suicide rate among patients was 100 times greater than that for a comparable normal population.

Although not discounting the importance of these dilemmas —many, indeed, have been raised by physicians themselves— the transplant surgeon is confident that the benefits already outweigh the hazards, and that virtually all problems plaguing the field can eventually be solved. Medically, they point out, the facts that one of the first kidney patients has lived more than seventeen years and five men have gone six years with a new heart show that rejection is not inevitable and that a new disease need not supplant the old. Research into the compatibility of body tissues is also making it possible to predict with greater accuracy whether the graft will take.

This, in fact, may be the key that unlocks the body's reluctance to accept a new organ. Such reluctance is known to be inherited. The white cells of every person carry four chemical molecules containing what are called histocompatibility antigens (HL-A)—two from the father and two from the mother. These molecules may include any combination of some thirty-two known antigens, and it is they that spark the rejection episode. The trick, therefore, is to find something that will neutralize or combat the HL-A reaction between the donor and the recipient's body.

The most promising drug is antilymphocyte globulin, or ALG. When the antigens of the donor and host are reasonably well matched, and when ALG is used to suppress the un-

matched or antagonistic antigens, the body has a good chance
of retaining the organ. In one study, a new super-pure ALG,
which permits much larger doses to be given, has shown an
80 percent survival rate with cadaver kidneys, compared to the
average rate of 40 percent. Dr. Shumway goes further; he pul-
verizes a small amount of the donor's tissue and injects it into
the heart candidate to create advance tolerance.

New discoveries concerning the body's immune system may
also reduce the drug-related side effects that produce malignan-
cies or calcium loss in the bones. As we learn more about the
effect of diet on transplant acceptance, strokes and coronary
disease need not be a common hazard. One reason the survival
rate will never be 100 percent is that recipients will continue
to die of accidents, or ailments unrelated to their primary
disease. But don't we all?

The Supply-Demand Gap

A more serious long-range problem is the shortage of spare
parts. For today, with tissue-typing closing in on the heroes and
villains in the blood sera, it is becoming easier to graft an organ
than to procure one. To ease this situation, the National Conference of Commissioners on Uniform State Laws established
the Uniform Anatomical Gift Act in 1968 to standardize various state laws that permit or forbid a person to donate all or
any of his vital organs in advance of death. Under provisions
of the act, the donor must be eighteen years or older and he
may revoke the gift at a later date. His decision, moreover,
supersedes any rights of the survivors to withhold the gift unless
a mandatory autopsy is declared. Physicians accepting such
organs are protected from legal action, and the time of death
must be determined by a doctor or board of physicians not
involved in the transplant.

Unhappily, the Gift Act has done little to ease the organ
shortage. Although 12 million donor cards have been distribu-

ted, it is estimated that no more than 200,000 people carry them, and figures compiled in 1971 showed that up to that time only three card-carrying donors had provided organs. Maryland and Illinois now issue driver's licenses which include space for the motorist to sign over his organs in case of death. The proposal has also been ma le that people carry cards, or wear tatoo marks on their body, only if they don't wish to be a donor. Blair Sadler, a lawyer who, with his brother, helped write the Uniform Anatomical Gift Act, states that "if we get to the point where we could show that lives are being lost, I would seriously consider giving medicine the right of eminent domain." Authorities would be permitted to condemn medically suitable bodies without permission of the donor or his family if it could be shown that a life might be saved. (Sweden, France and Israel are among the countries whose laws allow the government, in some cases, to remove organs without permission.)

Sadler, however, believes that for the United States the most promising course is educating the public to the need for organs and the social advantages of donating them. The donor card itself could very well include such information as blood and tissue type, the donor's medical history and similar data. Potential recipients—those with serious heart disease or renal failures—might also carry pertinent information about themselves: credit cards, in effect, that could help them buy a few more years of life.

Organ preservation may make such a drastic step unnecessary. Kidneys are now kept for as long as five days in a perfusion chamber; indeed, one was flown by Dr. Frederick Belzer from Denver to Holland and successfully transplanted, even after a delay in getting it through customs. Dr. Shumway packed one of his hearts in brine and flew it by helicopter from Oakland to Stanford. Logistics, too, are improving. At the University of California at Los Angeles, Dr. Paul I. Terasaki and his associates have established a national transplant communications network. Using data banks, teletype terminals search recipient and donor pools

throughout the country to coordinate the optimum tissue matching; the patient is then flown to the source of the organ. Within
the Common Market, Eurotransplant exchanges livers, hearts,
kidneys and other organs among ten countries. In spite of these
advances, Dr. Terasaki estimates that in the United States, out
of 100,000 potentially suitable cadaver kidneys that become
available each year, not more than 10 percent are harvested.

The New Miracles

Probably the most ingenious solution to the spare parts
problem has been advanced by Columbia University sociologist
Amitai Etzioni. Instead of cremating or burying bodies, Dr.
Etzioni told a meeting of the American Association for the
Advancement of Science in 1973, medicine could keep them
indefinitely alive by artificial resuscitation; the body need not
die until it has been suitably cannibalized. "These cadavers,"
writes Dr. Willard Gaylin in Harper's, "would have the legal
status of the dead with none of the qualities one now associates
with death. They would be warm, respiring, pulsating, evacuat-
ing, and excreting bodies requiring nursing, dietary, and general
grooming attention—and could probably be maintained so for
a period of years." Such neomorts, as Dr. Gaylin calls them,
would be especially useful for blood and tissue typing, since this
could be done well in advance of transplantation.

Cadaver farms are not an immediate prospect. One reason,
Dr. Gaylin points out, is that people have a natural revulsion to
exploiting the newly dead. "Sustaining life is an urgent argument for any measure," he writes, "but not if that measure
destroys those very qualities that make life worth sustaining."

A far less objectionable procedure would be the transplantation of animal organs into human beings. More than ten years
ago, Dr. Keith Reemtsma, at the Tulane University Medical
Center, grafted the kidneys of a twenty-five-pound rhesus mon-
key into a thirty-two-year-old housewife. The organs did not

take, were removed ten days later, and the woman died. Dr. Reemtsma next transplanted a chimpanzee kidney into a man who, after surviving two months, died of pneumonia. Now at Columbia-Presbyterian in New York, Dr. Reemtsma continues his laboratory experiments in cross-species grafting—from dogs to rabbits, for example—in the belief that the matching and rejection problems should be licked before renewing attempts on human beings. "In many primates, such as chimpanzees, we do know that the immunological barrier is not insurmountable," he says.

Chimpanzees, however, are expensive to catch and keep, and although baboons are cheaper, "they fight like hell to keep their kidneys," N.I.H.'s Dr. Donald Kayhoe declares. Dr. Denton Cooley, at University of Houston Medical Center in Texas, once tried transplanting a ram's heart into a dying patient. It failed immediately. The team had a pig standing by, but by the time it was chased around the room, caught, bound and anesthetized, it was too late. Dr. Reemtsma, however, says that in the long run he is "still hopeful for such heterografts." Should that day arrive, the animal ranch may eliminate the need for cadaver farms. Genetically homogeneous animals would be bred purposely for their human organ compatibility, much as race horses are now bred for stamina and speed. The supply of organs could easily be geared to human requirements.

In the case of the heart, even this may prove unnecessary. According to the American College of Cardiology, as many as 50,000 people with heart disease might be saved by transplantation. Since not that many donors are available, the quantum leap at present is toward the Totally Implantable Artificial Heart. Funded by the N.I.H.'s Heart and Lung Institute, models of this workbench organ have already been tried in animals with fair success, and the institute hopes that a human version can be made practical within the next ten years.

The Totally Implantable Artificial Heart—or T.I.A.H., as its inventors like to call it—is a miniaturized pump with a Saran

Wrap-like lining and rigid plastic parts. In one battery-powered prototype, the "business-man's special," energy is stored in the patient's vest pocket or carried in an attaché case. In another version, batteries are implanted just beneath the skin and can be recharged at night. The most promising long-range model, however, is the nuclear-fueled heart; a small cannister of plutonium-238, carried inside the body, would be good for at least ten years. At death, with the heart still beating, the fuel would be recovered and allocated to someone else.

Like real-organ grafts, however, the T.I.A.H. threatens to introduce its own social and psychological side effects. Too many nuclear-powered hearts could be dangerously radioactive. One atomic scientist whose views were solicited by an N.I.H. panel wrote, "My main worry about a plutonium–238-powered heart pump is that one day on a transpacific flight, economy class, I will be seated between two of them." Most scientists discount the radiation hazard, pointing out that it is unlikely that very many artificial hearts would be concentrated in any one place. A married recipient, however, would not be able to sleep in the same bed with his spouse.

The institute's Artificial Heart Assessment Panel does anticipate certain practical and philosophical difficulties. "The prospect of a recall of artificial hearts for repairs is, to say the least, disturbing," the panel points out. Expense is a factor, and the nuclear fuel might have to be financed through a bank or loan company. The fatal heart attack, considered a boon to many who have reached old age, would no longer take place, providing "a much greater probability of a lingering and painful death." And should Medicare do for the heart what it does for kidneys, cost would be enormous. The public may look to government as the giver of life itself.

More problematical is the effect of the T.I.A.H. on one's sense of identity. With technology implanted at the very center of man's bosom, would the fundamental symbolic role of the human heart be altered? The panel suggests that it might, and cites what it calls the Tin Woodsman syndrome, referring to the character in *The Wizard of Oz* who fell into a depression while searching for a real heart.

Organ transplants hold out the tempting promise of eternal life, but would man lose something in this Faustian bargain? Theologians, if not physicians, are inclined to think so. From an idolatry of the whole body, they say, we have moved to an idolatry of its individual parts. Life is reduced to a set of replaceable functions. Man needs a sense of closure on his life. If obsession over "staying alive" by all means supplants the deeper meaning of life, man can never experience the transcendence that guides the spiritual side of his nature. It is only when we accept the inevitability of death that we attain meaning and balance in our lives. In performing miracles on the dying, the radical Catholic priest Ivan Illich has said, modern medicine is depriving man of a natural vision of death. And it is this vision, he thinks, that adds meaning to a life that is more than mere biological existence.

THE AMERICAN COLLEGE OF SURGEONS MAINTAINS A TRANSPLANT REGISTRY. AS OF JULY 1, 1975, THE FOLLOWING NUMBER OF OPERATIONS AND THEIR OUTCOMES HAD BEEN REPORTED TO THE REGISTRY.

	HEART	LIVER	LUNG	PANCREAS	KIDNEY
Teams	64	40	21	15	296
Transplants	280	238	36	46	21,803
Recipients	273	229	36	45	19,637
Still living	49	23	0	3	9,000 (approx.)
Longest survival	6.7 yrs.	5.9 yrs.	10 mos.	3 yrs.	19 yrs.
Longest current survival	6.7 yrs.	5.9 yrs.	0 mo.	3 yrs.	19 yrs.

CHAPTER III

The Search for Longevity

IF WE ARE not yet ready for composite man, is it possible to extend human life by ordinary rather than heroic measures?

In April 1970, experts in the fields of gerontology, biology and the behavioral sciences met in Santa Barbara, California, to explore this possibility. Sponsored by the Center for the Study of Democratic Institutions, Project Life Span concluded that by 1990 an additional decade of "healthy and alert life" would be possible for everyone.

The biological time clock has already been set back through better nutrition, medical care and an improved environment. From 1960 to 1970, the proportion of old people in this country grew nearly twice as fast as the total population, and those seventy-five and older increased at three times this rate. By the end of the century, almost a quarter of the total population will be sixty-five years and older.

Project Life Span sees this as just a beginning. A better understanding of the aging process and, possibly, biological manipulation of human genes, raises the prospect that, strictly speaking, no one need ever die of old age. Dr. Alex Comfort, the leader of the conference, believes that even a small breakthrough would open up new discoveries that might give people a normal life-span of 100 to 120 years. In the words of one participant, ". . . the prospect of eternal life would begin to glow on the horizon. . . . It is no longer strictly in the realm of science fiction to contemplate a time when one would need to request permission to die."

Already, in remote enclaves around the world, an astonishing number of people "beat the averages" and outlive most of us by many years. In 1971, Dr. Alexander Leaf, of the Harvard Medical School, visited three such regions: in Ecuador, Hunza and Russian Georgia. High in the mountains, in the village of Vilcabamba, Ecuador, he found that 16.4 percent of the aged population lived to be sixty or more, compared with 6.4 percent in rural Ecuador as a whole. One man was 121 years old. In all cases, since these villagers were Christians of European descent, age was verified by baptismal certificates in the local church. The significance of these figures can be seen if they are measured against life expectancy in our own country. Although taken as a whole, this expectancy is still much lower than in the United States, once a citizen of Vilcabamba has survived the struggles and diseases of youth and middle age, his chances of living to be 100 is about 1 percent, far in excess of the seven out of 100,000 who live to be centenarians in the United States. While our elderly people die chiefly of heart disease and cancer, a disproportionate number of Vilcabambans seem to go on living until they literally wear out.

Why this should be is puzzling. Dr. Leaf points out that rural Ecuadorans "live without benefit of modern sanitation, cleanliness or medical care." Many of them bathe once every two years, and one man had gone ten years without a bath. Chickens and pigs share their primitive living quarters. For the most part the men are heavy smokers, although there is some question about how much they inhale. On the other hand, they are universally hard-working, and despite the altitude—4,500 feet—spend much of their day scratching a living from the mountain soil. Scientists from Quito who studied this unique group also found that most elderly adults averaged no more than 1,200 calories of food a day, a minimal diet by our standards. Perhaps more important, this diet was extremely low in animal fat and protein; cereals were the main staple. On the whole, Vilcabambans had been toughened by years of physical labor right up to the end; disease had eliminated the weak. Those who survived did so with a vengeance.

Another group of centenarians studied by Leaf live in Hunza, a principality "hidden among the towering peaks of the Karakorum Range" on Pakistan's border with China and Afghanistan. Leaf describes Hunza as "one of the most inaccessible places on the earth." These people, too, work at high altitudes, possibly strengthening the heart muscle to almost superhuman capacity so that it remains healthy far beyond the normal span. Their diet is very low in meat and dairy products. Dr. Leaf speculated, however, that their longevity is the result of genetic isolation from the outside world; generations of inbreeding among a small, homogeneous group of people had suppressed the "bad" genes that are life-shortening and produced, in effect, a race of superannuated men and women. Extreme old age, in this case, could be the outcome of natural selection.

This was not the case in Dr. Leaf's third area of study, Abkhasia, on the shores of the Black Sea. Here, a heady mixture of Georgians, Russians, Jews, Armenians and Turks exhibit remarkable longevity, and for the Caucasus as a whole the figure is scarcely less impressive. According to G. Z. Pitzkhelauri, head of the Gerontological Center in the Republic of Georgia, the 1970 census places the number of centenarians for the entire Caucasus at between 4,500 and 5,000. In Georgia, 39 out of every 100,000 people live to be 100; in Azerbaijan, the figure is 63 per 100,000 or nine times the American rate.

Because the Caucasus historically has assimilated many races from both East and West, genetic isolation is probably not an important factor in longevity. Nor does the diet of these people match the other groups in frugality. They do, however, maintain an active physical regimen. Furthermore, the proportion of elderly people increased at higher altitudes. At sea level, for example, the incidence of atherosclerosis was twice that found in the mountains.

Perhaps the most important impression that Dr. Leaf gained from his three visits, however, concerns not biological but social factors. For one thing, the inhabitants of these remote farms and villages are unaffected by the stress of modern life. War and political tensions are largely unknown. Competition and aggressiveness play a small part in their lives. The people are remarkably even tempered and optimistic. But even more crucial, in Dr. Leaf's view, is the role of elderly citizens in their society. They live at home rather than in institutional storage bins. Pitzkhelauri reports that of 15,000 persons over eighty whose records he followed, more than 70 percent maintained active lives, often doing physical labor on the state or collective farms. Like the very old in Ecuador and Hunza, the Caucasians "continue to be contributing, productive members of society . . . there is no fixed retirement age." Equally important, in Pitzkhelauri's research, is the factor of marriage. The fact of being married, and a prolonged sex life, seem to go hand in hand with extreme old age.

The Limits of Longevity

To ask why some people live so long is also to ask why others don't live longer than they do. If 120 years is possible for a few, why not for many? Is there no biological cutoff point at which life is simply no longer possible?

In a famous series of experiments conducted many years ago, Alexis Carrell attempted to demonstrate that animal cells *in vitro*—removed from the body and placed in a solution—might never die. At any rate, he kept chick fibroblasts alive and multiplying for thirty years, far longer than a chicken's life expectancy. More refined experiments since then, however, indicate that immortality of *normal* cells is not possible. (It is thought that when Dr. Carrell's chicken cells were fed, live tissue was inadvertently introduced into the culture.) Although cells from mice—and even humans—have proliferated outside the body for more than twenty years, and show no signs of dying, they are highly abnormal, grow rampantly, and are similar to malignant tumors.

The most persuasive evidence against biological immortality comes from a series of experiments conducted by Drs. Leonard Hayflick and Paul S. Moorhead of the Stanford University School of Medicine. Using lung tissue from human embryos, these two scientists were able to grow cells in a nutrient culture for a considerable period, but never beyond a certain limit. Their fibroblasts doubled about fifty times, and if they had not used samples from each doubling to continue the experiment the original seeding would have grown to about 20 million tons of cells! This Sorcerer's Apprentice phenomenon, however, always came to an end after about the fiftieth division, when the cells died.

Hayflick and Moorhead then attempted a more elaborate experiment. They put some of the cells in cold storage—similar to the cryonic principle of freezing human bodies—to find out if life could be suspended and then revived. They found that it could. When cells that had been suspended for as long as six years were taken out of cold storage, growth resumed. But rather than start anew, so to speak, growth picked up at the point where the original doubling had been interrupted. Cells that had been stored at the thirtieth division went on to double about twenty more times. The tissue always finished out its "program" and then stopped.

If fibroblast cells have a predictable life-span, does this necessarily mean that other cells that make up the human organism are also limited in their ability to reproduce? Hayflick thinks they are. Actually, no two organs die at exactly the same rate, which partly explains why some parts of our body wear out faster than others. In fact, brain cells do not reproduce at all, but since the brain matures with an excess of cells this doesn't seem to make much difference.

But long before reproduction stops, it begins to slow down; cells become physically larger and divide in a peculiar fashion. Biologists think that this explains many of the characteristics of aging, such as dry, wrinkled skin, stiff joints and reduced circulation of blood. Even our sense of taste diminishes as the number of taste buds per papilla of the tongue drops from an average of 295 in young adults to 88 in the elderly. Nature seems to have supplied a genetic blueprint for the gradual diminution of each organ, just as it "instructs" the organ how to function.

What happens to cellular reproduction that not only prevents the process from continuing indefinitely, but slows it down as we grow older? Recently, it has been theorized that "copying errors" might occur in the DNA, or genetic instructions, as the cells approach the limit of their reproductive lives. If microbiologists can uncover these errors it might be possible to reverse their inevitability. This, at any rate, is one tack in an approach to cell immortality.

Another view holds that the body's natural immunity in later life rejects the newly formed cells much as it tends to reject a transplanted organ. With medicine's ability to suppress such immunological activity, this rejection of cells might be forestalled; and, although such a course would not necessarily guarantee immortality, there seems little doubt that it could prolong life and make growing old a less painful time.

The evidence at present, however, is that nature never intended us to live much beyond our reproductive years, and old age is simply a bonus. This is demonstrably true of lower-order species which exhibit a fixed life-span. The May fly lives a single day, the frog, about six years, and the dog, fifteen.* This is also

---

* Such limitations, in rats at least, have been modified rather dramatically. By restricting the caloric intake of young rats while supplying all required nutrients, experimenters were able to slow down the rate of growth during the formative period of development and extend life in the mature period. Some rats lived to be double their expected age.

characteristic of human life, but on a less rigid scale. As we have seen, on average people live longer than ever before. Primitive man died young, largely because of a hostile environment. Even in Roman times, average life expectancy was twenty-two years. But modern man, with more control over both his environment and himself, has extended the possibility of living longer. He has foiled nature with his brain.

This ability to outlive one's biological purpose in life, in the opinion of some gerontologists, is precisely the dilemma of old age. Dr. Alex Comfort compares the human body to a space-probe vehicle which has been designed to pass Mars "but has no further built-in instructions once it has done so, and no components specifically produced to last longer than that." It will travel on, he notes, but its guidance and control mechanisms steadily fail, "and this failure of homeostasis, or self-righting, is exactly what we see in the aging organism." Human beings have extended life beyond its evolutionary need—extended it, so to speak, into a vacuum. Unlike youth and the middle years, old age seems to have no intrinsic meaning. Old people simply get in the way.

Comfort's thesis is by no means accepted by many other professionals. The problem, they say, is as much social as biological, for social activity, as we have seen in the case of the centenarians of Hunza and the Caucasus, seems to have distinct physical benefits. One biologist, Harry Sobel, believes that even the individual cells—especially those of the nervous system and the brain—are stimulated by our everyday actions. When stimulation falls off, when there are insufficient challenges (in the form of new experiences, for instance), the functioning of these cells declines.

This may be one reason why sedentary people tend to live generally shorter lives than more active people. "Exercise is the closest thing to an antiaging pill now available," one gerontologist maintains. Experiments with healthy, young volunteers who were immobilized for six to eight weeks showed that the body became increasingly weaker, that muscle weight was lost while fat was added. Among the elderly, a vigorous program of exercise for one hour, three times a week, resulted in improved circulation and lower blood pressure. Golfers have long known that one's ability to drive the ball far does not diminish with age, provided one plays regularly. And most of us have learned that in our daily lives fatigue is more likely to occur from doing too little, rather than too much.

Social involvement can also reduce the physical effects of aging. For many elderly people, senescence results from lack of stimulation or contact with others. And in our society this tends to be the case. No longer employed, often segregated, the aged are usually pushed out of the mainstream of life, and the result is physical, as well as mental, deterioration. (Of course, physical changes which have little relationship to lifestyle do take place; a narrowing of the blood vessels in the brain due to atherosclerosis diminishes intellectual vigor. But even these changes need not be wholly irreversible; witness the stroke victim who learns to talk again.) One approach to the prolongation of human life, therefore, would seem to depend on a change in social attitudes—a change that would enable the aged to retain their self-esteem and their identity as contributing members of the community.

The challenge theory receives convincing support from our observations of people who do remain vigorous and creative well into their eighties and nineties. The spry old man who chops wood at ninety and the woman who bakes apple pies at eighty-seven is lmost always an individual with a zest for life and a role to play. Emotionally, too, they are needed, and appreciated. They receive warm and positive feedback. Of course, it can be said that they might still go on living if they were sickly and inactive, but the evidence points to the fact that much sickliness in the elderly is the direct result of lack of stimulation and challenge.

Jung believed that to grow old was not to decline but to

mature. Ideally, we should get smarter because we have accumulated a larger store of experience. Dissection of the brains of people who died at seventy or later reveals exactly the same number of neurons as in the young person of twenty-five. Whether these are used as effectively among the old is another matter. The physiology, at least, is reasonably unimpaired. Verdi composed *Otello* at seventy-three and *Falstaff* at seventy-nine. Goethe wrote the second part of *Faust* between seventy and eighty. Galileo at seventy-four was still contributing valuable scientific information to his time. G. B. Shaw, a "superman" whose own conception of the Life Force anticipated, in a highly speculative vein, much of today's thinking about the immortality of the human psyche, was still writing plays at ninety. These titans were, above all, intellectual woodchoppers.

But how applicable to the average person is this kind of data? Few of us are Goethes or Shaws. Is there some special combination of factors that enables genius to prolong creativity while the rest of us wither on the vine? Or, barring accident and disease, is genius itself a guarantor of long life? This is highly unlikely. What does seem to be true is that we have a better chance of living longer if we work longer. Dr. Roy M. Hamlin, a research psychologist at the Danville, Illinois, Veterans Administration Hospital, thinks that by staying at some kind of job beyond retirement age people retain a sense of competence, which in turn lengthens life. If a person keeps on working to the age of 100, Dr. Hamlin theorizes, he may live to be 120 to 140 years old.

In 1955, the National Institutes of Health intensively studied a group of healthy elderly men whose mean age was 71.5 years. Some of the major findings are worth noting here:

The body's metabolism and blood circulation in the brain showed little if any relationship to chronological age or duration of life as such. In this respect, most of the men examined did not differ significantly from a group of normal men fifty years younger. When blood flow and the consumption of oxygen were reduced, it could be attributed to arteriosclerosis. But this condition is far from inevitable, and the brain itself does not seem to undergo organic changes as we grow older.

The EEG rate, however, did slow down somewhat, regardless of health. Older people put out less electrical energy; in the case of the elderly men, however, this did not seem to affect their "mental flexibility and alertness."

In one respect, verbal intelligence, these men were significantly superior to young adults. They were more articulate, more logical in their thinking about the everyday world. What psychologists call psychomotor and perceptual ability, however, had declined. Reflexes and ability to respond to external cues undoubtedly slow down as we grow old. Physicians at N.I.H. think this is not necessarily the consequence of physical aging, but rather the result of extraneous factors: in some cases, high blood pressure, in others, a change in the environment as elderly people experience fewer challenges and social contacts.

Much of what we now describe as old age has no real meaning. We are not even sure how to label it. The Social Security Administration variously refers to the elderly as senior citizens, older folks, the aged, and older Americans. The euphemism Golden Years is often used by the promoters of retirement communities. The American Association of Retired People accepts applicants for membership at fifty-five. Many localities give discounts on buses, and a reduction in taxes, when a person reaches sixty, thus officially defining old age at this point. Yet a good many men and women of sixty are just getting their second wind.

Predicting Longevity

People can be chronologically old but functionally young, and this tells us something about how many more years are left for them. Dr. Erdman B. Palmore and his associates at Duke University Center for The Study of Aging and Human Development studied 268 "normally healthy community volunteers" for thirteen years. Their ages ranged from sixty to ninety-four. At the end of the period, 121 subjects had died. By measuring certain characteristics of both the deceased and the survivors, Palmore devised a longevity index. What he found was that physical condition had a great deal less influence on life expectancy than did psychological and social factors. He was able, in effect, to predict longevity in a far more accurate fashion than is now done by the actuarial tables used by life insurance companies, who base their predictions almost solely on the basis of physical health.

The most important predictor, of course, was the person's age at the time of the initial interview. In short, a man of seventy could expect to live a greater number of years than a man who had already reached eighty. General good health proved to be a reliable sign. Use of tobacco made a significant difference for people between sixty to sixty-nine, but not for those seventy and over. A man who survived tobacco until that age might just as well go on smoking. For men, physical functioning had little effect, although for women up to age sixty-nine this was the single most important indicator of how long she would live.

Did a person's income make a difference? Very little. High-paid and low-paid people showed no variations in life expectancy. What did matter, Palmore found, were the nonmaterial rewards of a job, what he calls work satisfaction. An eighty-one-year-old white man who could be expected to live another 5.6 years according to the life insurance tables rated "highest possible" on his work satisfaction. Palmore's equation predicted he would live 9.5 years. He actually lived another 11.6 years, more than double the actuarial prediction.

By eliminating the current age of his subjects, and concentrating on the remaining factors, Palmore worked out a longevity quotient that was even more accurate. He found that "performance intelligence"—the ability to do things well—leisure activities, work satisfaction and overall happiness proved more important than physical health, exercise or the use of tobacco. In sum, "a useful and satisfying role and a cheerful and contented view of life" were the best guarantees of outliving the actuarial predictions.

Palmore's final conclusion was that heredity by itself tells us almost nothing about our chances of outwitting Father Time. By comparing the survival rate of his subjects with the ages at which their parents died, he found virtually no correlation, contrary to the popularly held view that the best way to live to be eighty-five is to have a father who lived to be ninety. This bit of folklore was also challenged in an extensive study made by the Institute of Gerontology of the USSR Academy of Medical Sciences at Kiev. Of the 40,000 superannuated individuals aged 80 to 100 who were studied by the institute, fewer than half had blood relatives who had reached extreme old age.

Before we accept these findings as the last word on the subject, however, it should be noted that not all researchers arrive at similar results. A study by the Veterans Administration Outpatient Clinic in Boston, using 149 veterans of the Spanish-American War, indicated that heredity may be an important factor in long life. These men, ranging from seventy-two to ninety-two, reported parents who died, on the average, at seventy (fathers) and seventy-two (mothers). These parents had been born when life expectancy was under forty.

Educational level, social class and marital status were also found to enter in. Sixty-eight percent of the veterans were in skilled, white-collar or other categories, and 92 percent were married, although only 60 percent were currently living with their spouses. The genetic factor at work, according to the author of the study, Charles L. Rose, may not be physical but mental. An above-average IQ would account for the higher educational level, which in turn would reflect the occupational and socioeconomic standing. These factors are also associated with an environment favoring longevity. Perhaps these linkages

are more applicable to the United States than Ecuador or
Georgian Russia. In any case, Rose's study indicates that there
is more than one way to live to be 100.

Old Age and the Spark of Life

When organs cease to function, death comes physiologically.
But before that—sometimes long before—the person we knew
has already begun to surrender the qualities that made him
human. The spark of life, the pilot light in all of us, has gone
out even though bodily functions go on. Today, a few farsighted
physicians and psychiatrists are treating not only the physical
process of aging, but this lingering flame of the self. In this
opaque region, impervious to X-ray and IV tubes, the final secret
of death may be unlocked.

A generation or two ago, death was so thoroughly physical
that any effort to equate it with a state of mind or a spiritual
reality would have been viewed as little more than wishful
thinking. The insights of psychoanalysis have already shown us
how untrue this mind-body dualism is for the functioning person. Psychoanalysis began as a scientific investigation of the
unconscious and demonic forces of the mind on behavior. Later,
it came to realize that these same influences profoundly affect
physical health. Certain types of ulcers are said to be psychosomatic; so is fatigue. Some medical researchers even believe
that proneness to cancer can be traced largely to psychological
stress. It is almost certain that the body's natural resistance to
disease is weakened by a sense of hopelessness. Pining away, or
the broken-heart syndrome, common to nineteenth-century
young women, represented the body's surrender to an emotional
defeat.

Is the converse true? Can people prolong their lives beyond
a somatic limit through sheer willpower? That this is apparently
so was brought home to me dramatically in the case of a friend
who died of lung cancer. Always a man of great perseverance,

when death was inevitable he fought it off with remarkable courage. Bedridden for the last seven months of his life, he strove to complete a book he was writing. It was finished four days before he died, on the morning he entered the hospital for the last time. The doctors had written him off months earlier.

A man in our community was diagnosed as having an advanced case of Hodgkin's disease. Unlike many physicians, his doctor made no effort to conceal the severity of the illness, and the patient set about putting his affairs in order. "It will take me about six months," he said. His biggest problem was his wife, a highly dependent person who needed time to prepare herself for widowhood. The man's business was liquidated, a trust fund set up for his family, and a small apartment located into which the wife could move when the time came. Everything was done with an eye toward making her comfortable and financially secure. At the end of six months, this man entered the hospital and died, but one wonders if he would have lived a year, say, if that much time had been necessary to complete his personal affairs.

Such incidents might be dismissed as coincidence, but evidence points to the contrary. In a survey of the death dates of more than 1,200 famous Americans, the sociologist David P. Phillips, of the State University of New York at Stony Brook, reported that terminally ill people tend to hang onto life until they reach some date that is important to them—a wedding anniversary, a birthday, a religious holiday. This appears to be particularly true for the famous because of the attention they receive on such occasions. Phillips found that these notables were less likely to die in the months preceding their birthdays, and that they died most frequently in the three months following them. It is interesting, for instance, that both Thomas Jefferson and John Adams died on July 4, fifty years after they had signed the Declaration of Independence.

Extending his survey to the less famous, Phillips found that in Budapest, which had a large Jewish population between 1875 and 1915, the death rate declined significantly during the month just before the day of atonement, Yom Kippur. The same phenomenon was also observed in New York City between 1921 and 1965. For the United States as a whole, the death rate dipped markedly in the week preceding every national election between 1904 and 1964. It would appear that many dying people literally prolonged their lives to see how the elections would turn out!

Fascinating as such statistical indications are, a more important avenue for investigation involves the influence of mental states before the terminal period begins. Does what a man thinks about his life become more important than his physical condition in putting off death? Can people prolong their lives by finding meaning and value in existence?

This, rather than biologically based longevity, now intrigues an increasing number of researchers. By showing how mental health affects the aging process, they have already identified many of the psychic variables underlying a long life. As we shall see in discussing bereavement, the loss of a loved one significantly reduces one's chance of survival. This explains why widows and widowers are more likely to die within a year of their bereavement than the nonwidowed of the same age. And it suggests a reason for the high incidence of premature death among the recently retired. These people have lost the central focus of their lives, the thing that gave it meaning. The growing practice of mandatory retirement at age sixty-five is almost certainly a prescription for foreshortening the life-span. Even moving to a new location, one study tentatively indicates, reduces chances of survival, although the new home may be physically more desirable.

Death and Social Influences

Sudden and unexplained death has always been a puzzle to medicine. The most spectacular examples are the voodoo killings found among primitive peoples in which the victim drops dead through mental suggestion. Psychologists theorize that for a superstitious person to be socially condemned in this way is so frightening that the heart literally stops beating. We do know that extreme stress has this effect on animals, and it is not unlikely that the human organism reacts in a similar fashion. To be frightened to death is not wholly a figure of speech.

Some years ago, C. P. Richter performed an experiment with rats that shows how strongly threats to their well-being influence physiologic functioning. After trimming the whiskers of thirty-four wild rats, he put them in turbulent water where they "swam around excitedly on the surface for a few seconds, dove to the bottom, obviously searching for an avenue of escape, then continued to swim around below the surface until they suddenly stopped swimming and died." Autopsies revealed that none of the rats had actually drowned, but had died, apparently, from fright. Richter attributed their deaths to hopelessness. Finding no escape, they literally gave up. When rats were taken from the water prior to death they recovered very quickly.

It is always risky to use animal activity to explain human behavior, yet hopelessness does seem to hasten death in people too. From North Korean POW camps came reports of many American soldiers who gave up and died, even though their physical conditions remained relatively good. Studies of the Bergen-Belsen concentration camp indicate that, bad as conditions were, it was depression that ultimately led to the deaths of the 70 percent of the inmates who died there in their first year of captivity; they simply became too indifferent to carry on the battle. And Bruno Bettelheim, himself a survivor of a concentration camp, has remarked that in his unit the Seventh Day Adventists showed the best survival rate because of all the groups they exhibited the most disciplined morale, literally reinforcing one another with the will to live.

The forces that influence the social death of a person are usually prolonged and subtle, and they are frequently hidden, often from the person himself. In exploring this aspect of dying, Dr. Avery Weisman, of the Harvard Medical School, and psychologist Robert Kastenbaum, of the University of Massachusetts, coined the phrase psychological autopsy. If the physical cause of death can often be determined by dissecting the body and analyzing the affected organs, they asked, why cannot the social and psychological factors that influence a person's death be examined just as scientifically? More important, to what extent were these factors the immediate cause of death?

Weisman and Kastenbaum's initial investigations were begun in the late 1960s at Cushing Hospital, in Framingham, Massachusetts, an institution devoted exclusively to the care of men and women over sixty-five. At the time of the study, the hospital averaged 640 patients and the mean age at death was untypically high at eighty-three years. It was quite apparent that a majority of these old people had come to Cushing to die; their mode of dying, therefore, and the degree to which they "chose" the time of their death, was crucial to the study. The authors write: "What people die *with* is not the same as what they die *from*. . . . What prompts a person to become ill, enter the preterminal phase, and die at a particular time and in a particular way cannot always be ascribed entirely to the disease process. The final illness is a psychosocial as well as a medical event. . . ."

Indeed, some patients at Cushing, without visible organic disease, appeared to will their deaths. In one premonitory situation, a seventy-six-year-old widower, described as "alert, enthusiastic and convivial," declared one day, "My time is almost here." He consulted his lawyer and sold his house. Three days later he died. There was no seeming change in his physical condition to account for this, although some evidence did exist that he worried about death.

Kastenbaum, who headed the project, noted many instances in which death appeared to follow enforced changes in the patient's lifestyle. A ninety-year-old widow with extensive cultural interests was active and alert until she was transferred, for administrative reasons, to another ward. There, the staff did not play up to her sense of self-importance and social status, and within a month she died. Another patient illustrated Phillips's "anniversary reaction" theory and remained alert until just after he celebrated his one hundredth birthday. Declaring that he would rather die than deteriorate further, "he refused food and drink and stayed in bed as long as possible each day." Kastenbaum adds that the man's mental state was clearer at death than when the final illness had begun two weeks earlier. "The attitude was that it was time to die, despite the absence of serious illness."

With other patients, certain precipitating events seemed to hasten death. One eighty-five-year-old man, who was far from being in a terminal stage of illness, eagerly anticipated going to his son's home for Thanksgiving. When the day arrived, he got dressed and waited for someone to come for him. Sadly, no one did. His decline set in rapidly, he kept more and more to himself, accepted minimal care, and within a few weeks was dead.

The Cushing psychological autopsies were held weekly. Participants included nurses, doctors, social workers and chaplains. A recently deceased patient was discussed at each session in an effort to reconstruct the person's frame of mind and psycho-social functioning as a clue to his death. This information was then used to enhance the lives of other patients. One approach was to make it easier for these elderly castoffs to become more sociable and interactive. Kastenbaum and his assistant at the time, Philip E. Slater, devised a simple, yet, for a hospital, rather daring experiment. They organized a cocktail hour and compared the effects on those who drank wine with a control group which received grape juice. Neither group was told at first what it was drinking, although we may speculate that three ounces of sherry (the maximum served) will not go unde-tected by anyone who drinks it. After a six-week period, the two groups were reversed.

The results were interesting. When the patients were allowed to choose which of the two drinks they preferred, fifteen of the twenty selected wine, three opted for grape juice and two chose neither. Perhaps this is not surprising. Although it is a depressant, alcohol stimulates sociability. The wine sessions lasted longer than the juice sessions and the "winos" mixed more with their colleagues. But even with grape juice, there was a notable boost in morale. Kastenbaum and Slater suggest that what was drunk may have been no more important then the setting. In effect, these patients had formed a drinking club, and their behavior was comparable to healthy people who retreat to the corner bar for their good times. Moreover, for the elderly, wine and perhaps even grape juice is perceived as better medicine than the commonly prescribed stimulants and tranquilizers. "Pills," Kastenbaum writes, were often seen as a form of punishment "for being a burden. Wine conveys a heartening psychosocial message to the patient. . . ." He is less likely to look for an excuse to die.

While far from definitive, such studies point up the increasing role that institutions play in prolonging, or shortening, the lives of the elderly. And it is in institutions that an increasing proportion of our old people spend their final years.

The modern family has little room for excess baggage in the form of aging parents and maiden aunts. Old-age specialists have taken over this function, at a price, reassuring us that the trials of the infirm will not be our trials. The geriatric home is one way Western society keeps its dying out of sight.

Convincing evidence exists that merely entering an institution for the aged shortens life. Dr. Morton A. Lieberman, a professor of psychiatry at the University of Chicago, spent several years observing and testing people between the ages of seventy and ninety-five. Comparing residents in institutions with a similar group of like background who remained in the community, he found that the risks of dying rose sharply for those who entered a home, at least during the first six months. Out of 1,000 patients, 24 percent died within the half-year; of the outside group, only 10 percent died: a 2½ to 1 ratio. Lieberman concluded that it was the crisis of entering the home, perhaps involuntarily, and of being torn from a familiar environment, that made the difference. Their demise was essentially psychological.

Yet it appears that a very substantial percentage of those whom society defines as old do not so regard themselves. A number of studies report that people in their sixties and seventies classify themselves primarily as middle-aged, and in one survey a bare majority of people eighty and over admitted to being old. Perhaps this is unrealistic, a fighting-off of old age by denying that one has attained it. Yet, psychologically, it indicates a state of mind and even bodily health that contradict society's arbitrary classification system. A century ago, people in their sixties and seventies were old, not only because life was harder and medicine less effective, but also because the elderly represented a much smaller proportion of our population. They stood out. Ironically, as these factors have changed, the definition of elderly is being pushed further down the scale—into middle age—largely for reasons of social convenience. Whether we like it or not, more and more of us are going to be called old at a time when the physical limits of life are actually extended.

In his Cushing Hospital studies, Kastenbaum found that the dividing line between age groups was not primarily physical condition but frame of mind and the restrictions imposed by others. A majority of the patients he interviewed, all sixty-five or more, considered themselves middle-aged. Only one in ten thought that chronological age was a true basis for deciding who was elderly.

It is not only the old whose psychological situations make them candidates for premature death. To find out just how prevalent nonphysical factors might be in everyday settings, the psychiatrist Edwin S. Schneidman has proposed what he calls death investigation teams that would go into the community and interview persons who knew the deceased: "the spouse, grown children, parents, friends, neighbors, co-workers, physicians and so on, and attempt to reconstruct his life style," particularly in the period just prior to death. The data obtained from interviews, Schneidman believes, could tell us not simply *how* a person died but *why*—and why at a particular time. Out of such data professionals would be able to identify certain recurrent predictors of death.

The often depressed or bizarre behavior of the suicide, of course, is one obvious predictor; suicide prevention work leans heavily on detecting these signs in order to provide help. But with natural and accidental deaths, the warnings may be more subtle—the psychological role, as Schneidman puts it, that a person "may have played in his own demise." It would not be sufficient, as at present, to list a cause of death as heart disease; also included would be the patient's attitude toward his illness. If he continued to smoke, was this because he really wanted to die? Or was he perhaps a gambler by nature, betting on the odds? Through such information, Schneidman believes, "public health officials and social scientists could assess the mental health of any community. It is obvious that the number of deaths that are caused, hoped for, or hastened by the decedents themselves is a measure of the prevalence of psychological disorder and social stress."

One community has already put the lethality intention test into practice. The Marin County, California, coroner's office classifies such intention as high, medium, low and absent. Excluding suicide, one-fourth of all deaths studied over a two-year period showed some degree of intention, although the individual may not have been aware of it. Forty-four percent of accidental deaths were psychologically implicated; for homicides (often considered accidental) the figure was 54 percent.

In many cases, professionals believe, a person loses his will to live. In extreme form, this can lead to suicide; more frequently, it undermines the body's physiologic resistance to disease and even seems to cut short the life-span of otherwise "normal" individuals. In a test of 108 retired steel workers, this will to live correlated highly with individuals who remained active in other endeavors and found a role for themselves in society. Those who did not were more likely to give up and regard themselves as in poor health. Retirement had alienated them from life. The early deaths of many retired people, whether blue collar or white, stems partly from the fact that the goal of retirement, once achieved, is irreversible and may not be replaced by another. For millions of people, there are simply no more goals left.

One conclusion that emerges from these studies is that many —perhaps most—people die prematurely: the very elderly, because social alienation is often mistaken for senescence; the middle-aged, because they fear this very alienation. "Normal" death, in the view of the German pathologist Rossle, results from a harmonious wearing out of the body, at a different genetic rate, to some extent, in each of us. We suspect that there is a biological limit to the length of time the machine can go on running, but we also know that a majority of people seldom approach this limit. Medicine is only beginning to understand why healthy people die too soon. And in all probability, it is this approach, rather than the miracle transplants, that promises us a longer life.

CHAPTER IV

"The Doctors Did Everything Possible"

SEVERAL YEARS AGO, a publisher I knew telephoned his doctor to say that he was having severe pains in his chest. "I don't think we'd better take any chances," the physician said. "Why don't you go up to ——— Hospital and I'll come have a look at you." The publisher left his office and got a cab to the hospital, a semiexclusive place that was run more like a good hotel than a medical institution. He was admitted to a private room and went to bed. By the time his physician arrived, about an hour later, he had died. In fact, it was the doctor who made the discovery.

The heart attack that killed this man might not have been fatal had he gone to any number of municipal hospitals where staff nurses and a resident physician would have seen him immediately in an emergency ward. As a private patient in a hospital that did not cater to emergencies, however, he found himself alone and unattended in a room that now costs $150 a day. Paradoxically, he was neglected because he had money.

Miami, Florida's ——— is a large, public institution so crowded with patients that new admissions are often put into wheelchairs and left sitting in an emergency room until space can be found for them elsewhere. One Sunday morning last year, two of these patients were found dead. Voltan Jordan had been sitting in his wheelchair for three days; the other patient, Clarence Brinson, had waited two days. Both had died several hours before anyone noticed. At ———, these indigent ill—there were thirty of them "stacked up" at one time —are called boarders; they are fed by overworked nurses and nurses' assistants. Since some are not expected to live, about all that is done for them is to find a nursing home willing to take welfare patients. Little or no medical care is attempted. Unlike my publisher friend, they were neglected because they were penniless.

Between these two extremes, American hospitals exhibit astonishing differences in their treatment of the dying. On a Saturday night—peak time for auto accidents and big-city shootings—the emergency ward at many hospitals is so busy that the initial diagnosis of dead on arrival is made by the ambulance driver; victims are placed in the morgue until a doctor finds time to make an official certification. At this point not a few of these "dead" patients get a last minute reprieve.

A large New York City medical center has a private pavilion for terminal patients, but it studiously avoids this designation. "We always keep a few beds available for the recoverables; it reassures the patient and his family," a staff physician admitted.

Yet all hospitals increasingly find themselves in the business of terminal care. Seventy-five years ago, Americans, on average, died of an acute illness before they were fifty. Today, the predictable life-span is seventy-two years. Death comes slowly, from cancer, heart disease, kidney failure. During the next decade, the number of people over sixty-five who can be expected to die each year will double. Eighty percent of these deaths will occur in some kind of health care institution.

According to Dr. Laurenz White, of the University of California School of Medicine, hospitals are not the place for the dying. Their first aim, he says, is to handle acute illness, such as pneumonia, then "to make the doctors feel better, next to make the nurses feel better." And Dr. Charles H. Goodrich of Mt. Sinai Hospital in New York states that, although the physician should become the advocate of the dying person and to observe his wishes, "everything in education and in hospitals militates against it."

A few hospitals—very few, indeed—let the terminal patient die at his own pace, with a minimum of heroics and a maximum effort to make this final journey as dignified and human as possible. Municipal hospitals, as well as state and federal institutions, may also skip the heroics, but the care is likely to be routine and highly impersonal. (Exceptions are the "interesting cases" which invite a young, ambitious resident to try out the latest life-support apparatus, chiefly for the benefit of his own training.)

It is in the medical centers and teaching hospitals that dying can be most prolonged, where one fatal disease is held in abeyance until another takes over to finish the job. Physicians in these hospitals are captives of both the scientific gadgetry that surrounds them and the high expectations of their specialist colleagues; in these settings, what Lasagna calls frenzied doctoring can run rife.

One such procedure is known as coding, a kind of medical call to arms. To code a patient is to apply resuscitative procedures for the particular crisis that has overwhelmed him. A tracheotomy may be performed to ease breathing; electrical stimulation of the heart and an injection of adrenaline can coax an uncertain beat into a steadier rhythm; plasma infusions lift the blood pressure; catheters are sometimes threaded through the blood vessels of the neck or into the bladder.

Coding undoubtedly saves many lives, especially among the seriously, but not fatally, ill. Patients with reserve strength are successfully coded three or four times. But with the dying, the technique seldom buys more than a week or two of life. (I know of one case in a teaching hospital where an elderly woman's heart was restarted thirteen times by electric resuscitation, until the smell of burning flesh drove the nurses to protest.) A letter from a London physician to the *British Medical Journal* describes one such futile attempt at resuscitation, even though the patient requested that, if he had another collapse, no further steps be taken to prolong his life, for the pain of his cancer "was now more than he would needlessly continue to endure."

His wish notwithstanding [the letter continues] when the patient collapsed again—this time with acute myocardial infarction and cardiac arrest—he was revived by the hospital's emergency resuscitation team. His heart stopped on four further occasions during that night and each time was artificially restarted. The body then recovered sufficiently to linger for three more weeks, but in a decerebrate [unconscious] state. . . . Intravenous nourishment was carefully combined with blood transfusions and measures necessary to maintain electrolyte and fluid balance. In addition, antibacterial and antifungal antibiotics were given as a prophylaxis against infection, particularly pneumonia, complicating the tracheotomy that had been performed to ensure a clear airway. On the last day of the illness preparations were being made for the work of the failing respiratory center to be given over to an artificial respirator, but the heart finally stopped before this endeavor could be realized.

No wonder nurses are often the most vocal doubters of prolonged resuscitation. Valerie Lezoli, the head nurse of New York's Bellevue surgical intensive care unit says, "It's very rare that our patients die peacefully. Most have cardiac arrests, and an attempt is made to resuscitate them. Bellevue is a teaching institution and the doctors have to learn." A Mt. Sinai nurse is emphatic on the subject. "I don't want to be wheeled into the IC room if I'm a hopeless case." She added, only half in jest, that she planned to have the words *no coding* tatooed across her chest so that when the doctors prepared her they would know exactly how she felt.

Residents in hospitals for the elderly often call the intensive care ward "Death Valley," because so few who enter it come out alive. Studies have shown that many such patients experience "almost instantaneous psychological regression." With their clothes and possessions taken from them, they feel abandoned and helpless. Ironically, in some hospitals about the only way a dying person can gain admission to these units is to be labeled recoverable by the attending physician. And for a few patients, the very intensity of intensive care, at least in the mechanical sense, seems to summon up strength for only one purpose: to have done with it.

Psychiatrist Edwin Shneidman tells of investigations among elderly people suffering from a terminal disease who, "with remarkable and totally unexpected energy, succeeded in taking out their tubes and needles, climbing over the bed rails, lifting heavy windows, and throwing themselves to the ground several stories below. When the occupational histories of such individuals were studied, they were typically found to have one thing in common: they had never been fired—they had always quit."

Medicine, however, does not treat all the dying alike, as we have seen in the case of Miami's Jackson Memorial Hospital. In general, the charity patient is allowed to die more peacefully than the man or woman who pays, chiefly because the charity patient is more likely to be neglected. David Sudnow, writing of a large county hospital on the West Coast, states that most of the patients there died unattended. "Aides typically made every effort to avoid discovering a patient was dead, partly because as soon as they informed the nurse it meant more work for them." People brought in for emergency care ran a greater risk of being declared dead on arrival if they were obviously from a lower-class background. "If one anticipates having a critical heart attack, it is best that he keep himself well dressed and his breath clean if there is any likelihood of his being brought into the County Emergency Unit," Sudnow advises.

Even in private hospitals, a patient thought to be dying who lingers too long, or even improves, can upset the routine of the staff. For the impoverished it is especially important to die on schedule. Machines cost money. California sociologists Anselm Strauss and Barney Glaser describe the case of one man who was accepted as a charity patient by a private hospital where he had been a frequent paying patient for thirty years, on the doctor's assurance that he had no more than four hours to live. "He did not die immediately but started to linger indefinitely, even to the point where there was some hope he might live. The money problem, however, created much concern. . . . Paradoxically, the doctor continually had to reassure the hospital administration that the patient (who lived for six weeks) would soon die. . . ."

Dying Is a Lonely Business

Most hospitals in this country share at least two characteristics: they do their best to conceal from the patient the fact that he might be dying, and when the fateful time draws near they isolate him from family and friends.

Telling the truth has long been considered destructive to the patient's morale. In many cases, however, it has been found to be therapeutic. Herman Feifel, in a study of sixty elderly people with terminal illness, found that 82 percent of them wanted to know about their condition in order to get their personal affairs in order.*

Deception is only half the problem. Abandoned to the care of intravenous tubes and oxygen tents, the patient has little

---

* The problem is apparently not confined to the United States. Studying hospital care in Great Britain, Ann Cartwright found that "patients were more critical about the difficulty of obtaining information than of any other aspect of hospital care . . . 61 percent described some failure of communication." Her study, however, was not confined to the terminally ill.

chance to express his feelings; he is psychologically, if not physically, isolated from those around him. And when all else fails, as it frequently does, he is spirited out of sight of others and into a room in some remote section of the hospital where no one will see him die.

Researchers say this gradual withdrawal from the terminal case results in a form of social death. The doctor spends less time at the bedside; consultants are no longer called in; nurses take longer to answer the call light. At a large county hospital described by Sudnow, the fact that a dying patient had no visitors for a few days was taken as a signal to wind down the case and discontinue further treatment. Some of these men were even dressed in postmortem diapers and had their feet tied while still living! One nurse always tried to close the patient's eyes before death, because "this made for greater efficiency when it came time for the ward personnel to wrap the body."

Another investigator, Richard Kalish, made a study in 1966 comparing the attitudes of people toward those who were known to be dying and such discriminated-against ethnic groups as Jews, blacks and Mexican-Americans. He found that the dying are more often avoided, even though they might be friends or neighbors.

One does not need to be a sociologist to know that in our culture dying is a lonely affair. And the loneliness, one suspects, is not because we fear death when the time comes, but because death has been made complicated and dehumanizing.

All this seems quite curious when we look back to a time as recent as the nineteenth century. For our grandparents, death was a common intruder. Historians have remarked on the great number of poems about death that filled the pages of *McGuffey's Readers*, as if to prepare the child for a premature mortality. A recent book, *Wisconsin Death Trip*, reveals the precariousness of life as it was experienced in a small midwestern community in the 1890s. Whatever their reasons, these people faced the fact of death squarely; indeed, they celebrated it. Tears of grief flowed more easily, and death seemed less final. One reason for this greater acceptance of an unpleasant fact was simply that, in those days, people died at home.

In North African villages, it is not unusual for a person to die, in the presence of not only his family, but of his goats and donkeys; all crowd into the tiny room. For these people, death is a social occasion. Such a custom is hardly practical for Americans, and, even if it were, such behavior would almost certainly be regarded as bizarre, an invitation to call in a psychiatrist rather than one's pet dog. For the message that emerges from our own experience is quite different: in a highly developed country, people are expected to die at a level that is appropriate to the prevailing technology. To do otherwise defies the mythology of the age. Thus, to the definitions of neurological, biological and social death, we can add a fourth: technological death, the impersonal, machine-monitored death of the modern hospital.

This in itself, Dr. Vincent Collins thinks, may actually shorten life. ". . . a preoccupation with sophisticated diagnosis and advanced instrumentation" obscures whatever spiritual resources the patient may have at his command for fighting the illness. Precisely this conclusion is implied in a study that Robert Kastenbaum conducted among a number of elderly men and women who entered a geriatric hospital in Massachusetts. Those who were assessed by the doctors as having a strong will to live actually did live longer than was predicted by a diagnosis of their physical condition. They were not, however, living on machines.

One interesting by-product of machine medicine is the rapid growth in malpractice suits. Dr. John Pecorino, claims administrator for Aetna Life and Casualty Company, thinks that machines, in effect, have diminished the old doctor-patient relationship. "Without the close relationship," he says, "there is less reluctance to sue." The use of machines, moreover, has raised the expectations of family and patients, who no longer accept mistakes. At the same time, there are more chances for things to go wrong. The Aetna Company in 1974 had twice as many malpractice suits pending against it as it did ten years ago.

In a sense, the modern hospital is a victim of its own success. It performs exciting cures on the young and middle-aged which are of little value when applied to the elderly. In its pursuit of a value-free scientific approach, it has lost touch with the human aspects of patient care. "On a surgical ward," Dr. Avery Weisman has written, "even a renowned scholar might be reduced to the status of his diseased organ. He would be, say, a carcinoma to his doctor, a complaining voice to his nurse, an open mouth to the dietician, and an unpaid bill to the front office."

Echoing this view, the Swedish gerontologist J. S. Bockoven thinks that medicine tends to "regard human individuality and personality as distinct from one's biological functions as superfluous, obsolete and expendable." He adds, "It is contributing to the undoing of its own efforts to the extent that it participates in demoralizing its patients and undermining their will to live."

We should look at how this tendency applies to the dying process, at the games that are played by those involved: physicians, the staff, family and the patient himself.

The Doctor's Game

Mr. Oldman is dying but I must be careful not to let him know this. He asks too many questions. I wouldn't want him jumping out of the window if he found out the truth. Besides, I can't be absolutely sure myself; there are miracles in this business. It's not likely in his case, of course; a man eighty-three with cancer and a bad heart doesn't recover. Besides, he's comfortable. The drugs keep him drowsy most of the time. And none of us are going to live forever, are we?

It's when he's awake that he gets curious about himself. If he

would just leave the treatment to me. He's a child, really, someone you have to pamper. Why do you think I run all these tests?
Mr. Oldman is fascinated with tests. They keep him busy, keep
him from worrying about himself. . . . I suppose he thinks we're
still trying to find out what the trouble is. They don't tell us
anything but they do keep his hopes up. I'm not going to let
him fall into a depression.

But those questions! I really dread calling on Mr. Oldman.
Why do I swing my stethoscope when I go in his room? It
distracts him. As I say, he's like a child. But I don't lie to him
outright; the words I use, like eschemia and pancreatic tumor,
don't seem to mean much to him. And the words he does understand, like inflammation, are quite appropriate to explain his pain.

The family is bringing pressure on me to operate. It won't
save him, but it might help control the symptoms. And it will
let the patient know we're doing everything we can. I think he
rather enjoyed his last operation. I hope it doesn't kill him. I've
already lost three patients this month. . . . It may sound odd for
a doctor to say, but death frightens me. I suppose I see too
much of it. And if it frightens me, what does it do to others?
No, Mr. Oldman must not find out that he is dying. If he keeps
up those questions, I'll order a suction tube for him. That way
he can't talk. And what with the tests and maybe an operation,
he'll be too preoccupied to care. There's no reason why his last
days shouldn't be as comfortable as possible. Thank God, I'm
being paged; I can leave now. Remind me to ask the chaplain
to look in on Mr. Oldman more often.

Mr. Oldman and his doctor are composites, but they are not
untypical of the terminal care relationship between many a patient and physician. The essence of the doctor's game is to maintain a clinical distance from the person, as distinct from the
illness. In many institutions, it is not uncommon for the patient
to be referred to in staff conferences as "the kidney" or "the
CBS" (chronic brain syndrome) rather than Mr. Jones or Mrs.
Smith. The doctor sees his patient as a case rather than a person
—necessarily so, in a sense, for he has been hired to treat an

illness, not make a friend. The specialist or surgeon may never meet his patient until the disease is far advanced, and the bedside manner all but disappears in hospital wards, which do not lend themselves to an exchange of confidences. In any event, the doctor is usually busy and resident physicians are continually being paged. "About the only time I see my resident," one man said, "is when he brings a group of medical students in to study my case."

The dying patient is often subjected to a final, and needless, operation. One surgeon, Charles G. Childs III, points out that 13 percent of all exploratory operations of the abdomen end in death on the operating table or soon afterwards. And it is fair to say that for elderly patients the rate is probably much higher. "The procedure is sometimes little more than the last rite of a terminal illness (in which case its economic justification ought perhaps to be questioned)." Twelve to fourteen thousand dollars is not unusual for an operation with its attendant hospital costs. The elderly patient who survives may indeed gain a few weeks or months of life, but at an astronomical cost.

Whether this is the reason or not, it pays the physician to operate, whatever the prognosis. Godfrey Hodgson, in his comprehensive study of health care in this country, found that members of group health plans were operated on only half as often as subscribers to Blue Shield, through which the surgeon is paid a fee for each operation. ". . . those American surgeons who earn a fee every time they operate perform twice as many operations as British surgeons [under socialized medicine]. And worse, when American surgeons had a financial incentive to operate, they did so twice as often as when they had none." Citing a study by Dr. John Bunker in the *New England Journal of Medicine*, Hodgson notes that twice as much surgery is performed in proportion to the population in the United States as in England and Wales.

In charity hospitals, where the fee incentive is not a factor, operations are often performed simply to give the resident-in-training more experience. David Sudnow, in the observations referred to earlier, found that patients not yet abandoned, who were given but a slight chance to recover, often served as an excuse for "gaining eperience in techniques that could not be attempted on healthier patients with similar problems."

Operations, as well as other forms of treatment (cobalt, radiation, blood transfusions and chemotherapy), are often performed without the patient ever being told what is wrong with him. This is particularly true in critical illnesses. One survey of 444 doctors found that 70 percent of them either never, or usually did not, inform the patient that he might be fatally ill. The figure was even higher for a group of 219 doctors who were treating cancer victims: 88 percent said they would not tell the patient, and this was true even if the patient were himself a doctor. The most surprising information to emerge from this study, however, was the desire of these physicians to know the truth themselves; 60 percent said they would like to be told if they had a fatal form of cancer.

Doctors argue that the patient usually does not want to know, and that, in any case, it is important that he not be unnecessarily discouraged—a dose of hope may be better treatment than another X-ray. Psychiatrist Samuel L. Feder, of Mt. Sinai Hospital in New York, says that people dying there of cancer are often given the diagnosis inflammation, tumor or arthritis. My next-door neighbor, who had a lung removed for a malignancy, reentered our local hospital for the last time after being told that she was suffering from a bad back.

Yet the evidence suggests that few dying people are *not* aware of the gravity of their condition. Two midwestern professors of medicine, Russell Noyes, Jr., and Terry A. Travis, elicited answers from 1,600 Iowa physicians and found that 81 percent of them thought that their terminal patients frequently seemed to realize that they were dying, even though few of them brought up the subject. Many discover, or suspect, the truth for themselves, often in the roundabout way that a man finds out that his wife is unfaithful.

One of the first clues, according to Barney Glaser and Anselm Strauss, is a change in attitude on the part of the hospital staff. Questions are answered evasively, and conversations between doctor and nurse are carried on out of the patient's hearing. New visitors are discouraged. The attending physician may order more tests, but he makes fewer stops at the bedside and leaves sooner; he is likely to maintain more distance from his patient, often behind the protection of a mask and with the aid of obfuscating medical terminology. At Billings Hospital, in Chicago, the chaplain told me, "Nobody wants to talk to a dying person because they simply don't know what to say." He corrected himself. "We do have some people who are not like that—the cleaning women. They don't have to put up a front."

Although the rationale for concealing the truth is usually that it is in the patient's interests, some investigations indicate that, on the contrary, the doctor may be unconsciously acting in his own interests. In many cases, death represents a defeat he does not wish to admit. By denying this unpleasant fact to the patient, he denies it to himself. Society has always imputed magical powers to the physician, who is seen to be above personal sickness and fear. This is a role he unconsciously wants to believe in.

But deeper down, the doctor may be more fearful of death than the average person. And considering that he confronts it more often, it is not surprising that he is continually reminded of his own mortality. Dr. Herman Feifel compared the death fears of eighty-one doctors, ninety-five persons who were healthy and ninety-two hospitalized patients, more than half of whom were critically ill and suspected that they might die. His results were quite revealing. Physicians, Feifel discovered, were "significantly more afraid of death than both the physically sick and the healthy normal groups." In endeavoring to find out why this might be, he queried his subjects on their values and beliefs. The doctors, it appeared, were not as likely to believe in personal immortality as the other groups, and they perceived death in basically materialistic terms.

Similar research supports the belief that physicians are, in fact, more vulnerable to death anxiety than people in other professions. The rate of suicide among M.D.'s, for instance, is twice that for all white American males; 28 percent of the doctors who die before the age of forty do so by their own hand. True, on the dire, or critical, wards, physicians become inured to death; they are more callous, but it is agreed that these doctors are also more likely to become alcoholics or drug abusers. (Among all professions, medicine has the highest rate of problem drinkers.)

Psychiatrists are apparently among the most fearful of all medical practitioners, and surgeons are the least. This hypothesis was put forward by Dr. Peter B. Livingston and psychologist Carl N. Zimet in a study of 116 men attending the same medical school. The investigators found that the more authoritarian types showed the least anxiety, while the inverse was also true— less authoritarian students were likely to be anxious about death. They suggest, too, that people are drawn into medical specialties on the basis of their personality. The authoritarian individual finds surgery congenial because, among other reasons, it is a technological, scientific and cold-blooded means of controlling his own personal anxieties. The surgeon, in fact, may be suppressing his fears—and seeming to be free of them— because of the precise nature of his work. Other physicians, who must struggle with the more shadowy areas of medicine, are not so fortunate.

Another Veterans Administration psychiatrist, Dr. G. F. Seacat, surveying resident physicians in this country and abroad, found that doctors who don't tell their patients that they are fatally ill are likely to be those with a greater fear of death themselves. Seventy percent of his group would tell the patient only if the information is important for making plans.

The significance of these various studies is highlighted when

measured against the patient's own desire. The great majority
of critically ill people say they want to know the truth. In 1971,
Psychology Today sent a "death questionnaire" to its subscribers. Thirty-thousand were returned, breaking the record
previously set by the same magazine's sex questionnaire. Of all
the respondents, seven out of ten replied that they would want
their physician to tell them if they had a terminal disease. But
eight out of ten said that, even if it were possible, they would
not want to know the exact date on which they were going to
die.

Other surveys have confirmed this overwhelming vote in
favor of plain speaking. It might be argued, of course, that
people in good health are willing to discuss their mortality more
freely than the seriously ill, but this does not seem to be the
case. The University of Southern California's Gerontology
Center surveyed a sizeable group of men and women between
fifty and eighty-six. Using psychological tests, the researchers
found that more than 90 percent of these people showed good
adjustment to the prospect of their own deaths. And two-thirds
favored withdrawal of treatment when death becomes imminent, "except for measures to maintain comfort and reduce
pain."

The conspiracy of silence is based on the assumption that
most people don't want to think about death, especially their
own. But if the studies we have cited mean anything, the opposite is more likely the case; most people are willing to think,
and talk, about it, even though they may not welcome the idea
of dying. One survey of 260 persons sixty and over found that
only 10 percent answered the question, "Are you afraid to die?"
in the affirmative. The authors believe that the high percentage
of those who said they were not afraid can be accounted for by
an almost as high (77 percent) number of persons who pro-
fessed a belief in some kind of afterlife. But they add that a
positive attitude toward death can also be a form of denial: "It
won't happen to me." They see this as "a very important
mechanism for dealing with anxiety in old age."

Somewhat similar conclusions were drawn by Wendell M. Swenson, of the Mayo Clinic, who studied 210 over-sixties. Using a "death attitude" checklist and forced-choice questions, he rated only 10 percent of his sample as fearful of death. He too found that persons with more fundamental religious convictions and habits had more positive and forward-looking attitudes toward dying than those for whom religion meant little. Like denial, faith is one way of handling anxiety. But this does not mean that old people want to die; they are simply not afraid to discuss their own mortality. A striking exception was found in homes for the aged. Swenson reports that people in these institutions did, indeed, look forward to death more than those on the outside. Seemingly, they have little else to look forward to.

What happens when people who do have a terminal illness are told of their condition? A few will go to pieces and even commit suicide. But most apparently become reconciled to the truth and are better for it. A study made at the University Hospitals in Minneapolis, Minnesota, revealed that 86 percent of the cancer patients were aware of their diagnosis and approved of knowing. Four-fifths of those who were seriously ill thought that others in the same condition should know. In their own cases, it actually gave them peace of mind; there was less anguish when one did not have to play the game. This appears to be particularly true of older patients. Clearly, however, not everyone should know. Dr. Kübler-Ross states flatly, "Never tell the patient he is dying. Let him tell you." Nevertheless, she believes that a far greater number of people benefit from an awareness of their impending death, however they learn it, than are harmed.

The Nurse's Game

Mrs. Oldwoman keeps asking me why she doesn't get better. Even if I knew, I don't think I'd tell her. Dr. Busy doesn't tell me anything either; besides, I think the patient knows more than she lets on. It's hell on the geriatric ward. You can't really make contact with these people. They're like little children. You know they're going to die, so why bother?

Oh, I feel sorry for them all right; I do my best to take care of them—that's my job. But that call light is always blinking, and you just can't stop what your're doing and run in every ten minutes, especially when you know they've got about three days to go. Mrs. Oldwoman doesn't need those tubes anyway; she's just hanging on.

Do you want to know what I think? I think she's taking too long to die. We need her bed. I just hope to God the doctor doesn't expect me to pull the plug—that's his job. Well, I'm not going to code her, that's for sure.

Nursing is a game for steady nerves. For it is not the doctor but the nurse who watches people die. Torn between a pillow-patting joviality and her vulnerability to the patient's anguish, she too is unwilling to enter into an honest discussion of death. The patient is treated like a child: "nurse knows best." Lesser members of the staff take their cue from her. Many—perhaps most—dying people are kidded into thinking they are going to get better. "It's what the patient wants," is the standard claim. But we have seen that this is not usually the case.

Kastenbaum asked approximately 200 attendants and licensed practical nurses at Cushing Hospital for their responses to two hypothetical statements from patients: "I think I'm going to die soon," and "I wish I could end it all." Their answers followed four strategies:

The fatalistic turn: "We're all going to die sometime," or "It's God's will." Curiously, for people who are trained to save lives, nurses themselves seem to have a fatalistic attitude toward death. Most agreed that "no matter what you do, when it's your time to go, you go."

The denial approach: "You're going to live to be a hundred." This is done ostensibly to keep the patient's hopes up, or at least to deflect his suspicions of the truth.

Change the subject: "Let's talk about someth
shall we? Who brought you those pretty flowers?"

Sympathetic understanding: The nurse is willing
the patient talk about his feelings, to find out "what's
him."

Kastenbaum found that fatalism and denial were
predominate. Only 18 percent of the nurses said they would
sit down and discuss the patient's feelings on a commonsense
basis. "The clear tendency was to 'turn off' the patient as soon
as possible."

In effect, the nurse is also turning off. Like the doctor, she
abandons the patient psychologically while attending to his
bodily needs. Consciously or not, the nurse may view the elderly
person as someone with a low priority on her attention. One
group of nurses was asked to indicate the time and energy they
would give to saving the life of a twenty-year-old youth, an
eighty-year-old patient and a pet dog. Not surprisingly, the
nurses in this survey would work harder to save the life of a
twenty-year-old, as compared with an eighty-year-old person.
But they also indicated they would make greater effort with a
pet dog than an elderly patient!

Jeanne Quint, a nurse who has written widely for health
journals, says that most nurses don't enjoy taking care of the
dying. Patients who are angry and demanding are avoided, as
are those who don't know their diagnosis—the nurse is uneasy in
their presence. Laurel A. Copp, supervisor of nursing research
for the Veterans Administration, states flatly: "We trade good
care for good behavior."

Of course, nurses do have feelings. What seems to happen is
that their natural compassion gets entangled in the bureaucratic
procedures of the hospital. "We're not supposed to discuss
the patient's illness with him," says Jennie O'Neill,* a nurse
in Greenwich, Connecticut. "That's the doctor's job."

* pseudonym

Like many nurses in this country, Jennie came here from Ireland. "In a way, dying was rather beautiful in our hospitals," she commented. "The patient was almost never isolated; he might be one of twenty-seven on the ward. When it was obvious he was dying, one of the sisters came in and said the rosary. A lot of the other patients would join in. There wasn't any attempt to hide what was happening. And then, of course, the body had to lay untouched for an hour. Here, I get a call from the admitting office: 'Send that body down to the morgue. We need the bed!' "

With patients in resuscitation, it is the nurse who must sometimes terminate the power flow. Dr. Charles K. Hofling describes the case of a postoperative patient whose surgeon decided to discontinue treatment. After giving instructions to the resident physician, he left the room. The resident repeated the instructions to the intern, and he too went out. The intern thereupon turned to the staff nurse. The doctors were writing off the patient, he said, and she should discontinue the intravenous fluids and the oxygen. Alone, she followed instructions, the patient died, and the nurse suffered an acute anxiety breakdown, ending up in the care of a psychiatrist.

As we shall see in Chapter Ten a more personal attitude toward care of the dying is growing among nurses. In numerous seminars around the country, nurses make up a large proportion of those who meet to discuss this neglected phase of medicine, usually on their own time. (In this respect, they are far ahead of the doctors.) Said Karen Ward, a nurse at Billings Hospital, "We've got to be available to the patient and willing to listen." And Mrs. Dorothy Cutler, Director of Medical Nursing at Billings, added, "Some people find in dying what they missed out on in life—affection, understanding. By relating to them, you make this possible. What can you say? A little thing like, 'It's okay to cry.' That way you make the next step possible."

The Family's Game

Dad looked pretty bad today. He keeps asking me why he doesn't get better. I tell you I'm at my wit's end thinking up excuses. I should have been a doctor. He's had cancer for two years. Thank God nobody ever told him. . . . Sometimes I come into the room . . . he doesn't even recognize me. He just lies there staring at the ceiling. It's like he had something on his mind. When he does come to, all he talks about is going home, but that's out of the question. The children wouldn't understand an old man like that lying up there in the bedroom dying; it's too hard on them. And their noisy ways would drive dad crazy. He's forgotten what kids can be like. Plus the fact that Dr. Busy doesn't make house calls anymore, except in emergencies. And the neighbors wouldn't understand it, either. Let the old man die at home? They'd think I was trying to save money.

I've asked Uncle Charlie to come for a visit. I know Oklahoma is a long way off, but he and dad were close. He ought to have one last look at him. It will cheer the old man up. . . . And I'm going to talk to that new psychiatrist in town, ask him to explain that this dying thing is all in his mind. No one in our family has ever needed a psychiatrist, but there's no getting around it: dad's in a bad frame of mind. Well, there's a first time for everything. And the Reverend Meek has promised to look in at least once a day, even though he pointed out that dad hasn't been to church in forty years. Well, he might as well get to know him before he conducts the service.

The essence of the family's game is pretense. This is why the experience of dying is often more difficult for the survivors than for the patient. Appearances are kept up; there is much small talk and forced cheerfulness while the basic feelings, the things that cry out in the heart, go unsaid.

Long before the end, the fatally ill person begins to notice subtle changes in the attitudes of others toward him. At first, the family may be too solicitous. ("They've never treated me this way before.") If he is observant, he may sense that this kindness is rather remote and formal. Some people avoid him altogether. And almost everyone wears a social mask which makes person-to-person contact difficult. Just as a white uniform serves the nurse and the chaplain has his black suit, the family members don their own masks, playing the role of visitor who must not tire the patient by staying too long. Visiting hours are limited, and one has to be careful not to interfere with hospital routine.

If the patient is transferred to an intensive care unit, the distancing is even greater. In Dr. Avery Weisman's phrase, the dying person now occupies a kind of "sacred space." "It seems required that visitors put on a special face before entering, walk softly, speak in hushed and respectful tones, be ever so careful about what is said and done. . . ." The care of the patient is surrendered to elaborate instrumentation, reducing the chance for human contact. Family members are reassured that they are not needed, indeed, that they are in the way. One can hardly visit with an oxygen tent or a coil of intravenous tubes. The modern hospital makes pretense easy. "Play the game with us professionals," it says to the family.

Dr. Michael Rohman, professor of surgery at New York Medical College, says, "As soon as you are dishonest with a patient he loses faith in you and in his family. You make actors of everyone. He feels somehow that his family is 'handling' him. Dishonesty in any kind of relationship is wrong."

Family trust is one important reason why most people express a desire to die at home. Unfortunately, relatives of the dying are often not inclined to share this view. One study in England revealed that, although a majority of those questioned believed that hospitals were the best place for such a person, they did not want to be sent there to die themselves.

One factor favoring hospitals is the widespread purchase of medical insurance. It does not "pay" to die at home, since coverage for care outside the hospital or nursing home is seldom included in the policy. Perhaps the most common reason for hospitalizing the seriously ill person, however, is reluctance on the part of the family to assume the burdens of patient care, but the degree of care required is often exaggerated. A study of cancer patients in Sheffield, England, who were cared for in their own homes showed that fully half were managed without difficult nursing procedures.

More than eighty-five years ago, the famous teacher Sir William Osler reported that of 500 deathbed cases he studied only 18 percent suffered bodily pain and only 2 percent exhibited mental apprehension as death approached. With modern drugs, this ratio is even lower. The *British Medical Journal*, reporting in 1973 on a survey done through general practitioners, noted, ". . . something like half the cancer patients dying at home had no significant pain, no suffering and no distress. Something like a third of the patients dying of cancer at home had problems, but for less than six weeks. . . . Those who needed hospital care were something like 17 percent. . . ."

Dr. John Hinton, of London's Middlesex Hospital, writes that, "the suffering of the cancer patient that we read about is often that, not of the disease, but the treatment." He thinks that hospitalization exacerbates pain because of the complexity, impersonality and anxiety-provoking elements in the setting. When morale is high, he says, when easygoing, confident relationships exist between the patient and those caring for him, fewer drugs are needed. It is a fair assumption that the person who is attended at home experiences less suffering simply because there is more regard for him as an individual. Even good nursing homes, in Hinton's view, are probably better for the dying patient than hospitals. "Fewer people are involved and there is an atmosphere of greater intimacy. . . ."

Hospitalization is one way the dying person is abandoned, although, of course, it represents other things, too. In fact, abandonment often begins long before this final stage. As far back as 1915, Freud noted both the conscious and unconscious reasons why people avoid those who are marked for death. And although dying has been "professionalized," the professionals, too, gradually withdraw, along with friends and family. This may occur well before the terminal stage.

Sending a person to a hospital to die is sometimes a form of exile. In a death-denying society, relatives don't want to be accountable for the dying. The hospital assumes this malevolent function. ". . . the mysterious collapses of patients following hospitalization resemble nothing so much as the equally mysterious collapses and deaths of sorcery victims in primitive societies. . . ." writes Prof. Philip Slater.

The Patient's Game

Nobody ever tells me anything. I must be dying—why else would they be so secretive? But I mustn't let them suspect I know. . . . I'll just pretend that everything is all right.

Dr. Busy was in this morning long enough to order some more tests. Thank God I've got major medical insurance; this place costs a fortune. I asked the doctor what the tests showed, but he wasn't much help. Why can't he talk English? He doesn't spend much time with me anymore. The nurses do everything now—when they're around. Miss Starch is nice, but when I try to talk to her she says, "Don't worry, everything is going to be all right." If that's the case, why don't they let me go home?

Well, she must know something I don't. Come to think of it, I've felt better these last few days. The inflammation seems to have died down some. That's what Dr. Busy called it. God knows I don't want to die. Sometimes I get goddamned mad at the whole idea; other days I'm depressed. Lying here watching daytime television is no fun. Reverend Meek tries to cheer me up, but I'm not about to get religion at my age. And that headshrinker—what was he doing here? My boy sent him around. He saw right off that my marbles were lined up all right. I'll say this, he didn't kid around like the rest of them. "Mr. Oldman," he said, "you're very sick and it's quite natural to feel frustrated and depressed about things. I could give you some drugs, but I don't think that's what you want. And you don't need psychotherapy; you're what I call pretty well adjusted. But you've got to make allowances for your situation, show them you're not afraid to talk about what's on your mind." I tell you, I felt pretty good when Dr. Brain left. He said he was going to have a chat with the boy. . . .

But talk about what's on my mind? Who's going to listen? They treat me like a child. I may as well be in the nursery. Well, drinking out of a straw and with these diapers they put on me, why not? But I'm not a child, I'm an old man. There's nothing wrong with my mind, whatever else may be the trouble. No, sir, nothing at all, but you wouldn't know it the way they treat me. And my hearing is still good. Why don't they talk?

Those two cleaning women, Mrs. Bucket and Mrs. Broom, they're nice to me. Oh, the nurses are nice, too, but Mrs. Bucket and Mrs. Broom are different. They come right out and laugh and tell jokes. They're so good-natured . . . natural. It's like being at home. I'd like to put in a word for the Gray Ladies, too, even though they keep bringing toothpaste. Don't they know I've got false teeth? Maybe when you're not paid anything it's easier to talk to a dying old man.

Dying? I really don't know. Maybe I don't want to know. Hell, I'm no braver than the next man. I don't seem to be getting better—a little worse, if anything, in spite of the operation. I'm getting sleepy again. There's not much pain, but maybe that's the pills and injections. Miss Starch is very particular about that. As long as they don't move me into intensive care I'll be all right. Death Valley, that's what the other patients call it. Nobody comes back from there. It's the end of the road. I'll know for sure if they put me in that place. If they don't, I'll just go on playing the game—I'm not one to hurt people's feelings.

And if they do send me there? I'll spite the doctors: I'll die!

The patient's game is difficult because he is playing by someone else's rules. At the same time, he plays his own private game with death. Not infrequently, he discovers the truth, however reluctantly, from other patients. They have sensed what he has not.

Dr. Harold Levine recounts the case of John and Bob, two "partners in death" who occupied a cancer ward in the Cook County Hospital in Chicago. John, an alcoholic from a white, middle-class background had "hit the skids" and was a charity patient. Bob was a black man and an ex-convict who had been made tough and resilient by the struggle to survive in the face of death. These two men at the end of the road shared one thing: they were dying of the same disease. "Our fingers were mashed in the same place," Bob said.

It was Bob who told John what was wrong with him—on charity wards, the news travels fast. John never quite accepted the truth and continued to regard the doctor as a parent-protector, a magical healer with omnipotent powers, a role Dr. Levine decided he must play for the sake of the patient's morale. He visited with the two men almost daily, often bringing them a little liquor (against regulations) as a token of his friendship. The partnership was enlarged to three. When Bob was discharged to be cared for at home, he returned faithfully to visit his erstwhile ward-mate. A dependent type, John needed all the support, and all the illusions, he could muster.

Dr. Levine's point is that no two people face death in identical ways, even when they confront it together. We bring to dying what we have brought to living, "the unresolved feelings from one's own lifetime and its inevitable conflicts." For many, indeed, denial is the answer, a basic psychological defense as natural as the wish to avoid pain.

Freud believed that it is impossible for a person to conceptualize his own dying—that one cannot imagine what one has not already experienced—even though a death instinct is at work to bring about death. The inability to imagine one's own death, however, does not seem to interfere with people's willingness to talk about dying and even their expressed desire to be told when it will occur. Elderly patients who have been interviewed on this subject are quite sincere in saying they want to know when their time comes. But they may be equally sincere in denying the truth when that moment arrives. Psychiatrists point out that it is normal for the human psyche to protect itself against bad news, and that this inclination may actually be strengthened at death.

Yet there is a point beyond which denial may no longer serve as a useful defense mechanism. The dying person will gradually digest as much information as he can handle. For these patients, an awareness of their condition often contributes to peace of mind; it removes the burden of uncertainty, and, in those fortunate cases when donkeys and goats are figuratively brought into the room, a degree of ease of communication is made possible between patient and survivors that is never achieved through pretense.

Europeans of peasant background seem to be particularly uninhibited in the face of death; they are less fearful of it and certainly not as awed by the formalities of the hospital. Edwin S. Shneidman tells of a Greek patient who was dying of leukemia at the age of fifty. "He took stock of his life and counted his blessings." Family and loved ones trooped into his room "to convey to him their appreciation, love, and sense of what his death would mean to them. . . . There was much talk, even laughter, around his bed." A by-product of this somewhat joyful approach to death was the improved medical and nursing care this patient received. He was no longer a case but a living person.

The sociologists Barney Glaser and Anselm Strauss have devised a more typical, if theoretical, model of "dying awareness" which posits four possible sets of relationships between the patient and those who are caring for him.

Closed awareness: This is described as "keeping the secret." The patient does not know that he will probably die, but family and medical personnel do. On the supposition that the patient will cooperate better if he thinks he is going to get well, the medical staff invents a fictional future which will elicit his trust. Probably most dying situations follow this pattern. It is not that doctors lie to patients; they simply scatter misleading clues. The object is to reinforce the person's own will to believe, to let him deceive himself.

Suspicion awareness: Dr. Avery Weisman says this middle awareness comes into play when the patient breaks through the staff's secretiveness and begins to suspect the truth. He gets hints, he may even get the message. He sneaks a look at his medical charts; he asks questions that are difficult to brush aside. Often the patient doesn't really want to know too much at this point, but he suffers from uncertainty. By being canny and clever, he tries to catch the doctors and nurses unaware. What he really wants is to have his suspicions disproved, and, with the staff's cooperation, this may work for a time.

Mutual awareness: This is described as the "let's-all-pretend" strategy. It is a ritual drama, or masquerade, as Glaser and Strauss call it, in which the patient, as well as family and staff, keeps the secret. He is pretty sure that he is dying but doesn't want to spoil the play, to be thrown back on his real feelings. He speaks the proper lines, knowing that if he falters others will furnish the cues. He dresses neatly, often carries on his work in bed. The family talks of the future, not the past; but mostly they talk of unimportant things. Mutual awareness is the third stage in knowing, and those who reach it may prefer it to a more forthright stance. Acknowledging one's impending death is not easy, and pretense on the part of the family may be the better part of love. In such cases, the things that go unsaid can matter most. Feelings form bridges where words fail. This kind of pretense has its own special way of getting at the truth.

Open awareness: This is putting all the cards on the table. The patient admits he is dying, tidies up his affairs, gives last minute instructions and may even plan his funeral. He becomes intellectually, if not emotionally, resigned to death. The family grieves *with* the dying person rather than simply *for* him.

But this kind of awareness presents problems. The patient becomes the director in the drama, supplying the cues to others.

He is the "master of his fate" and may want to hasten death (as we shall see in the next chapter) by refusing treatment. There are further difficulties. In Robert Neal's words, "How is the patient going to present his dying self to the world?" As the rebel who goes down fighting?; the well-behaved, cheerful and composed person he may not have been during his life-time?; the brave, silent and stoical individual who is simply doing what is expected of him? Open awareness asks him to play a difficult role, to find an identity at a time when the self is in process of dissolution, when physical pain diminishes one's ability to think and act normally, let alone heroically.

Yet, as in any crisis, it helps to have one's anguish shared by others. The important thing is that the person himself must decide that this is what he wants. In Dr. Kübler-Ross's words, he should be psychologically ready for the truth. But he must not be deceived. The Catholic Church is explicit on this point: both for practical reasons and reasons of faith, it is forbidden to lie to a patient, who is entitled to put his spiritual affairs in order and attain whatever peace of mind may follow a final confession.

In Dr. John Hinton's view, the truth should always be tinctured with a measure of hope. Many people are willing to accept the fact that they are dying but don't want to know when or how soon. Moreover, the physician himself can seldom produce a timetable for death, since it will be affected somewhat by the course of treatment. A few more days or weeks are valuable to the dying, and nothing should be done to diminish the little pleasures that are still possible: the visits from one's family, the reliving of memories, the sense that one is still partly in control of his life. The doctor might say, "Yes, your illness is incurable. But we don't know when the end will come, and, in the meantime, we will see that you are comfortable, that this final period, however long or short it may be, will be as good as we can make it." This realizable hope, as opposed to the false hope of miracles, enables the patient to keep up his morale and, with it, his self-esteem and identity. In any case, hope is a relative thing. What the dying cling to is the prospect that their last days will not be too painful, that those they love will be on hand, that each day will bring its own little fulfillments.

But this capacity to cherish the last days of life is difficult for the heavily sedated patient, whose mental faculties might otherwise remain quite intact until the comatose period preceding death. A study of sixty-one geriatric patients in the terminal stage of their illness revealed that these old people were much more aware of things than their physical condition would seem to indicate; they were also responsive to human contact. When small amounts of mind-stimulating drugs were administered, a majority of them "returned to life" in a manner that astounded the physicians, indicating that the dying person is usually written off much too soon.

It is difficult to generalize about an experience that can never be described first hand. And not everyone, of course, dies peacefully. Acceptance is much more difficult for persons in the prime of life, for those who have unfinished business, for young people whose careers are just beginning. And dying presents a particularly acute problem for the child, whether it be his own impending death or that of a sibling or parent.

Children and Death

Until a couple of generations ago, the young were not customarily shielded from death. As children, my mother and her sisters were sent off to the cemetery to scrub the gravestones in the family plot. Hearing them tell of it later, I learned they rather enjoyed this chore, sometimes extending their efforts to the graves of others nearby that needed cleaning up.

Childhood death was itself more common, but it was apt to occur swiftly, by "brain fever," spinal meningitis or a host of contagious diseases which medicine was far less effective in dealing with than it is at present. Today, a young person is much more likely to die slowly and painfully, a victim of such linger-ing diseases as leukemia and cystic fibrosis. Often, the treatment for these conditions can be protracted, difficult and expensive, particularly when experimental drugs are used. The experience becomes a trying one for other members of the family.

Doctors and psychologists who work with children define three major problems that arise from the fatal illness of a child. What is the effect on the parents?; how much should the brothers and sisters be told?; and what do you tell the ill child himself?

Unlike the patient, the mother and father are almost always given a truthful diagnosis, but they are not always endowed with the maturity and emotional strength to deal with a pro-longed crisis. In unstable marriages, according to Dr. Jesus Nahmias, a psychiatrist who works with children and their families at Memorial Hospital in New York, the dying child is often used as a weapon or bargaining point in conflicts between husband and wife. Guilt sometimes plays a part: the tragedy is seen as a form of punishment for not giving Johnny the things he needed and wanted, or for favoring a younger brother. Mother and father take out the child's illness on each other. Madeline Petrillo, a nurse who specializes in the emotional health of children at New York Hospital, estimates that 75 percent of parents she has observed who are not given psychi-atric help during this crisis period are later divorced or sepa-rated. Nonetheless, in some cases, perhaps a minority, the crisis binds up old wounds. "Two people crying together can achieve real communication," Dr. Nahmias says. In larger families, the grief can be shared by others, although when young children are involved this presents a problem. Should nine-year-old Johnny be told that twelve-year-old Susie is going to die? The question is not really, should he be told, but, in what way. It is generally agreed that a brother or sister should be prepared for the loss of a sibling; death, when it comes, will be less traumatic. Without this knowledge (and, to some extent, even with it), healthy brothers and sisters might resent the extra attention lavished on the sick child, the new toys that they are denied. In an interview with a New York Times reporter, a Long Island couple whose six-year-old daughter died of spinal cancer said they foresaw the danger that might grow out of the rivalry among children when one of them got excessive attention. "He [the older brother] might at some point say to him, 'I wish she would die.' And then she does die and he feels guilty and wonders, 'Did I make my sister die?'" One way the mother handled this problem was to mete out punishment with an even hand. "When Jean [the ill child] needed a spanking, she got it."

The Center for Preventive Psychiatry in White Plains, New York, handles many problems that affect children when a member of the family is critically ill or dies. Its director, Dr. Gilbert Kliman, discusses the reactions of two sisters, Barbara and Carol, to their brother Charles' leukemia. Carol, eight years of age, began pilfering from other members of the family. In interviews with the therapist, she said she wanted to become like Charles and be able to complain about physical pains. At a later stage, her feelings shifted between wanting her brother to get better and wishing that he would die and end the family's suffering. Barbara, the younger of the two, was angrier; fantasies of vengeful ghosts appeared to her.

Intensive treatment during the terminal stage of Charles' illness gave both sisters a more realistic grasp of their brother's plight, a sense that he was, indeed, dying and that this was something they must try to understand. Charles' symptoms, his medication and his worsening appearance ("His eyes looked like they were out . . . they weren't really out, but they looked bigger.") were discussed openly. The girls were encouraged to express their sadness. When the end came, Dr. Kliman believes, it was more accepted and less damaging to these young survivors. He calls this approach to an impending death immunization; in many illnesses, a small, controlled exposure to the disease marshals the body's defenses. In this case, the sisters were helped to organize the feelings unleashed by a terrifying and unknown event simply by talking about them before death actually occurred.

Most psychologists think that, although young children do not fully understand death and probably are not affected by it as strongly as adults, they are quite capable of making it part of reality. One of the easiest and most common methods of explaining death to a child is to say that God has intervened, but, according to Dr. Robert Furman of the Center for Research in Child Development in Cleveland, blaming the loss of a loved one on God is a sure way of producing an atheist in later life. This approach is often the result of a mistaken belief that the child does not realize the finality of death and that the less he knows, the better. It is true that, up to the age of six, death is seen as reversible, part of a child's fantasy world in which he creates and destroys at will. Death is a separation but not necessarily a permanent one. David Hendin quotes the remark of one five-year-old: "I know Daddy is dead, but why doesn't he come home for dinner?"

The psychiatrist Gregory Rochlin studied a group of children between the ages of three and five by observing their play through a one-way mirror and listening to them through hidden microphones. Death, he concluded, was commonly part of a child's play, entering into their games at many levels, but it was never final. "Dead animals can take medicine and be restored. . . . Planes would crash with no effect on the passengers." This suggests that the youngster is aware that death exists, but that he does not accept it in the concrete sense. Many youngsters attribute supernatural powers to the dead, who are seen as observing and watching over others, moving and acting with a freedom denied to the living.

Hide-and-seek is a way for children to experiment with non-being and death. Disappearing has a fascination because the child anticipates being found by, or himself finding, a playmate.

Halloween, with its skeletons, ghosts and goblins, provides an imaginative ritual by which one plays with and defies the notion of being carried off by evil forces. In general, children of pre-school age are frightened of death, but they do not quite believe in it; or, at least, they are not convinced that it applies to them.

By the age of seven, however, the child is capable of perceiving death on a more mature level. Some experts think this is because fantasizing about death reaches its peak a year earlier. After seven, fantasy no longer plays an important role in the child's handling of this notion, and he begins to seek other explanations, with an increasing belief in spiritual immortality taking the place of return to life. Interestingly, the seven-year-old is more likely than the ten-year-old or the adolescent to accept death as total cessation, according to a study of 548 young people from five to sixteen years of age in Omaha, Nebraska. Older children, of course, see more of death—if not in person, on television—and, no doubt, have more anxiety about it.

Dr. Kübler-Ross believes that the earlier a child is exposed to death in the family, the greater will be its appreciation of death as a less terrifying and more natural part of life. She tells of an elderly bachelor uncle who lived in her home and died, after an extended illness, in his room. (Dr. Ross does not think that most people should be sent off to hospitals to die.) Her own young children were taken in to see the body shortly after the man was pronounced dead, and they later accompanied their mother to the funeral home when she selected a coffin—much to the consternation of the undertaker.

One opportunity to discuss death with children comes with the loss of a pet. In our own family we have, over the years, witnessed the death of dogs, cats, goldfish, a parakeet, a rabbit and a hamster. For our children, these were shattering events. They were soon forgotten, it is true, but I like to think they were nevertheless valuable opportunities, in some slight way, to prepare my children for the intense pain of human loss. Except for the fish and rabbit, all of these pets were buried with little ceremonial rites, the dog in a homemade casket. The loss of a pet, of course, is no substitute for the death of a parent or sibling, but, when properly ritualized, it does enable the child to handle some of his anxieties and fears in the family context.

Equally important to a healthy understanding of death is what the child is *not* told. Rabbi Earl A. Grollman gives these don'ts for parents:

1. Don't explain death in fairy-tale terms: "Now grandmother is up in the sky with a beautiful pair of shining wings so she can fly away." Only the very young would believe this.

2. Don't tell the child what you yourself do not accept. If the parent does not believe in eternal life, he or she should not impose this view on the child. Children quickly see through hypocrisy.

3. Avoid unhealthy explanations of death. Such statements as, "Mother has gone on a long journey," or "God took Daddy away because He wants and loves the good in heaven," suggest that journeys are dangerous, or that a reward for goodness may be to die prematurely.

4. Don't equate illness with death. Most sick people recover. And don't suggest that death is just a form of sleep. This might create a pathological fear of bedtime. The child's prayer, which includes the well-known lines "If I die before I wake," is cited by many experts as both bad psychology and bad theology.

The problem is far more difficult, of course, when a child must come to terms with his own possible death. There is some indication that nature shields the very young from the worst of the blow through the power of fantasy. These children, as noted, seldom comprehend the seriousness of their condition or even the finality of death. As a concept, it hardly exists for them. Older children come to terms with it in a way that is less painful, and, since they have fewer ties to the world and less responsibility than adults, their mental suffering is not as acute.

Mother, I Knew It All Along

Should the child be told he's dying? Even though he might come to his own conclusion about an illness, Dr. John E. Schowalter thinks it is wrong for the doctor or parent to confirm it. "It is easier for him to deny his own judgment than that of his doctors or parents." Hope is essential to good treatment. New drugs are performing remarkable feats in prolonging the lives of youthful cancer and leukemia victims, and pediatricians know that children who fight their illnesses respond better to treatment than those who give in to them. Fear of death, says Dr. Audrey Evans, a pediatrician at the University of Chicago, is not unreal (like many fears), but real, and cannot be dissipated by discussion. In her own work with leukemia patients, Dr. Evans tells young people that they have anemia or tired blood, and that they will get well. Indeed, she says, he will likely have a remission and seem well. Why worry him prematurely?

There is probably no single answer to this problem but the trend in the United States among many doctors is to prepare the child for his possible death when there is no chance for recovery. Hope, these pediatricians say, should not be based on deceit. If the child is old enough, he will probably discover the seriousness of his condition from other children on his ward or read the truth in the anguished faces and oversolicitude of his parents. At the City of Hope Medical Center, a hospital for seriously ill children in Duarte, California, where the young patients are deliberately shielded from their prognosis and even the deaths of other children, it is reported that many become depressed and withdrawn.

Precisely the opposite reaction was observed at the National Cancer Institute in Bethesda, Maryland, where, in an experiment with fifty-one leukemia victims who were told frankly of a death on the ward ("Johnny died last night. He was very sick."), all the children were able to function normally, and depression and withdrawal were infrequent. What dying children worry about, say the authors of this study, is not only their condition but the wall of secrecy that is erected around them. Said one eleven-year-old to her mother, "I know there is no cure for leukemia, but at least I'm glad you told me what I have." And a sixteen-year-old boy (not part of the experiment), who was told of his fatal condition only twelve hours before he died, expressed great relief. "Mother," he said, "I knew I had it all along."

Far more important than shutting off the child's questions at this point is to reassure him that everything possible is being done to effect a cure, or at least an alleviation of the illness. But this should not be aimed at raising false hopes. Dr. Paul Patterson, of the Albany (New York) Medical Center, advocates confronting children suffering from cystic fibrosis with their eventual death from the beginning. In this disease, which begins early in childhood, daily therapy is necessary. Although life can be extended for several years, it is Dr. Patterson's view that the child should be prepared psychologically for a fatal outcome. Such an approach, he believes, provides healthy relationships for all concerned, including the child himself, who is less likely to be dependent upon others.

This view is shared by Dr. Gilbert Kliman of the Center for Preventive Psychiatry. Even children as young as six, Dr. Kliman thinks, are capable of appraising their condition realistically, if encouraged to do so. Charles, the younger brother of Barbara and Carol, discussed earlier, was four when his leukemia was diagnosed. His problem was not only the disease, but excessive femininity and transvestite tendencies that apparently resulted from an overly dependent relationship with his mother. These symptoms disappeared in treatment as Charles was induced to talk frankly about his illness. "The . . . personnel were particularly moved by the child's ability to state that he knew he was going to die. We were sustained in our own anticipatory grief by the fact that the child's new-found ability to make such truthful statements was associated with marked clinical improvement and strengthening of his character."

In the terminal phase, Charles even kept watch over his oxygen regulator. His last words were, "Mommy, I think I'm dying now. You better call the doctor."

CHAPTER V

The Right to Die

WOULD CHARLES, the young boy doomed by leukemia, have been better off if the oxygen regulator had been stopped before he died? With recent medical advances, and longer life-spans, we have seen how difficult dying can be. Having wired people into eternity, we now face the problem of pulling the plug. If machines are the villains in needlessly prolonging human life, isn't the solution to turn them off?

Passive euthanasia, the withholding of treatment, is increasingly popular with ministers, doctors and others who see no advantage in extending what they consider a meaningless existence, yet who do not approve of actively putting a patient to death with drugs. It is somewhat less popular with those who are most concerned, the patients themselves. Euthanasia has become the standard borne by a new breed of civil libertarians for whom the right to die is one of the last unresolved issues in the battle for all human rights. From the malformed infant to the moribund old person, it is seen as the answer to intractable suffering and survival of the unfit.

If dying is difficult under present conditions, it is no less so with euthanasia, which asks us to make life-and-death judgments about the value of human existence. It attempts to give legal standing to that cloudy region of medical treatment which separates murder from mercy. It gives awesome responsibility to those who are empowered to make the decisions, including the patient, who voluntarily becomes an accomplice in his own death.

Like most people, I do not look forward to spending my final days in a torture chamber of life-support equipment. Yet neither do I want to be written off—especially by myself—for the sake of medical convenience. The great danger of euthanasia is that it can be premature, performed to ease not the suffering of the patient but the anguish of the survivors.

The expression euthanasia is Greek for a good or easy death, but, oddly, the Greeks had no word for it, however much or little they may have practiced the concept. We know, for instance, that they drank the hemlock on occasion, but we also know that they held an essentially stoical attitude toward dying; and there is no evidence that an easy way out, voluntary or otherwise, ever became a general policy in classical Greece. (It was even less acceptable to the early Christians, who taught the positive virtues of suffering. Only God could call a man from this life.) The term, in fact, is a neologism first used, according to the Oxford English Dictionary, in the seventeenth century. It implied the hope that the patient would die without protracted mental and physical pain.

The euthanasia movement began in England in 1935 for the purpose of advancing legislation to "make the act of dying more gentle." In the United States, the Euthanasia Educational Council, founded in 1938, seeks to educate the medical profession and the public on "the ultimate reality of death, . . . [to] examine procedures, teaching and attitudes towards patients in terminal illness . . . [and] to seek ways of humanizing death." In the last four years, the society has grown from 600 members to over 35,000 and has distributed literature to many thousands more. One of its efforts has been a petition to the United

Nations asking that the right to die be included in the Universal Declaration of Human Rights. The UN did not adopt the measure.

Euthanasia advocates cite numerous horror stories of dying patients who are harrassed by X-rays, catheters, IV tubes and other paraphernalia in a vain effort to keep them alive. It is the quality of existence, they say, not a few extra days, that matters for the dying. They stress the cutoff point at which life ceases to have meaning. Thus, it is often argued that people who have lain in a coma for years should have intravenous feeding stopped so they may be permitted to die. Because such patients are not suffering, however, it cannot be said that they are put out of their misery. Euthanasiaists attempt to endow such action with an *a priori* sanction: Long before they are ill, people are asked to consent to their death, should the outlook appear hopeless.

The implications of practice, however, go far beyond a "good" death for the patient. Perhaps the most troublesome aspect of voluntary euthanasia is that it sets up standards of suffering that must be decided by someone other than the patient. In a world burdened with too many unproductive people—and too much medical technology for keeping them alive—the idea becomes a potentially sophisticated population regulator, a means of shutting off a threatening quota of congenital misfits at one end of the scale and of useless old people at the other. Euthanasia *could* be one of society's ways of coping not only with the Malthusian pressures on the food supply, but with the notion of human fitness. There may be a case for euthanasia, as many people believe, but, even in its limited sense, it has little to do with mercy.

In its passive form, euthanasia is one way a physician says, "I've done all I can. We'll stop the intravenous feeding (or turn off the machine). The patient isn't going to recover and the cost of continued treatment will only bankrupt the family." Is such an attitude unusual? Apparently not. In a poll of the

Association of Professors of Medicine, 80 percent of those responding said that they practiced passive euthanasia, and 87 percent approved in principle. Only 15 percent, however, voted to intervene "positively" to hasten death. A considerably larger proportion of fourth-year medical students (46 percent) and staff physicians (27 percent) in another poll did come out for a more active approach. In any case, these figures probably understate the actual employment of life-shortening techniques. Rare is the physician who does not at some time prescribe pain-killing drugs which he knows will speed up the dying process.

Almost all euthanasia in this country takes place in hospitals. And it occurs mainly on three wards—obstetrics, intensive care and geriatrics. The first instance might be called a screening operation, in which the grossly malformed, the monsters and, often, the mongoloids are frequently weeded out with little ceremony. Intensive care units deal with the critically ill who cannot be kept alive by ordinary means. If there is a case to be made for shortening the life of one who suffers hopelessly, it is in this kind of situation. Geriatrics is another matter. The problem here is that old people take too long to die.

Babies Can't Speak for Themselves

Doctors don't talk much about infanticide, and, for obvious reasons, hospitals don't specify euthanasia as the cause of death. Thus, no one knows how many deformed, brain-damaged and poor-risk "preemies" who might be coaxed into life are allowed to die, or are chloroformed outright. When two physicians at the Yale-New Haven (Connecticut) Hospital reported in the *New England Journal of Medicine* on forty-three infant "mercy deaths" at the hospital's special-care nursery over a two-and-a-half year period, so great was the outcry that Sen. Edward M. Kennedy convened a "right-to-survive" hearing in Washington to look into the matter. He found the situation worse than suspected. Nationwide, the number of severely handicapped babies left to die each year, according to Dr. Raymond Duff of the Yale University Medical School, is several thousand. And Dr. Lewis B. Sheiner, of the University of California Medical School at San Francisco, testified that "a literal interpretation [of the Biblical injunction against killing] may be possible for most of us but it is no longer possible for the physician: The apparent exceptions have become too numerous."

When almost everyone was born at home, infanticide was rarer. But the hospital, by its very sterility, gives a curious sanction to such deaths. It speaks for society. When a parent does not want the damaged child, or when a physician decides that the world needs no more monsters, the hospital staff not infrequently omits the usual feeding orders. Starvation is seen as more merciful than outright suffocation. Yet it takes a long time for even a newborn baby to starve.

A few years ago, in a Chicago hospital, such a mongoloid was rejected by its parents; although physicians could have saved his life, parental consent would have been necessary for the operation that would make it possible for him to ingest milk. Instead, the baby was placed in a side room where its cries would not offend others. Nurses, torn by this decision, went in from time to time to hold and rock the infant as they might any normal baby. They did this for the eleven days it took the child to die.

Because the baby lacked normal intelligence, doctors decided against appealing the parents' wishes by taking the case to court. In our society, the potential value of a human life is judged more and more on the basis of IQ. (This has ominous implications for future population policy!) Apart from this, both doctors and nursing staff, in subsequent interviews, strongly indicated that it would have been clearly illegal to hasten death —say, with medication. And finally, why a side room? From the point of view of the doctors, who would have preferred to operate, ". . . our own desires [have] to be separated from the decisions we're making." It is clearly better not to observe the consequences of one's actions.

On the face of it, the decisions made by these doctors were

rational; they were "best for everybody." The difficulty is that it is seldom possible to determine at what point continued life will no longer have human value. There are 6 million mentally retarded people in the United States, three-fourths of whose difficulty cannot be traced to organic brain damage. Since their lower intelligence did not show up on X-rays or other tests at birth, they slipped through the net, so to speak, before their condition was diagnosed. Many of these people are productive, most are as happy as the rest of us, and only a small minority of them live in institutions. A variety of acquired childhood diseases prove far more crippling than mental retardation, but they are without the stigma.

Mongoloids of one degree or another comprise 3 percent of our population. Because the condition is evident at birth, the mongoloid baby is a likely candidate, if not for euthanasia, almost certainly for life in an institution. What is not apparent at birth is the great variability among mongoloids in mental capacity and potential for being trained. They need stimulation and companionship, and if raised in understanding families, can be quite happy. Society tends to frown on this; "What are you doing to the other children in the family?" is a common reaction. (In most cases, one is helping to show them what it means to love.)

Probably the most vocal proponent of euthanasia in this country is a Miami, Florida, physician and member of the Florida State Legislature, Dr. Walter W. Sackett, Jr. Dr. Sackett has introduced two right-to-die bills in the legislature and, although his primary concern is over the elderly patient whose life may be needlessly prolonged by extraordinary means, he would also do away with severely retarded, institutionalized cases. Fifteen hundred such patients, he contends, will cost the state of Florida $4–6 billion over their life-spans, money that could be better spent on keeping normal people healthy. Although this doctor does not advocate killing them outright, he would withhold treatment for infections and like ailments—in a word, let them die the hard way.

This cost-benefit approach is not often stressed by euthanasia advocates, although it will loom larger as Malthusian pressures on the world population make the "unfit" increasingly vulnerable to social decisions.

"My personal feeling—and I don't ask anyone to agree with me," writes Millard S. Everett in his book, *Ideals of Life,*

> —is that eventually, when public opinion is prepared for it, no child shall be admitted into the society of the living who would be certain to suffer any social handicap—for example, any physical or mental defect that would prevent marriage or would make others tolerate his company only from a sense of mercy. . . . Life in early infancy is very close to nonexistence and admitting a child into our society is almost like admitting one from potential to actual existence, and viewed in this way only normal life should be accepted.

The problem here is predictability. Tests that reveal a structural abnormality of the brain can seldom forecast the outcome of this damage. Severely retarded children are about three years old when the diagnosis is certain, and the mildly retarded may be ten to twelve. Until recently, it was assumed that the premature, two- or three-pound baby who survived would grow up to be mentally retarded. Very small babies commonly stop breathing for a few minutes, with consequent brain damage. Because something like 83 percent of such infants experience this problem, the tendency was frequently to write off the two-pound "preemie" at birth. But a British study now indicates that it is the doctor who is usually premature in this decision.

Dr. V. I. Fairweather, director of obstetrics and gynecology at University College Hospital, London, found that babies who were artificially stimulated when they stopped breathing were ten times as likely to survive without a defect over those who were given no special care. He followed for five years ninety-five intensive-care babies weighing three pounds or less; nine out of the total did have some kind of handicap at age five, but the others were quite normal.

Not a few unfortunate children are the products of medicine's own mistakes. The thalidomide babies of a decade ago are well known. Other unintended prenatal effects, such as those of penicillin (suspected of causing growth retardation) and strepto-mycin (deafness) are being investigated. Although these drugs may not result in the gross deformities produced by thalidomide, the number of babies affected will certainly be greater. This in itself may create temptations to devise a more critical thresh-hold for marginal cases. The problem then becomes one of mere numbers, for society seems willing to tolerate at any one time only a relatively small, nonthreatening quota of congenital misfits.

The age of simple skills—the jobs that almost anyone, even the retarded, could do—is passing. Community care for these people is disappearing too. There is no longer a role for them in our society.

Eli, the "village idiot" in my home town, spent his fat, grin-ning existence delivering handbills door to door. (Today, this is forbidden by city ordinance.) Looey, another brain-damaged youngster, earned money rotating eggs in a chick hatchery, an operation now done mechanically. Looey went off to YMCA camp with us in the summer. It was all he could do to feed himself, and we had to dress him in the morning and undress him at night. Over the years, we grew quite fond of Looey.

In our specialized world, the grossly malformed and the re-tardate are quickly vetoed out. Always on the sidelines, they are, nevertheless, part of the scene, giving it a sense of whole-ness by their own incomplete existence; helping us see the interdependence of the sick and the healthy, mirroring in their misfortune our own marginal and precarious existence. With the more "rational" criteria that seem to measure survival in our world, this is no longer a practical view, let alone an ideal. We are tempted to solve the problem where it's easiest: in the beginning, before it haunts our sense of guilt.

Please, Doctor, Let Me Die!

A couple of years ago, at a conference on death and dying at New York's Columbia-Presbyterian Hospital, I met an attractive young woman whose name tag read, "Hi! I'm Betty L——." Betty was an out-of-town librarian, the kind, I suspected, who used these occasions to dress a bit more daringly than her job ordinarily permitted. In any case, a tight-fitting pants suit, neatly coiffered hair and bangles that clanked when she took notes, caught my attention. Everything considered, she was the sort of woman most men try to sit next to.

During the coffee break, when I asked Betty what had brought her to the meeting, she showed me a living will. This little document, which she carried with her driver's license, some credit cards and a Blue Cross membership certificate, gave her the right to die. Well, not quite, since it wasn't legally binding, but, just the same, when her time came she hoped people would take it seriously. Addressed to "my family, my physician, my clergyman, my lawyer," it expressed the wish that "if there is no reasonable expectation of my recovery from physical or mental disability, I, Betty L——, be allowed to die and not be kept alive by artificial means or heroic measures. . . . I ask that drugs be mercifully administered to me for terminal suffering even if they hasten the moment of death."

It was hard for me to visualize this vivacious woman in such a condition, and perhaps it was difficult for Betty. It all seemed so distant. But Betty, I found out, is not so unusual. Three-quarters of a million of these living wills have been distributed and thousands of people have signed them. I was reminded of the nurse at Mt. Sinai who proposed a no coding tattoo across her chest, and certainly that seemed a lot simpler.

To what extent may a mentally competent adult elect to hasten his death? The law is quite clear on one point: such a person can refuse further treatment, and no doctor who complies with this request will be considered guilty of murder.

One of the most widely publicized cases of this nature involved a seventy-two-year-old Cuban refugee, Mrs. Carmen Martinez, who was hospitalized with hemolytic anemia. The treatment for this disease is a series of "cutdowns," or surgical incisions into the skin, so that blood can be forced into the veins. After two months of painful transfusions, Mrs. Martinez begged her doctors to let her die. "Please don't let them torture me anymore!" she pleaded with her daughters. It was the doctor in this case who went to court to clarify his own rights and responsibilities. Judge David Popper of the Dade County, Florida, circuit court ruled: "This woman has a right not to be hurt. . . . She has a right to live or die in dignity." The transfusions were stopped, and one day later Mrs. Martinez died.

In Detroit, a thirty-three-year-old man who had lived on an artificial kidney machine for three years finally decided to refuse further treatment. "I'm taking myself off the machine," he told the doctor. "I'm ready to die. . . . I could put up with the blindness and the pain but the futility—I mean being inactive and with no chance to do anything—this is the worst of all." The doctor insisted on a waiver removing him from responsibility for further treatment. No one challenged the patient's decision and morphine was used to deaden the pain of his final days.

These are clear-cut instances of voluntary euthanasia; although one might question whether such deaths were "good," from what we know they appear preferable to continued suffering and a worse death to follow. But can the decision be made by another person—the doctor himself, a spouse or parent? Legally, it seems doubtful, and it certainly cannot when treatment might effect a cure. Such a case came to the attention of the supreme court of New Jersey when the mother of a twenty-two-year-old girl with an injured spleen refused permission for an operation and blood transfusion. Because she was a Jehovah's Witness, the mother contended, a transfusion was against her daughter's religious beliefs. But the John F. Kennedy Memorial Hospital applied to the courts to appoint a guardian for the patient. The order was granted, the operation carried out, and the patient survived.

Had the injured girl been in a condition to make this decision herself, however, it is probable that the court would have ruled against the hospital. This intriguing paradox is suggested by similar cases in which members of religious sects who oppose blood transfusions have refused them and been upheld. The supreme court of Illinois has ruled that compulsory treatment violates a person's constitutional right of religious freedom. The court then went on to declare that this First Amendment right should also apply to others. "Since a person may cause his own death by refusing blood transfusions for religious reasons, the equal protection clause should logically guarantee the same option to all persons." In New York, too, courts have construed the right to live or die to inhere in the individual concerned. "It is the individual who is the subject of a medical decision who has the say. . . ."

The right-to-die movement today comprises a cross section of Protestant social action groups, Catholic theologians, thanatology advocates and activist organizations such as the Euthanasia Educational Council, which now boasts 35,000 members, most of whom carry a living will. Although it has no legal force, one doctor, hearing about it for the first time, said, "Great, this makes it a lot easier for all of us."

Organized medicine is only slowly coming around to this point of view. A policy statement adopted in 1972 by the Medical Society of the State of New York, recommending the "cessation of the employment of extraordinary means to prolong life," is an exception. According to this statement, there must be "irrefutable evidence that biological death is inevitable," and the decision is to be made by the patient and/or family with approval of a physician. A more far-reaching declaration is the American Hospital Association's "Patient's

Bill of Rights," which includes the proviso that "a patient has the right to refuse treatment to the extent permitted by law." Unfortunately, most people entering a hospital are unaware that they have any rights at all and this fact is not usually conveyed to them.*

Nurses themselves tend to sympathize with the hopeless patient since they run the machines—and, ultimately, turn them off! A substantial majority of geriatric nurses who replied to a questionnaire sent out by the American Nurses Association believed the patient had a right to die "without undue harassment by the use of techniques to delay death temporarily." Theoretically, this makes sense; practically, it is not so easy to determine which technique is to be avoided. The oxygen tent? Barbara Allen Davis, a geriatric nursing specialist, does not consider it a harassment. She says, "I could not stand by and see a person having difficulty breathing and not do something to try to relieve it, even if it might temporarily add a few minutes or a few days to live."

In spite of these dilemmas—and a long history of antipathy to the idea of cutting life short—American public opinion seems to be swinging around to the idea of euthanasia as long as the term itself is not used. In 1950, the Gallup Poll asked the question, "When a person has a disease that cannot be cured, do you think doctors should be allowed by law to end the patient's life by some painless means if the patient and his family request it?" Almost two-thirds (67 percent) said no. But in 1973, when the same question was repeated to another sample of Americans, a majority (53 percent) answered yes.

A Harris Poll came up with somewhat similar results when it found that 62 percent of those queried believed that "a patient

---

* There are exceptions, of course. Some years ago, the Martin Luther King Medical Center in the Bronx began giving ambulatory patients an illustrated booklet, "Your Rights as a Patient." A similar pamphlet distributed by Beth Israel Hospital in Boston implies that a patient has a right to refuse therapy even if such refusal might result in death.

with a terminal disease ought to be able to tell his doctor to let him die rather than to extend his life when no cure is in sight." Only 28 percent opposed this view. (Ten percent had no opinion.) Interestingly, however, when the question was rephrased, and the term euthanasia used, 53 percent of those polled were against the patient's right to "tell his doctor to put him out of his misery." Apparently, one approach is seen as natural, the other as unnatural. But the difficulty, as we have seen, is that, under conditions of modern medicine, it is increasingly harder to die a natural death. A further, and perhaps fatal, problem with these surveys is that by the all-inclusive nature of their sample they are disproportionately weighted in favor of the young, the healthy and the middle-aged. No one has ever polled a cross section of the old and ill to ask how they want to die.

Whatever its application in practice, the right to die, under certain circumstances, finds a substantial theoretical sanction in present-day religion. In 1957, Pope Pius XII, in an allocution to physicians, expressed the view that doctors are not bound to use extraordinary treatment to prolong life in cases where the patient cannot be consulted. He went further: Life-shortening drugs may be used to lessen unbearable pain "provided no other means exist." Finally, there are financial considerations. If such attempt at reanimation is a burden on the family, the pope declared, "they can rightly insist that the doctor interrupt his efforts."

Jewish law, too, sanctions "the withdrawal of any factor . . . whether extraneous to the patient himself or not—which may artificially delay his demise in the final phase," according to Rabbi Immanuel Jacobovits in his *Jewish Medical Ethics*. However, it condemns any form of active intervention. In fact, all Western religions endorse passive euthanasia in theory, although the Protestant churches have done most to encourage discussion of the problem, usually under the rubric "Death with Dignity." It is hard to find a city parish today that has not staged at least one conference on death and dying, and the movement is filtering down to smaller communities.

Attempts in the United States and England to legalize euthanasia have not been successful. Bills submitted in the House of Lords were defeated in 1936 and 1969, and a similar bill in the House of Commons was shouted down. In this country, legislatures in three states have rejected similar bills. (It is interesting that in Florida, where there has been the greatest pressure for such legislation, an unusually high percentage of the population is old people.) Mercy killing, by whatever name, is illegal in all states, although out of eleven cases that have reached the courts, only one defendant (not a doctor) has been jailed. Nine others were freed on grounds of temporary insanity and the eleventh defendant received a six-year jail sentence with an immediate parole.

A few countries do make legal allowance for "compassionate" killings. Uruguay, for instance, provides that an act of homicide that follows the victim's own request, if it is motivated by compassion, is not a punishable offense. Germany has also changed the definition of murder by stressing the importance of motive rather than the act itself. Mercy killings are classified as homicide upon request, and, although punishable, they are subject to lighter sentences. Swiss law also provides for exoneration if it can be shown that compassion was the motive.

Under American law, such consent to homicide is no defense. Convictions, however, are rare. Probably the most publicized mercy killing in recent years was the case of Lester Zygmaniak, a twenty-three-year-old New Jersey resident who shot his brother to death three days after a motorcycle accident had left him paralyzed from the neck down. Twenty-six-year-old George Zygmaniak lay on a hospital bed when his brother entered the intensive care unit with a shotgun concealed under his coat. "I am here to end your pain, George. Is it all right with you?" According to Lester's testimony, the brother "nodded, yes." There were no witnesses. Lester was acquitted after an insanity defense.

Physicians, too, run afoul of the law on these matters, although they obviously employ more subtle means. A noteworthy case arose some years ago when Dr. Herman N. Sander, a country doctor in New Hampshire, was arrested on the charge of murder. Sander was an unlikely suspect. A Dartmouth graduate who had been captain of the ski team, he was a respected physician with an unblemished record, a family man and a regular churchgoer. Yet, according to the law, he had murdered a patient. Dr. Sander's crime was injecting a lethal air bubble into the vein of a fifty-nine-year-old Manchester, New Hampshire, woman who was dying of cancer. The end came within ten minutes and her suffering was over. The doctor's most unusual act, however, was to note on the hospital records what he had done. When this was discovered, he was reported to the authorities.

Prior to his trial, an overwhelming majority of the citizens of Candia, his home town, signed petitions in support of Dr. Sander's integrity. Ministers preached in his defense. Townspeople and colleagues offered to testify for him. Clearly, he had the sympathy of the community. He was acquitted when the prosecution failed to prove beyond a reasonable doubt that the patient was still alive when the air bubble was injected. His license to practice, however, was temporarily suspended by the state medical society and Dr. Sander was compelled to work as a farmhand at four dollars an hour to support his family.

Cases that do come to trial are unusual; most mercy killings go undetected—society's way of handling a problem medically when it cannot be handled legally. What jury verdicts, and public opinion in general, seem to be saying is that doctors should have the option of hastening the death of a suffering person as long as no one hears about it. In these instances, there is no malice, although deliberation and premeditation, two other conditions of first-degree murder, are clearly present. The Catholic theologian Daniel Maguire suggests that a way out of this dilemma is the Greek idea of *epikeia*—reasonableness or equity— "whereby it is reasoned that the law is too general to cover every particular case and that therefore there are valid exceptions which *epikeia* discovers. *Epikeia* discerns the primacy of the spirit over the letter of the law."

For many doctors, however, the question of euthanasia is not all that simple. Because death is certain and immediate, says Dr. Laurance V. Foye, Jr., of the Veterans Administration, does not mean that we have the right to make it more immediate. Yale's Dr. Jonathan H. Pincus thinks that homicide should never be among the medical alternatives. The doctor, he says, would then be "treating society, the family's feelings, their purse, but not his patient."

Other physicians go even further. Once treatment has been started, they argue, any interruption is itself a positive act quite different from withholding treatment. The doctor has a moral obligation to continue. There are today hundreds, if not thousan , of examples of the apparent futility of this point of view. A forty-five-year-old man, victim of a massive stroke, has lain virtually unconscious for four years in a hospital, unable to speak or eat. He is incontinent. A battery of sophisticated tests indicate that he will never regain normal consciousness. The cost of keeping this man alive (by tube feeding) amounts to $40,000 a year.

A California doctor cites a patient with irreversible brain damage who was kept alive for eight years with a catheter in his bladder. "Every eight hours a nurse would poke a tube down his throat and shoot some food in. . . ." Three special nurses were required and the cost of treatment for the eight-year period amounted to almost $200,000.

Dr. Richard Restak, writing in the Washington *Post*, describes the case of a young man who was injured in an automobile accident in 1966 and has been unconscious ever since. He is maintained by intravenous feeding. At one point, six years after the accident, the boy's father decided that it was time to quit, and, with the doctor's consent, plans were made to stop the feeding. Then, overnight, the father changed his mind. The son is still unconscious, and may remain so for a good many more years.

Unfortunate as these cases may be—and as costly to family or society—they demonstrate three of the difficulties that face medicine in deciding when death is the better part of treatment. None of these victims was in pain, nor were they suffering mentally. None was in a position to write himself off, so voluntary euthanasia was out of the question. And finally, none was terminal in any accepted medical sense.

The risks of voluntary euthanasia may be even greater when the patient *is* conscious and in pain. A "bill of rights" that gives him the option of refusing further treatment cannot be separated from the subjective context of the illness. In brief, the patient will not necessarily know his true condition. He might think he is dying when, in fact, he has good chances for recovery; he might be in a postoperative depression; he might worry about the financial burden to his family. None of these reasons justifies the termination of treatment. Doctors resist the patient's pleas to be allowed to die in such cases, even though the courts now seem to side with the patient.

Consider the case of a eighty-seven-year-old man who fell on the sidewalk, fractured his skull and became partly paralyzed. For three months after he was operated on, he did not speak rationally. When the first slurred and difficult words came forth, he said to his son, "Why didn't you let me die? That was my time. Now I'll be a nuisance to myself and a nuisance to you." This is an especially revealing case because the man in question recovered to live seven more productive years, only during the last one of which, according to his son, did he require special care.

Spectacular coma cases, in any event, are exceptional. Euthanasia proponents stress the numerous and well-documented examples of prolonged terminal illness—the dying by inches—that overtake more and more people as medicine finds new ways to thwart death. And, since the elderly comprise by far the largest number of these cases, it is in this shadowy realm that the elderly need be concerned. It is probably no coincidence that the Euthanasia Council's most numerous supporters are found in California, or that the most persistent efforts to legalize euthanasia take place in Florida. Both states have a disproportionate number of old people among their populations.

Old People Take Too Long to Die

When I was a student at Antioch College, the president of the school was Dr. Arthur E. Morgan, later head of the Tennessee Valley Authority. Dr. Morgan and his wife, Lucy, were Quakers. They lived an abstemious and clean life. No alcohol, no tobacco; coffee or tea was never served in their home—the best one could hope for was a glass of goat's milk or a cup of cocoa. Perhaps this is one of the reasons why both the Morgans lived into their nineties. Lucy died at ninety-four; Arthur, at ninety-six, is still active, and writing books! Not many years ago, he walked in a local protest march against the Vietnam war.

I mention the Morgans because Lucy once wrote of a friend who was senile that "one should be allowed to drink the hemlock in some dignified and simple way." The "prolongation of senility" during this woman's last four years, she added, had cost relatives, friends and friends' children "enough to care happily for at least three children during that time."

Tragically, Lucy Morgan herself became senile in her later years. She was blind, largely deaf, lived on baby food and recognized almost no one. But her pulse was strong and she was not in pain. I recall on one of my visits to Antioch seeing her husband lead her down the street as one might a small child. My first reaction was pity, but then I sensed something indescribably brave about these two people. It is very difficult to live one's whole life in the cause of humanity and then surrender this belief at the end. Lucy Morgan never drank the hemlock.

Arthur Morgan, appearing before the Senate Special Committee on Aging in 1972, agreed that death ought to be as humane as humanly possible. But he was even more emphatic in proposing safeguards for the dying. If we are going to have right-to-die legislation, he said, we also need right-to-live laws that will protect the patient.

What should be the criteria for terminating the life of a dying person? "An over-riding principle of theology or morality?" asks the Council for Christian Social Action. "Acuteness of the patient's pain and suffering? His desire to live or die? His ability to function physically? To function socially, i.e., to think, talk, contemplate? To have a spiritual life? Anguish of relatives? Financial costs and hardships of the family?" These are not easy questions to answer. Even the no coding approach—an accepted form of euthanasia—asks the doctor to play God. Other things being equal, age is frequently the main criterion; yet even here there is wide disagreement as to the cutoff point. When a number of physicians in Great Britain were asked to propose an age beyond which resuscitation should not be attempted, suggestions varied from sixty-five to eighty years! The lower age was cited because that is presumably the last year of productivity. England's Church Assembly Board for Christian Responsibility used another criterion: One important factor in the decision to allow a person to die, it declared, should be his Christian preparedness for death.

Do the aged approve of euthanasia? Dorothea Jaeger, co-author of *The Aged Ill*, thinks that, because the elderly "see an image of themselves as not useful citizens, they are likely to go tacitly along with euthanasia programs." But if the 35,000 members of the Euthanasia Council are typical, by far the largest bloc of support for a "good" death comes from the middle to late middle-aged. According to Mrs. Elizabeth T. Halsey, executive secretary of the Council, such a person "has experienced a long, very costly terminal illness in the family, is usually a parent and is sensitive about being an economic burden to his own children should he suffer a similar fate." Probably few of these people are faced with the near-term possibility of dying themselves.

Indeed, there is considerable evidence that the no longer "useful" citizens are less likely to want to die than they did when they were younger. Although suicides among white males increase with age, according to statistics compiled by the United States Department of Health, Education and Welfare, this upward trend stops at sixty-five, beyond which the rate does not noticeably increase. And for white females, the incidence of suicide falls off sharply after sixty-five. Paradoxically, too, the rate of suicide among the elderly is declining as people live to be older, and sicker. At least this is the implication of a study in Los Angeles County which showed that although 60 persons per 100,000 people over seventy committed suicide in 1965, 41 per 100,000 did so in 1970—a decline of about 32 percent. The authors of the study attribute this drop to better medical care for the elderly.

John Dalmas of the Gannett chain of newspapers, interviewing a number of residents of Rockland County, New York, found the most ardent supporters of euthanasia to be those who had the least contact with the elderly, the senile and the ill. The director of the county's Senior Citizens Council noted that the topic did not come up for discussion at council meetings or in organization-sponsored discussion groups. "It just hasn't been something we have felt was important," he said. At a Jewish home for convalescents, residents from sixty-three to eighty-five generally opposed euthanasia. "Talk to some young people," a man in his sixties told Mr. Dalmas. "They'll be glad to talk about it. You're not going to get much interest here."* What the old people did get excited about, however, was cryonics,

---

* Mr. Dalmas did talk to young people and found that the most enthusiastic supporters of euthanasia were teenagers.

freezing people at death in the hope that they could be thawed out later when a cure for their illness was found. It was living, not dying, that was uppermost on the minds of these institutionalized patients.

The alternative to an easy death need not be a difficult one. Nor is prolonged dying necessarily painful, except to the relatives. Thomas Bane, a chaplain at Grasslands Hospital in Westchester County, New York, says that in his three years there, and in ten years as a parish priest, no one has ever begged him to hasten death. "A woman in my parish had a stroke," he reported, "and as far as people could tell me she was completely comatose. They would talk in front of her as if she weren't there. I'd visit and hold her hand. Before she died, she partially recovered and told me she knew we were there. She appreciated what I had done. There was some kind of life experience that had meaning for her."

And Father Paul Duggan, of the Tagaste Monastery in Suffern, New York, says, "To deliberately seek a premature death just to avoid possible future physical pain is to despair." For one thing, the pain may not materialize, and, if it does, we may bear it with fortitude. Viewing the right to die more harshly than many theologians, Father Duggan identifies the movement with "the same mentality that embraces tranquilizers, alcohol and drugs."

But does one have a constitutional right to die, apart from his right to refuse treatment which may or may not lead to death? Some lawyers think that such a right is possibly inherent in the Ninth Amendment, which protects fundamental rights not enumerated in the first eight amendments. This raises the question, if the terminally ill person has a right to die, why not the curably ill patient who is simply tired of life, or wants his family to collect insurance? (It is not illegal to commit suicide, although one who assists another person in such an act may be guilty of homicide as accessory to the fact. Even here, the law has distinguished between handing someone poison and actually placing it in his mouth. It is administering the poison that constitutes the crime.)

Voluntary euthanasia is probably the least of the problem. Society's concern is increasingly with those who are not in a condition to make such decisions: the old man with a fractured skull, the prisoner of machines in an intensive care unit, the incurable psychotic who has already lost most of his legal rights. Who shall speak for them?

Prof. Cyril C. Means, Jr., of the New York School of Law, thinks that one possible way out of the dilemma is to set up committees of the person similar to those presently appointed by courts to manage an individual's affairs during periods of incompetency. Composed of the patient's attorney, his physician, his minister and his nearest of kin, they would perform essentially the same function as the "death committees" which now decide who is eligible for a kidney transplant. Professor Means points out that "what the law seeks to protect is not human life itself, but the human person. . . ." Under this interpretation, if consciousness is not present there is no person in the true sense, and the committee could act accordingly.

No doubt committees burdened with this awesome responsibility would act with discretion and, hopefully, more wisdom than committees frequently exhibit. One such, in fact, is in existence at Johns Hopkins University Hospital in Baltimore. Known informally as a God Council, its decisions to hasten death must be unanimous. However, no living will on the part of the patient is necessary.

Humane as this approach might be in certain circumstances, the risks of death by committee are apparent. Suppose the patient cannot pay his bill? His case may be an iffy one and the hospital could err on the side of death because it needs the bed. How much suffering must a person face before he is allowed to have his life curtailed, and who is to be the judge of the suffering? A majority of people don't die in pain, and the unconscious cannot be said to suffer mentally or physically. Suppose the patient's family has something to gain by his death? Suppose he has no family at all? Age itself, rather than the value of life, might be the determinant. In Dr. Sackett's proposed Florida legislation, if no family is available, a panel of three physicians would be empowered to decide when continued medical treatment would be useless.

Dr. Alfred Jaretzki III, of the Columbia University Medical School, points out that one does not really know whether the life-prolonging measures are useless until the patient dies. Sometimes, he doesn't; he recovers. With the help of drugs, a pacemaker and a defibrillator, Dwight Eisenhower lived through seven heart attacks, an intestinal blockage and pneumonia, most of these crises occurring while he was president. Nor can the decision to terminate be based on the law of averages; even if nine out of ten patients did die, this would hardly justify letting the one recoverable person go untreated.

A second problem is equally relevant. To whom does the doctor listen? If the family, which members? What if they disagree? More telling, patients themselves sometimes change their minds. A pharmacist with cancer of the throat exacted a promise from Dr. Jaretzski "not to let me suffer," then insisted on a whole series of operations when his illness became terminal.

Are committee-inspired deaths "good" deaths? From the individual's point of view, they might not be. From society's view, they might—one less old person (or deformed baby) to worry about. And if euthanasia were to become legal, would there, in Dr. John Hinton's words, "be just as great an impetus to improve further care of the dying?" He thinks not. What may appear rational to the doctor, family and clergy may actually reflect subconscious motivations, unrecognized feelings of sex, aggression or rejection. (Would an all-male committee be more or less disposed to hasten the death of a female patient?) Moreover, legal euthanasia provides a social rationale under which individual decisions can more easily be made. There is danger here—the danger of subtle social coercion. The patient may be made to feel society doesn't need him anymore; the right to die becomes a duty.

Voluntary euthanasia is equally subject to this danger. Men are filled with hidden, self-destructive drives which are easily encouraged by the right to die. In fact, exercising this right might represent an act of aggression against others, a way of punishing the survivors. The sick old person may really be crying out for help—as many do—and not death.

Those who would expedite the dying process almost always ignore the effect of such a death on survivors. Even under the most favorable circumstances, the loss of a close relative creates feelings of guilt; combined with normal grieving, the result can be emotionally shattering. One argument for "machine dying"—perhaps not a wholly convincing one—is that it gives the family more time to prepare for the loss of a loved one. In this view, prolonged dying is a boon to survivors, if not to the patient.

Euthanasia assumes that there are no dignified alternatives to the costly and laborious deaths to which many people are now subjected in hospitals. But given the right social setting, and pain-controlling drugs, this need not be the case. Some different approaches to dying will be explored in the next chapter. What matters to the dying is not the number of days that are left but the quality of those days: the love and care they get, the retention of personal integrity, the feeling that one is still respected as a human being. Many psychologists believe that it is social and psychological death, not physical death, that the old person fears most. Rejected by others, he rejects himself.

The remedy for this situation is not quicker deaths but a meaningful existence, insofar as this is possible, at a time when life is drawing to a close. Withholding treatment doesn't necessarily mean that a patient will die with dignity; it simply means he will die sooner. Dignity comes from within. "The living will is hard for me to swallow," says Dr. Austin Kutscher, of the

Foundation of Thanatology. "An individual signs it under circumstances when he is not concerned with his own death. It becomes operative at a time when he is 100 percent involved. There's no provision for cancelling out. I'd be much more satisfied with it if it were signed on a death bed."

Why not, asks Kutscher, form life conferences rather than death committees? Such groups, consisting of family, clergyman, doctor, social worker and psychiatrist, would be concerned with the patient on a daily basis, making certain that he enjoys both professional and human support in his passage from life. Emphasis would not be on ending treatment, but on strengthening the patient's morale, on making him feel wanted in this greatest, and last, of life's crises.

Can we establish the moment when life ceases to have any human value? For the hopelessly brain-damaged, the unconscious prisoner of machines, this may be possible. But to only a minute fraction of the dying can this be said to apply. Others cannot be written off so easily. It is these marginal cases for whom the prospect of a quick and easy death is made to seem beguiling. But in whose interests? The psychiatrist Felix Deutsch points out that "dying beautifully" is primarily for the benefit of those who are left behind. Euthanasia, he says, is "dying for an idea."

At present, euthanasia is widely practiced, although in a context of medical treatment that is socially acceptable. For most terminal patients, however, an unqualified and voluntary right to die is hardly a sign of progress. The real right of the dying—the human right—is to be treated as one of the living, with respect, good care, compassion and a measure of hope. Such an approach disturbs few consciences, minimizes risk and imposes no undue responsibility on society for deciding when people have lived long enough. The vast majority of us, even when old and ill, are in no hurry to die.

CHAPTER VI

The Experience of Dying

IN TIMES PAST, dying was something of a public event. The poor might die on the street or in a hovel surrounded by grieving relatives. Among the middle classes, a ceremonial was often arranged, with family, priest, friends and physician around the bedside. Dignitaries and heads of state enjoyed even greater sendoffs, with perhaps a bishop added to the entourage and a scribe to record the great man's dying thoughts. Did Gen. Ethan Allen, when told on his deathbed that the angels were waiting, really blurt out, "Goddammit, let them wait!" It makes a good story. Sir William Osler, the great nineteenth-century physician and teacher, is reported to have said, "I have been too far across the river to go back and have it all over again." John Keats, dying of tuberculosis in the arms of his good friend Severn, expired with, "Don't be frightened. Thank God it has come." For Gertrude Stein, a twentieth-century death was more difficult. "What is the answer?" she asked Alice B. Toklas, her companion of many years. Getting none, she asked, "Then what is the question?"

Whether legendary or true, these famous last words tell us something about how men and women were expected to die when death was not the private affair it is today. A patient in intensive care is hardly able to speak at all, and if he were, his words would likely be addressed to a battery of machines. What is preserved for survivors is not some final lucid revelation from the shadow of the valley but EKGs, EEGs and blood pressure readings announcing, "There is nothing more to be done." A person who has rehearsed some parting advice for posterity should make every effort to die at home.

On a more symbolic level, society no longer dramatizes death. Tristan and Isolde's drawn-out *Liebestodt* elevates dying to the status of lyrical passion, a "love death" that is rooted in a mythical, more poetic, past. Hamlet's dying words resonate the heroic attitudes of the Elizabethan Age; the great, tragic conflicts of life were reconciled at the end in noble language. Our expiring heroes today are allowed, at best, a few "ughs!" in scenes notable for their brevity and realism. The formal statement has been replaced by the gut reaction.

No doubt much of man's contemporary difficulty with death is his lack of belief in a life beyond. This book is not a plea for religion or faith in the supernatural; yet, it seems obvious that the experience of dying was somewhat easier in an age when most people believed in immortality. The Judeo-Christian faith in an afterlife provided answers, whereas today, like Gertrude Stein, we grope for questions. Perhaps it was easier then to depart this life with more confidence; finality did not seem quite so final. Today, man dies existentially, not quite sure who he is or where he is going. Far from being an adventure, ceremoniously arranged and socially launched, death has become an enigma. For the dying, what is there to say?

In truth, there is a great deal to say. If we have learned anything from the dying during the past few years it is that they are not as afraid of death as we had supposed. What frightens them is abandonment, if not physical, then social and psychological.

This chapter explores some of the ways the dying prepare

for and experience death. Talking about one's condition is one such method. Learning to grieve is another. Counseling and psychological therapy help people meet the crisis of death. Recently, the use of psychedelic drugs has been tried with astonishing, if inconclusive, results. Consumerism among the fatally ill has made some doctors, at least, more sensitive to the feelings of their patients. New hospitals are being built in which the emphasis is on not intensive care but intensive caring. Slowly—all too slowly—the indignities to which the dying have been submitted in our time are being abolished.

Where the Dying Teach the Living

"We had these medical books at home. They were out of date. My dad had something similar to this for three years . . . they treated him for nerves. . . . I actually didn't think there was much hope for me. This book says anywhere from two to four years. . . ."

Mr. R. has been wheeled into the little room with the one-way glass. His wife is at his side, and two chaplains in white hospital coats—a man and woman—adjust the microphone as he talks. A tape recorder sits on a table nearby. With its electronic equipment and glass wall, the room suggests an engineer's booth in a recording studio.

On the other side of the glass, the lights are dimmed; nurses, interns, social workers, a resident psychiatrist and chaplains-in-training at the University of Chicago's Billings Hospital pull out their notebooks. The room is hot. You have to strain to hear Mr. R.

"Things may not be as bad as they looked two weeks ago," says Carl Nyswonger,* the head chaplain, as he begins the interview.

---

* Since this account was written, the Reverend Nyswonger himself died, suddenly, of a heart attack.

"We both went to the medical book. . . . All our crises have always been together," Mr. R.'s wife says.

"Sometimes I feel we're too close . . . the separation is so hard. They really upset you emotionally, like Sunday with the children."

"Some families pull the blind down between them," Carl Nyswonger interjects.

"It's something you have to face. You've got to face up to the obligation."

"What kind of feeling has come out of this?" asks Shirley Herman, the middle-aged assistant chaplain who shares the interviewing with Carl Nyswonger.

"I said 'Why me?' I'm thirty-two years old. I've everything to live for. Where do you go from there? People come in and say, 'Oh, don't worry about it. You'll be all right in a few weeks.' But I'm in no mood for joking. . . ."

When Mr. R. is wheeled out of the booth an hour later, the class talks about his case.

Carl: "The doctor said he's a hard hat, but I had a gut feeling of real warmth. He may have a lot of time left. Let's cool it awhile."

Student: "There's an element of fatalism here. He says his father had it too—he's a chip off the old block."

Carl: "I sort of heard him saying, 'Don't push me. I don't know what it's going to be like when I get there.'"

Since 1964, more than 400 terminally ill patients have been interviewed at Billings as part of an accredited course called The Dynamics of Death and Dying, inaugurated by Dr. Elisabeth Kübler-Ross. There was Mr. B., who returned home, after twenty years overseas, with lung cancer. A nun, bedfast in her convent, had given up until the "D & D" staff went to work on her. (Near the end, her morale lifted; she wrote her own funeral mass.) A forty-year-old professor at the university, who had a heart attack while jogging, shares one of his last conscious hours with the class. Mrs. Y. came into the seminar years ago, but her illness was checked and she returns from time to time when there is an urgent need for a patient. Once, a dying opera star wanted to give a farewell concert to the seminar. She was persuaded to speak instead. And there is Mr. O. Flat on his back, he begins the interview with a formal "Ladies and gentlemen . . ." A professional entertainer in his youth, Mr. O. refuses to perform behind the one-way screen, wants to see his audience. The class is moved to an operating theater in the hospital, where the patient holds center stage. Here, because the tiers of seats are steeply pitched, he can watch the reaction of the students. "The man who laughed, please raise your hand," says Mr. O. "I like your enthusiasm." A hand goes up. "Thank you very much." When he is through talking, he asks for questions from the floor.

Years ago, a terminal patient in the seminar told the class, "I was dumbfounded to find that when I requested a chaplain in the middle of the night, there was no chaplain. I mean, this is just unbelievable to me, unbelievable. Because when does a man need a chaplain? Only at night, believe me. That's the time when you get down with those boxing gloves and have it out with yourself." Ever since then there has been a night chaplain at Billings. Nyswonger often slept on a couch in his office.

Ministers, of course, have always attended the dying. In the Catholic Church, priests administer the last rites. But, for the most part, the chaplain's role has been to cheer up the sick person, pray for him and console his family. When the end nears, the dying person is asked to face his Maker. The program at Billings, and a few like-minded hospitals elsewhere, is a scientific attempt to help both patient and family come to terms with death as part of the emotional crisis that attends all illness. For those who are able to face death openly, talking about it seems to remove much of the fear, the sense of isolation and the mystery of dying.

To some, this may seem like an arrogant intrusion into a

person's privacy at a time when he should be left to die in peace. How is this possible if the patient is hauled in front of a microphone, asked to submit to interviews and otherwise encouraged to let it all hang out? Perhaps the bluntest criticism of the Billings approach comes from Dr. Nathan Scott, of the University of Chicago Divinity School. He speaks of the "anguish and suffering that young seminarians pounce upon with a kind of scientific passion in exploiting people who are helpless." Scott thinks that public discussions with the dying—as opposed to private counseling—betray the sacredness and inviolability of the human person.

But others who are close to this kind of work disagree. The dying person in such situations, they point out, feels useful rather than useless; he is giving as well as receiving. And not least of all, he is getting things off his chest which, if left repressed, add to his anguish. In fact, most psychiatrists are of the opinion that people want to talk about their situation, whatever it is. In this respect, dying is different from other life crises only in its finality. Although the crisis cannot be resolved, it can be ameliorated. Peaceful death comes not when one is left alone but when one knows that he is being looked upon, and treated, as a living person.

Dying as a Peak Experience

Often it is not the physical but the psychological pain that makes dying so difficult—the knowledge that one will be separated from those he loves, from the world that seems increasingly precious as it begins to fade from his control. It is to this aspect of death that both the ministry and the psychiatric profession now address themselves in their effort to help the person achieve acceptance in his last hours.

Since death is an "undiscovered bourne from which no traveler returns," we can never be sure just what flickers through the mind of the dying person. For the unconscious, the confused and the heavily sedated, it is most likely that these final moments are meaningless if, indeed, one is aware of them at all. But for the mentally alert, it is quite possible that the transition resembles a psychedelic "trip"; indeed, there is evidence that death, when it comes suddenly, presents itself as an unbelievably glorious experience; not a return to the womb of Mother Earth, as some philosophers have speculated, but a flight into a totally new universe of sensation.

What makes us think this might be the case? Although it is true that no one returns from the dead, it is possible to be reprieved from almost certain death at the last moment and thus experience what goes through the consciousness of others not so fortunate—in a sense, to die, yet live to tell about it.

This intriguing possibility was first suggested in 1892, by Albert von St. Gallen Heim, an obscure geology professor in Zurich, Switzerland. Like many Swiss, Heim was an ardent mountain climber; and, like not a few of his colleagues, he sometimes lost his footing. Most of his falls were short and injury was minor, but on one expedition Heim found himself plunging from a sheer precipice into a crevasse several hundred feet beneath him with nothing to break the descent. He was headed for certain death, or so he thought. Actually, Heim landed in deep snow and suffered only a couple of broken bones. While waiting for a rescue party to reach him, he pondered on the remarkable flux of feelings that had accompanied his plunge. By his own account, he experienced his death on the way down. "Everything was transfixed as though by a heavenly light and everything was beautiful without grief, without anxiety, and without pain," Heim later told the Swiss Alpine Club. "I felt no conflict or strife; conflict had been transmuted into love . . . like magnificent music a divine calm swept through my soul. . . . Then I heard a dull thud and my fall was over."

But was this typical? After all, Heim's reaction might have been unique. Whereas he had entered an enchanted kingdom of peace, others might have plunged into hell. To check his impressions, Heim interviewed, over the next twenty-five years, many other survivors of alpine falls, asking them all the same question: What was your experience in the "last" seconds of life? Later, he included victims of railway disasters, rescued victims of drowning and others who presumed, for however long a time, that they were facing death. His findings confirmed his own subjective observations: The moment of death is not to be feared but to be embraced.

Heim identified three distinct phases of imminent death. One's initial reaction is to resist, to struggle against death. When it becomes apparent that this is useless, one passes quickly into a stage of acceptance and life-review. Those who think they are drowning often speak of seeing the whole of their life telescoped into a few brief seconds, as though one's past is to be taken on the journey. Finally, there is a feeling of transcendence. One lives outside of time, beyond past or future. "A sense of oneness or unity with other human beings and the entire universe develops."

Heim summarized his research in this way:

> No grief was felt, nor was there paralyzing fright of the sort that can happen in instances of lesser danger. . . . There was no anxiety, no trace of despair, no pain. . . . Mental activity became enormous, rising to a hundredfold velocity or intensity. . . . Time became greatly expanded. . . . In many cases . . . the person falling often heard beautiful music and fell in a superbly blue heaven containing roseate cloudlets. . . .
>
> We have reached the conclusion that death through falling is subjectively a very pleasant death.

In spite of Heim's persuasive account, we have reason to question his interpretation of this experience, at least to a degree. What one might really be experiencing, phenomenologically speaking, is not imminent death but the sheer sensation of falling through space, a distortion of the senses caused by rapid motion. Free-fall parachutists report some, although by no means all, of these sensations before the 'chute opens, and they, too, literally float above the world. Astronauts have recorded similar oceanic feelings upon seeing the earth from thousands of miles away. In brief, it may not be the anticipation of death that brings one into harmony with the universe but a temporary release from the ordinary bonds of life. Quite possibly, the mind is simply hallucinating under stress.

Yet the idea that dying can be ecstatic has haunted people through the ages. Dr. Russell Noyes, Jr., has remarked that "the rapturous, transfigured expressions observed on deathbeds a century ago and interpreted as tokens of beatific visions were, perhaps, accompaniments of a mystical state of consciousness." If true, this is obviously rooted in another age, when deep religious commitments, faith in the hereafter and mysticism were more common than they are today. It is easier to let go of this world if the next is envisioned as peaceful and roseate. In fact, Heim's imagery—his celestial music and heavenly light—bears the stamp of Christian belief. Would a Buddhist, falling through space, undergo this same transfiguration? Might he not rather experience a death that is much more closely attuned to earthly, though no less universal, sources?

Perhaps the details of imagery and feelings are not important; the essence of the experience is what matters. In any case, Heim's paradigm of death remained a curiosity buried in the obscure pages of the *Yearbook of the Swiss Alpine Club* until a few years ago, when psychiatrists began to probe the minds of patients dying under much more mundane circumstances. Dr. Kübler-Ross was one of the first to recognize that such a person, when he is free of physical pain, often achieves a serenity of spirit which is, if not ecstatic, free of psychological anguish.

Another doctor who has closely observed the mental processes of dying patients, E. M. Pattison, confirms many of Heim's subjective impressions of death by falling. (There is no indication, however, that Dr. Pattison has ever read Heim's account.) The dying person, he believes, "begins to return to a state of being at one with the world. . . . Existence is timeless and helpless, the individual and the outer world is [sic] no longer differentiated. At this point, one is rapidly approaching the surrender to the process of reunification of life and return to union with the earth out of which we have sprung." Pattison sees this psychic death as the true end, although the body may linger on in a comatose state. He did not, however, observe in his patients any of the heightened states of consciousness described by Heim. Death, instead, was a peaceful winding down of awareness, and it is this that makes possible the acceptance of the nothingness which one approaches.

There is some indication that women approach their deaths differently from men: they tend to fantasize it in terms of the sexual act. E. S. Greenberger studied two groups of hospitalized women; one consisted of women critically ill of cancer and the other, of women recovering from minor surgery. The former group had a strong tendency to see death as a form of punishment for illicit sex—seduction, affairs out of wedlock, adultery. These women were also much less likely to repress thoughts of death. At the same time, they experienced in their fantasies a thrill at the very idea of dying. Death was seen as the demon lover, which stands as a symbol of a woman's life urge. The women who were not dying reported almost none of these fantasies.

A more general, if equally Freudian approach is outlined by the European psychiatrist Felix Deutsch. Most of the pain of dying, Deutsch contends, is mental, and much of this, in turn, has to do with one's aggressive impulses, a desire to unburden oneself of guilt, a clinging to or abandoning of familiar love objects and persons. Above all, the individual seeks consolation in the "non-ambivalent relationships of another world." When these aggressive reactions subside, "when the fear of dying has been dispelled, and when there is no further question of a sense of guilt," Deutsch believes, the patient dies at peace with the world. He observes, too, that this is easier for those who have a strong religious faith.

Here, again, we see no evidence of a glorious entry into

heaven, with angels trumpeting and effulgent clouds lighting
the pilgrim on his way. Rather, dying requires a purge of psychic conflicts and for this is needed the guiding hand of our
twentieth-century priesthood—psychoanalysis. Clearly, such an
approach is impractical for most people. Even with the physically healthy but mentally anguished, classical analysis is a
drawn-out affair, and the average terminal patient would be
likely to die long before his analysis is finished. (There is some
indication, however, that a foreshortened life-span enables the
terminal patient to telescope much past experience that would
take years under other circumstances.) Obviously, if psychiatry
is to prepare a person to meet his Maker, in the figurative sense
that has taken the place of literal faith, some shortcuts are
necessary.

Here, in a roundabout way, we return to our percipient Swiss
mountain climber, Dr. Heim. Several years ago, the psychologist
Abraham Maslow, of Brandeis University, seeking a less clinical
and more humanistic approach to psychology, coined the term
"peak experience." Maslow wanted to put his science rather more
in the service of man, and less on the burden of stimulus-
response behavior that told us much about rats and pigeons but
little about the intact, nonexperimental experiences of human
beings. He believed, for instance, that man had a conscious will,
and that he could will himself into elevated, exciting states of
mind, much as a child becomes excited when told he will be
taken to the circus.

For Maslow, a peak experience is a mental reaching out, a
lifting of horizons, a grasping of one's immediate possibilities
with the whole of his being. The mundaneness of ordinary
life is thus transcended and made part of a deeper, more sen-
tient reality. To peak is to experience a kind of psychic intoxi-
cation. One figuratively ascends the alp, with all its breathtaking
beauty and challenge. He is on top of the world; he need not,
however, fall off, as our friend Heim did. Being on the peak is
its own reward. Consciousness is expanded and one joins the

eternal Now as the rush of new, tingling outer sensations blend with an inner heightening.

Maslow has never carried his notion into the realm of therapy, and he has probably never thought of dying as a peak experience. Yet, through an interesting coincidence, his peaking theory preceded by only a few years a much more dramatic development that achieved many of the same goals with greater intensity and variety. This was the accidental synthesis of the psychotropic drug LSD by a Swiss biochemist.

Not even its discoverers know quite how LSD works, but we do know what it does. A hallucinogenic drug, on the order of the natural substance mescaline but with much more powerful action, LSD figuratively takes one out of himself and thrusts him into a world so phantasmagoric that those who have made the "trip" have difficulty describing their full range of visions and feelings. The self seems to leave the body and penetrate the ultimate nature of reality. One might pass from terror to ecstacy. There are no inhibitions, no constraints (mentally, at least) on behavior. People "do" things under the influence of LSD that are quite impossible, and the "trip" often passes from schizophrenic nightmare to blissful serenity. Significantly, many people experience death and rebirth; one arrives at the kingdom within.

The drug is dangerous and should be used only under close medical supervision. A few physicians prescribe it in treating psychiatric disorders in the belief that it helps the patient cut through the layers of repression in the psyche that impair his functioning. It seems to reduce anxiety long after the effect of the drug has worn off. Although it is still highly experimental, psychiatrists are hopeful that, as more data are collected, LSD will take its place with such powerful drugs as thorazine in the treatment of the mentally ill. Possibly, its real value will be shown to be its fundamental reordering of consciousness. Whereas other drugs treat symptoms, LSD may very well work on causes.

This, at any rate, was an hypothesis adopted by a group of doctors at the Maryland Psychiatric Research Center in Catonsville, Maryland, near Baltimore. Led by Dr. Albert Kurland, these doctors used LSD on both mental patients and alcoholics in an effort to change profoundly ingrained patterns of behavior. Results were mixed, but whatever the outcome, one astonishing and consistent result was noted: the subjects reported "dying" while under the influence of the drug, and then undergoing a "rebirth." This new life persisted for some time afterwards and was characterized by a much more tranquil and well-ordered approach to life. Jerry Avorn, a Harvard medical student who observed the Catonsville experiments, reports on the drug session of one fifty-year-old homeless alcoholic to illustrate this transformation.

Now I found myself not as a person but as what I can only describe as my soul or spirit. I was part of everything ugly, dirty, and filthy. I traveled through intestines, garbage, dung, in and out of a rectum, and anything else you can imagine. . . . The further down I went, the worse it got. . . . I saw a vulture which I took as Death, or the Devil. When I got to the end, I was too terrified to look at it for fear of what I might see. Very much to my surprise, when I forced myself to look at the end, I found whatever it was I was afraid to look at was *nothing*. . . .

Having passed through the dream death, cleansed of what is clearly the symbolic imagery of the living death this man had experienced as an alcoholic, rebirth became possible.

After seeing all these horrible things, I came up to the beautiful and the wonderful. I continued to go higher, passing among billions and millions of minute spirits like myself. I felt a very, very small part of the whole thing. There seemed a small place above and beyond everything else, and I found myself being drawn to this place. After getting to this peak, I found who I thought was God. We were on the same level, looking down at this greatness. Something made me feel He wanted me to exchange positions with Him. This I didn't want to do because I felt unworthy. He insisted, so we made the change. It was a wonderful feeling to be there with Him, far beyond any of the ambitions of any astronaut—peaceful and wonderful—The closer I got to Him the less there was of me. This was a little terrifying, but I wanted to go to Him. Finally, when I got to Him I became Him. I was Jesus and He was me. We were one.

Did LSD do for this man what saints and mystics have spent years trying to achieve? It is not likely. Mr. Avorn notes that today, "if this sort of thing happens spontaneously, we call it an 'acute schizophrenic break with paranoid delusions and experiences of depersonalization.'" Induced by drugs, however, the outcome could be seen as the reintegration of an already disintegrated personality—at least temporarily. Psychiatrists don't know yet what the permanent effects of such treatment might be. They do know that insanity has its own insights into the nature of reality; the astounding number of geniuses, from Nietzsche to Van Gogh, who have wrestled with their private terrors to bring forth new intellectual concepts and great works of art bears this out. In its inducement of irrationality, LSD may well help us cope with a world that is overrationalized; it may help us to use all the senses, as our ancestors did thousands of years ago, in achieving a unity with our environment and coming closer to the source of the universe's mystery. This, of course, is mere speculation, but it is no less necessary to penetrate inner, as well as the outer, space if man is truly to know himself.

Our story might end here—and would hardly deserve a place in a book on dying—were there not a sequel. In 1965, a young research assistant at Catonsville was diagnosed as having terminal cancer. One of the doctors on the staff, the late Walter Pahnke, had helped pioneer the early experiments in the use of LSD. Why not employ the drug, he asked, to alleviate the distress of dying? In this respect, Dr. Pahnke had unusual qualifications; as a doctor of divinity as well as a physician, the soul, as well as the body, was his concern.

Pahnke's experiments are not wholly conclusive—he died in a scuba diving accident before they were completed—but the outlines of a new approach to terminal illness are apparent. LSD, for patients with intractable pain, is far more effective than morphine and its derivatives. More significantly, it seems to mask the terror of death, even to bring about a willingness to die. For some, dying becomes a peak experience.

Pahnke's work at Catonsville was taken over by a forty-one-year-old Czechoslovak-born psychiatrist, Dr. Stanislav Grof, who had used LSD in his native country as an adjunct to psycho-analysis. In observing its effect on terminal patients, he began to seek an explanation for its efficacy. One possibility, he thinks, is that "death, instead of being seen as the ultimate end of everything and a step into nothingness, appears suddenly as a transition into a different type of existence for those who undergo the destruction-rebirth cosmic-unity experience. . . . The patients who have transcendental experiences develop a rather deep belief in the ultimate cosmic unity of all creation and experience themselves as part of it without regard to the situation they are facing."

Grof found, for example, that people with widely differing religious backgrounds (or none at all) seemed to have "plugged in" to a universal set of religious insights that could not be accounted for by their previous experiences. Beliefs associated with Hinduism, Taoism, New Testament Christianity and Buddhism were reflected in the instant mysticism that accom-panied the psychedelic experience. These beliefs, Grof suggests, are buried deep in the unconscious of the human race (com-parable to Jung's archetypes and collective memories); they surface under the releasing power of the drug.

Not every patient, of course, went through this transcendental conversion, but even for those who did not the benefits of LSD were notable: a lessening of anxiety and depression, a greater willingness to participate in social activities, a more stable mood, a diminished fear of dying. Of the sixty patients who volunteered for the original Catonsville project, about two-thirds settled for something less than a peak experience; results, nevertheless, were considered therapeutically valuable.

The drug is also being used at the Menninger School of Psychiatry in Topeka, Kansas, where Dr. David V. Sheehan has reported that LSD does have value in alleviating the feeling of doom and destruction that hangs over the dying patient. "Patients on LSD were so strikingly unconcerned about death or any other anticipatory concern," he notes, "that death seemed unimportant . . . the imagery and aesthetic stimulation of the drug seemed to create a new zest for experience. . . ."

Psychedelic death is not without its critics. To some of these, Dr. Grof's "death and transfiguration" is closer to the old-fashioned deathbed conversion of the sinner than to the insights of the genuine mystic; and in any event, they ask, what point is there in converting a lifelong atheist at the last minute? Personal integrity would be better served by letting him die with his own convictions. And the truly religious person may not need LSD. Moreover, one might ask if the psychedelic psychiatrists are not simply manipulating the mind in the way that some medical doctors manipulate the body with their life-prolonging machinery? The person ceases to be himself and becomes a puppet of medicine, hostage to a drug-induced mysticism—or perhaps some fanciful delusions—that separates him from the *real* reality of life in which pain and sorrow are necessary concomitants. Since death is the final trip for all of us, why distort it with a synthetic "trip" that is wholly illusory?

LSD advocates respond to these criticisms by pointing out that their patients have experienced no psychologically harmful aftereffects from the drug, and that, in any case, its primary purpose is to prepare people to accept death within their own psychic framework. If morphine can be used to control bodily pain, why not LSD to lessen mental anguish? If this also opens up a new order of reality—a peak experience—so much the better.

We simply don't know enough about LSD and its effects to provide final answers to these questions. Until we do, its value as an adjunct to dying will remain largely conjectural.

Altered states of consciousness need not be drug-induced. For some years now, Dr. Herbert Spiegel has taught self-hypnosis to terminal patients as one means of lessening pain and blotting out much of their anguish. Hypnosis, he believes, is one of nature's tranquilizers, but without the unpleasant side-effects of psychotropic drugs. It is easily taught and helps the person maintain contact and communication with family and doctors. It is a far cry from a psychedelic awakening or peak; indeed, it is almost the opposite. In Dr. Spiegel's words, its main characteristic is "meditative respose." The dying person is not given a new world in living color, but is enabled to see his present world, no matter how troubled, from a more tranquil perspective.

In one sense, he goes into a trance in which painful thoughts of dying, and pain itself, are excluded. One physician, who had taken Dr. Spiegel's course in hypnosis, happened upon a seriously injured boy pinned under an automobile following a highway accident. Not having his medical kit, this doctor hypnotized the victim where he lay and remained with him in the ambulance until surgeons could take over at the hospital.

Patients who have learned to hypnotize themselves find that much less medication is required for the control of pain. This, in turn, enables them to remain in better contact with the outside world—in Dr. Spiegel's words, to hold on to the "glow of living." One young woman reported, "Dying is beautiful even the first time around, at the ripe old age of twenty. It's not easy, but there's a real beauty to be found in knowing that your end is going to catch up with you faster than you had expected. You try to get all your loving, laughing and crying done as soon as you can."

Physical pain is often not a problem for the dying, as we have noted, although mental anguish is seldom absent. Philosopher Jacques Choron distinguishes three types of death fear which may exist in any combination: (1) the fear of what comes after death, (2) the "event" of dying, and (3) the fear of "ceasing to be"—death's finality. Can these fears be reduced by encouraging people to face up to, rather than avoid, them?

Some psychologists think they can—if the death fears are associated with pleasant, nondisturbing stimuli. If this resembles the behavior modification technique used to treat alcoholics and some criminals, indeed, it is not much different. Whereas the alcoholic is given an unpleasant, or aversive, stimulus to counter the effects of something he enjoys (drinking), the dying patient is provided with pleasurable experience in association with that which he fears (death). He is, in effect, desensitized to his own forthcoming death. Hopefully, he finds that anticipating death is not as dreadful as he had imagined.

The technique for desensitizing a person is relatively simple and can be handled by a nurse-therapist. The patient is first taught deep muscle relaxation, lying comfortably, with eyes closed. He is told to tense different groups of muscles, one group at a time, then to relax them for twenty to thirty seconds in association with certain pleasurable sensations of his own choice. The exercises are repeated until he has learned to relax at will. Relaxation itself, however, is not intended to reduce anxiety, but to provide a base line by which it can be measured. For such people, the intrusion of a "death idea" produces quick tensing of muscles that have been relaxed. The therapist can then determine the effectiveness of the treatment as less tension is experienced.

She begins by showing slides or photographs of people in mildly threatening situations—a man, for example, undergoing diagnostic tests for suspected cancer. These are matched by pleasant or enjoyable scenes that counter the anxiety created by the earlier slides. On the second try, a somewhat more dangerous situation is shown, possibly a woman who has narrowly missed being run over by a car. This, too, is countered by a pleasure-reinforcing image. One man who found the idea of walking past a graveyard particularly disturbing was reassured by the picture of a chocolate ice cream cone—something he had always liked. Gradually, the scenes come closer to the patient's own situation, and as each new exposure becomes progressively more "lethal," it is paired with even more enjoyable associations. In this way—in theory at least—the patient is "inoculated" against his fears.

Still experimental, behavior modification is time-consuming, and to say the least, a mechanical approach to deeply rooted attitudes. Moreover, it doesn't work for everybody. For those who react favorably, it is an effective means of dealing with the dread of illness without resorting to LSD or sedatives. The technique is being simplified by a device that automatically regulates the slides and their auditory accompaniment according to the patient's response. If he tenses up, scenes revert to less arousing situations. It is the patient who decides how far he wants to go.

The Language of Dying

Interesting as this approach promises to be, behavior modification has found little support among psychiatrists. Fears that are expressed verbally, they say, may mask or distort more important things that are being said symbolically. This is especially true of the dying, because few such people are prepared to discuss their condition objectively, and many deny that they are afraid at all. The therapist, therefore, must be able to reach his patient on a deeper level of communication. To do this, he must understand what the person is trying to tell him.

Dr. Kübler-Ross was one of the first psychiatrists to interpret the dying person's "hidden" language as a precondition for counseling. From hundreds of interviews with terminal patients, she has identified six stages, or moods, which most persons experience during their last weeks or months of life. Their reaction to the bad news usually begins with outright denial—"It can't be me."—and is followed by feelings of anger—"Why does it have to be me?" In the next step, a bargaining period sets in, during which the patient offers his life for some worthy cause in return for a few more years on earth. One of Dr. Kübler-Ross's subjects pleaded for enough time to attend her son's wedding. Dressed in her best clothes, and given an extra dose of pain-killing drugs, she left the hospital for what everyone was sure would be the last time. She returned with a gleam in her eye. "Don't forget, Dr. Ross, I have another son," she announced. Sooner or later, according to the Kübler-Ross scenario, the dying person will fall into a depression. This silent, or preparatory, grief is his attempt to express sorrow, and it becomes a means of helping him into the stage of acceptance. At the very end, he will ideally attain a tranquil, even a hopeful, mood.

By recognizing the emotional rungs to which a patient clings, both family and medical staff can help him through his struggle and, in a sense, teach him how to die. At the same time, they also learn to manage their own reactions. In the case of the family, feelings of guilt frequently make death harder on the next of kin than on the dying.

Dr. Kübler-Ross has been criticized for arranging the dying patient's feelings into overly neat categories. Untangling the moods of the terminally ill is not easy. For one thing, they may not follow the script; indeed, the denial stage may last right through to the end. In some cases, too, the patient will decide to repeat Act II of the drama (anger) after he has been through Act III (bargaining); or he may jumble three or four acts into one big scene. The dying person, in a word, is seldom aware of the didactic role he is playing and may simply prefer to be himself.

Throughout his shifting moods, however, the patient will speak to those around him in at least one of three "languages." Some adults want to talk openly; this Dr. Kübler-Ross terms plain English, and it is probably the least common. "Am I going to die?" is a question not often asked; people who say when they are healthy that they want to know often don't want to know when they are ill. The question may really be a bid not for truth but reassurance. Nevertheless, some patients—probably a small minority—are willing to discuss their impending death frankly and openly and with these the task of the psychotherapist is comparatively easy. The therapist may, in fact, strengthen the will to live rather than the will to die! (We will see, later on, how one therapist handles such patients with great skill.)

Far more common is the second of Dr. Kübler-Ross's languages, which she terms symbolic nonverbal. The patient acts out his feelings. Anger at doctors and nurses, the deliberate breaking of infusion tubes and similar difficult behavior tells the therapist more than words can about a person's attitude toward his illness. Refusing or interrupting treatment is often a sign of despair, a way of saying, "I know I'm going to die." The person is saying, "I can't talk about it yet," or "I don't want to believe it." Action makes possible the release of feelings that are too painful to put into words.

Dr. Kübler-Ross's third category is symbolic-verbal language. Words are used, but not in the literal sense. The problem for the therapist is to determine what they do mean, and to reply in language that is elliptical yet supportive enough not to give the game away; or at least not until the patient is ready for a more direct confrontation.

One of Kübler-Ross's patients was a thirteen-year-old boy who had been hospitalized for a year while waiting for a kidney transplant. As time went on, he became restless and impatient and went around the children's ward with an imaginary gun shooting the other patients by pointing his finger at them and shouting, "Bang! Bang!" The staff observed that only girls were shot, and, of these, the prime targets were those who were critically ill. It took some time for Dr. Kübler-Ross to interpret this strange behavior. Like most thirteen-year-old boys, this patient "hated" girls, but, more significantly, he wanted their kidneys. His action was a symbolically desperate plea to live.

Adults will often talk about things related to their treatment rather than the illness itself. Or they may make plans for a trip. A new degree of tenderness may be shown toward the spouse. The ambulatory dying—a cancer or leukemia victim who may be on his feet until the last few weeks of life—often carry on their work as though nothing were wrong with them. A friend of mine who died of lung cancer never spoke of the possibility of his death, although he was careful during the last few weeks of his illness to have friends look into such practical matters as the Social Security payments his wife and child would be entitled to, and to otherwise tidy up his affairs. All of these actions were symbolic-verbal means of communicating to others his awareness of dying. More direct language would have been painful to everyone and, perhaps, less effective. This man was an example of someone who was able to control his dying almost to the last.

Children often find it easier to draw their feelings than to talk about them. At the University Neurological Clinic in Zurich, Switzerland, critically ill children are encouraged to express themselves with paint and pencil. These drawings help doctors interpret the course of the illness; as for the child, simply being able to express himself in graphic, spontaneous terms seems to make the ordeal easier.

A few years ago, two of these children, Peter and Priska, each with a life expectancy of two-and-a-half months, accounted for more than 300 drawings. What is remarkable about them is the clue they provide to the children's awareness of their steadily deteriorating condition. This awareness is largely metaphorical, or symbolic, a way of handling, without too much agony, the certainty that one is dying. Both children forecast their decline with awesome and precise timing.

In the first pictures, drawn soon after their admission to the hospital, Peter and Priska saw themselves involved in a struggle, with the outcome still in doubt. Their pictures reveal this in a series of ambiguous "happenings." A menacing, fairy-tale world seems to hang over them but there is still the chance of escape. For Priska, there is a rebirth of hope as the flowers in her drawing each toward the sun. For Peter, the hospital becomes a fortress, shielding him from the battle. Both of these moods change sharply after the children have returned home, and are then re-admitted: the hospital shrinks, the flowers "grow backwards." As the end approaches, the illness is no longer symbolized by objects but as belonging to "people," although it is projected onto others—in Peter's case, a snowman. Both children have reached some acceptance, if not comprehension, of what is taking place.

Are these drawings messages for the doctor—unconscious, perhaps, but messages nonetheless? "I hope these pictures may serve as a warning signal," writes Dr. Susan R. Bach, of the Neurosurgical Clinic, "when, in face of a 'lost life,' we might feel tempted to try out new methods of treatment and so prolong a patient's life unduly when its natural span has clearly come to an end and we should stand by him and, if we can, let him go in peace."

We have come a long way from our picture of death as a somber public event, or a phantasmagoric, drug-stimulated peak experience. Most people, we know, do not go out with the bang of LSD nor, necessarily, a whimper of loneliness. They may, in Dylan Thomas's words, "rage, rage against the dying of the light." More likely, they share the confusion, the grief and sometimes the panic of those who witness their final moments. Except for the sudden heart attack, death can, perhaps, never be made easy. But it can be snatched away from the bureaucratic and institutional nightmare that it is for most people in the United States today.

CHAPTER VII

"We Who Now Mourn and Weep"

JUST BEFORE MIDNIGHT on November 29, 1942, a Boston nightclub, the Cocoanut Grove, caught fire when a waiter's match accidentally ignited one of the artificial palm trees. An estimated 850 patrons were in the club, many of them soldiers and sailors home on leave. Panic spread through the lounge as the dense smoke filled the room and people scrambled for the exits. Most of them never reached safety. By the time firemen reached the building and began combing it for survivors, 499 people lay dead; it was the second worst disaster of its kind in the United States. One of the victims was a young girl trapped in a telephone booth; apparently, she had tried to call someone to come and help her.

Ambulances from twenty-two hospitals raced to the scene, and at least 200 survivors were taken away for emergency treatment. Not surprisingly, they were in a state of deep shock. At Massachusetts General Hospital, a young psychiatrist, Erich Lindemann, working with residents and interns, observed that even weeks later many of these patients exhibited bizarre symptoms which could not be explained by their physical injuries. After all, they had escaped when others had died. And this, he concluded, was precisely the problem. Insomnia, panic attacks, feelings of guilt, exhaustion, and numerous bodily disturbances all contributed to what Lindemann decided were symptoms of acute grief. Most of these patients had lost relatives, fiancés or spouses, and their loss was intensified by the quirk of circumstances that enabled them to survive. What right had they to go on living? One of these was a man who experienced a curious hallucination in which he saw his daughter in a telephone booth trying to talk with him.

Lindemann's patients improved remarkably under treatment, and out of this experience came his now classic paper, "The Symptomatology and Management of Acute Grief." Above all, it alerted doctors to the commonplace yet disguised nature of grieving and the tricks that death plays on one's emotions. Today, psychiatrists recognize survival syndrome as a well-defined medical entity whose symptoms may continue for some time after the precipitating event.

When record floods hit the Buffalo Creek Valley, in West Virginia, early in the morning of February 26, 1974, 118 people were drowned and 4,000 made homeless. In the weeks that followed, hundreds of distraught, depressed and fear-ridden survivors turned up in doctors' offices complaining of strange symptoms. Some could not remember what had happened, others were unable to sleep or eat. One man would not go to work when the sky was cloudy. A woman insisted that she was responsible for the deaths of her son and a neighbor who had been swept away in the current.

Some of these symptoms could be traced to the disorganization of community life which followed the disaster, but many were simply expressions of intense grief. For almost a year, psychologists and mental health professionals worked with these people to help them overcome the painful memories and bodily complaints that plagued them. As in the Cocoanut Grove fire, the intense and prolonged reaction stemmed partly from the nature of the disaster. The syndrome is more likely to occur when the situation demands competition for escape.

Even when the death of someone is expected, one's grief for such a person can assume many disguises. Physical illness is common, and some doctors think that even cancer may result. Hallucinations are frequent. Social workers and juvenile authorities recognize that some cases of childhood delinquency are really an acting out of grief; in one study, 30 percent of the youngsters who had lost a parent engaged in violence, theft or promiscuity. Among very young children, who may not comprehend what death means and are unable to resolve their feelings in a healthy fashion, there is a tendency to regress to an earlier stage of development—to lose some of their manual skills and learning ability. Suicidal impulses, such as running in front of cars and attempting to fall out of a window, frequently appear. Such behavior is both a cry for help and a protest against the overwhelming sense that punishment has been meted out by the death of a parent.

Physicians now speak of grief as the hidden illness and think that it accounts for many of the physical symptoms they see in the course of their daily practice. Indeed, the ultimate symptom, death, is one of them. This, at any rate, is one conclusion that can be drawn from the higher-than-average mortality rates for widows and widowers in the first year of their bereavement. According to the National Office of Vital Statistics, a white man between twenty-five and thirty-four who has been widowed for less than one year runs twice the risk of dying than does a married man of the same age. And although total deaths among women are lower, the risk of death for widows during the first year of bereavement is two-and-a-half times that for married women.

This situation is apparently not unique to the United States. In 1967, a Welsh doctor, W. Dewi Rees, writing in the *British Medical Journal*, traced the connection between grief-stricken survivors and their untimely deaths. Working with a statistician, Sylvia Lutkins, Rees followed the history of close relatives of residents of Llanidloes, Wales, who died over a six-year period. He compared them with a control group of nonbereaved of

about the same size. They, too, died, but not as frequently—
there wasn't the same risk.

Nearly 5 percent of the bereaved close relatives died within
a year of the death in the family. In the nonbereaved group,
the rate was .68 percent, or about seven times less frequent. If
a husband or wife died, the first-year mortality among the survivors was even greater: 12 percent, as against 1.2 percent in
the comparison group. Interestingly, the risk of a widower dying
was about twice that of a widow.

Rees and Lutkins also found that the mode of death is a
crucial factor in this broken-heart syndrome. If the family member died in a hospital rather than at home, the risk of the
survivor dying within one year was doubled. If death took place
suddenly or accidentally outside the home or hospital, the bereaved ran a five times greater chance of dying within a
year.

Using a more diversified population, Michael Young and his
colleagues in England followed the history of 4,486 widowers,
fifty-five years and older, for a nine-year period beginning in
1957. Two hundred thirteen of these men died during the first
six months of bereavement. This was 40 percent above the
expected rate for married men of the same age. An interesting
feature of this study was the immediate cause of death. This
was traced to heart and circulatory disorders in two-thirds of
the cases. Men of this age, increasingly vulnerable to coronary
disease, found their grief an additional stress; a period of mourning might well have precipitated the fatal heart attack.

Even more dramatic evidence that bereavement can be fatal
was shown by Jane Bunch, a sociologist at England's University
of Southampton. Studying a cross-section of persons who had
recently lost a parent or spouse, she found five times as many
suicides as in a comparable group of the general population.

What can we make of these figures? To begin with, it is
apparent that far more bereaved people live than die; they
become reconciled to their loss, in one way or another. And
for those who do not, death or illness may be only indirectly

grief related. In many cases, the stricken person goes to pieces: he neglects himself, turns to alcohol, doesn't eat properly and becomes vulnerable to physical disease. But in seemingly far more cases, the illness is literally a reaction—a protest—to an emotional loss. In one study of patients with ulcerated colitis, doctors reported that thirty-three out of forty-one such patients developed the complaint soon after the death of a person important to them.

The suspicion that an acutely bereaved person might even develop cancer intrigued the psychologist Lawrence LeShan. From 1954 to 1966, he studied 450 cases of malignancy in terms of the emotional background of the patient. His conclusion: ". . . the loss of a central relationship and a sense of utter despair" was present in 72 percent of the cases before the disease developed. By comparison, only 10 percent of patients who suffered from some other ailment reported a recent death in their family.

A striking confirmation of this finding was discovered in predictions of malignancy among hospitalized women. At Rochester, New York's Strong Memorial Hospital, Dr. Arthur Schmale interviewed a number of women who were suspected of having cancer of the cervix. No diagnosis, however, had been made. Dr. Schmale found that if the patient had suffered a recent loss, and had reacted to it with feelings of hopelessness and depression, her chances of having cancer were high; when such symptoms of grief were not present, however, the risk was low. Physical tests proved Dr. Schmale to be correct in 75 percent of his predictions!

These are not isolated examples. Leukemia and lymphoma appear to be especially prevalent in those who have recently lost a parent. Researching these types of cancer, psychiatrist W. A. Greene found that 85 percent of his sample group of patients suffered from separation stress just prior to the onset of the disease. And two other researchers, Muslin-Gyarfas and Pieper, compared women who had malignant breast tumors with those who developed benign lesions. The malignant group were conspicuous for the fact that a large proportion of them were recently bereaved. This was not the case among the others.

Cancer might literally be caused by grief, it is theorized, simply because any strong emotional stress brings about chemical changes in the body. An overproduction of corticosteroids reduces our natural immunity to disease, especially those triggered by viruses, and many forms of cancer are suspected to be viral in origin.

Many other ongoing illnesses are thought to be highly vulnerable to grief reaction. The British psychiatrist, Dr. C. Murray Parkes, probably the world's leading authority on bereavement reactions, reports that the consultation rates for many physical symptoms increased by 50 percent following a death in the family, and that the most common grief-exacerbated illness was osteoarthritis. Tuberculosis is another disease that is seemingly reactivated by the onset of grief. Writes Dr. Jerome Frederick, a biophysiologist, "There seems to be little doubt that people undergoing unresolved grief, who at one time had arrested tuberculosis, during or shortly thereafter undergoing bereavement redevelop active tuberculosis."

It is even more apparent that psychological disturbances are brought on by the death of someone who is important to us. Dr. Parkes, for example, reports that seven times as many women enter psychiatric care following the death of their husbands as would have been expected if there had been no loss. (With men, such illnesses were only four times greater than expected, which may tell us something about male attitudes toward their wives, or simply about a culture in which men are reluctant to accept psychiatric help.) The death of a spouse can produce feelings of panic, loneliness, despair and even guilt. A child's death often results in the parents' divorce. By one estimate, 80 percent of the parents of leukemic children had either divorced, or were about to do so, in the first year following their child's death. In enabling us to adapt to stress when it comes to the death of someone we need and love, nature seems to have fallen down on the job.

Grief Wears Heavy Shoes

To lose someone dear to us is to lose something of ourselves. A person who has been a part of our life is gone forever, to be revived only in memory. Memories themselves are often painful because they remind us of what once was and can never again be. This is bereavement: the irretrievable loss of another person whose existence has been closely bound up with our own.

Grief is our response to this loss and, naturally, it is most acute in the period immediately following death. It need not, however, always be connected to death. Under certain circumstances, people grieve for themselves; this sadness derives from disappointments, lost opportunities and even the existential *Weltschmerz* celebrated by the German Romantics. Individuals grieve for things as well as people: the child, for a lost pet or toy; adults, for familiar objects or heirlooms that mean much to them. In all cases, the thing is somehow tied to pleasant associations and, perhaps, a sense of one's own security. In a perceptive study of the relocation of slum residents in Boston's West End during the city's urban renewal program, sociologist Marc Fried identified the major readjustment problem for these people as one of simple grief. They were, as the title of this study suggests, "grieving for a lost home."

Mourning defines the ways in which we deal with grief. Until two or three generations ago, widows weeds were worn by women and black armbands by men to announce, in effect, that the wearer was grieving (or was supposed to be) and that any melancholy or oddities of behavior they exhibited could be explained by their bereavement. Perhaps more important, these markers, and the sympathy they elicited, helped the person to experience grief. They made it easier for him to express his feelings, to cry if necessary, to be irritable; in short, to work through the shock that follows death.

Modern man has long given up most of the individual rituals that once attended grief behavior, and society is beginning to deceremonialize mourning and relinquish its support for the bereaved. As we shall note in the following chapter, funerals aren't what they used to be—indeed, they are often omitted entirely—and the custom of visitations and wakes is giving way to memorial services at which the deceased is out of sight (and, all too often, out of mind). Much of the difficulty people in mourning experience today, psychotherapists believe, can be traced to the absence of social sanctions for expressing one's feelings. It is de rigeur not to cry, and the stiff upper lip has become the norm. People are expected to handle rationally what is essentially an emotional burden.

However society chooses to handle reactions to death, it is clear that bereavement, grief and mourning must be understood as a set of intertwined experiences. These, in turn, are rooted in the very psychological and biological nature of man. In his paper, Mourning and Melancholia, Freud theorizes that because all close relationships are characterized by ambivalence—feelings of both love and hate—the loss of a loved one creates an unconscious sense of guilt. Since we don't want to hate the person who has just died, we hate ourselves instead, and this leads to depression. In a majority of cases, this phase of grief is short lived, and the bereaved shifts his psychic energy to others. Mourning is part of this cathartic process that enables us to gradually reassume our old way of life and to form new relationships.

Later psychoanalytic theory has modified Freud's position considerably. Melanie Klein, for example, recognizes the guilt factor in grief but attributes it to quite another cause. Adults who are bereaved, she writes, become like children who have lost a precious object. Not only do they protest (by grieving), but they blame themselves for what has happened. The person must have done something bad to have had his beloved relative taken from him. Grief, in this view, is a form of regression to primitive, childhood reaction.

This approach helps explain much of the childlike behavior that we see in grief-stricken people—the uninhibited weeping and even wailing, the rage at fate that such a thing could happen. They protest vehemently, through tears and screams, finally, if temporarily, turning their rage on themselves. Often, they say they can't believe it and refuse to accept the loss as real. Psychologically speaking, it may not become real for many months, or even years.

Many studies have shown that the bereaved do, indeed, hang on to their loved ones long after they have died, often by hallucinating their presence. The Cocoanut Grove survivor who saw his daughter calling him from a telephone booth is typical of such an experience. Dr. W. Dewi Rees, in his study of the Welsh bereaved, reported that 47 percent of the 293 people he interviewed had experienced hallucinations and more than a third of them continued to do so, even ten years after the event. Not surprisingly, people who had happy marriages were more likely to have these reactions than the survivors of unhappy marriages. Sometimes these states were visual; at other times the husband or wife might hear the dead spouse, or simply sense the deceased's presence. "Very often he is by my side," one woman told Dr. Rees. A man who had lost his wife sixteen years earlier said, "I find hearing her breathing disturbing, but I like the feeling she is in the house." A young widow explained, "He speaks quite plainly. I often hear him walking about the house." In fact, 11 percent of Dr. Rees's sample reported that they had talked with their dead spouse.

Much of this unusual behavior probably serves a useful purpose. At least, this is a conclusion we can draw from the fact that younger women, who hallucinate less than older ones, are more likely to die during the first year of bereavement. Holding on to the deceased is not only comforting; it helps ease the transition to a final acceptance of death. Although these reactions are by no means universal, they do occur frequently enough to indicate that they are effective coping mechanisms for some people. Dr. C. Murray Parkes thinks such actions are part of a built-in tendency to search for anything important to us that has been lost. Charles Darwin noted that animals engage in this search when they are separated from their mates or offspring, and the lost call is a common one among monkeys. In Parkes' view, adults reenact this biological behavior on a higher level; what appears as the mind playing tricks is really an expression of dependency—sometimes a healthy one—and a useful part of the grieving process.

Carried to an extreme, suicidal fantasies and suicide itself are sometimes an attempt to rejoin the dead lover or wife. More typical are the reactions of widows interviewed by Parkes who reported mingling in crowds in a futile quest for their dead husbands. "Everywhere I go I am searching for him. In crowds, in church, in the supermarket. I keep on scanning the faces. People must think I am odd." A surprising number of people become afflicted with the symptoms experienced by a dying relative during his last illness. "Mrs. H., for example, when told of her husband's death, immediately lost the use of her voice for ten days," Dr. Parkes writes. "Her husband had died from the second of two strokes, the first of which had left him unable to speak." Psychologists see this as an attempt, usually unconscious, to identify with the deceased; in less extreme forms, people may adopt the mannerisms of those they mourn—their style of walking or certain habits.

In a sense, these are all adjustments to death. As in neurosis, the person creates certain defenses against an unpleasant and unacceptable reality. Beyond the rather commonplace and, for the most part, harmless reactions, however, bereavement can pose a serious threat to one's health, as we have already noted. And the danger seems to be greatest in the months immediately following death. If grief is not resolved during this period, or if it is deliberately repressed, the risk of later illness is increased. One of Dr. Erich Lindemann's most trenchant insights was that the longer one postpones mourning, the more severe will be his symptoms later on.

This delayed reaction is partly the fault of society. Custom, especially in large cities, no longer pays much attention to mourning, and the individual is left to flounder on his own. Half of us are not affiliated with a church, and even for those who are, ministers, like doctors, don't often make house calls. Absent, too, are clear-cut social guidelines. This, in the view of sociologist Robert Blauner, "results in an ambiguity as to when the bereaved person has grieved enough."

To compound the problem, modern families are scattered; the widow or widower is likely to live alone, and it's rare that such a person is on close terms with his next-door neighbor. During the critical sinking-in period, when help is needed most, it is least likely to be forthcoming. The finality of death, with all its psychosomatic overtones, catches up, and it is the physician who gets the case. Yet, whatever the symptoms, grief is the disease.

All researchers in this field agree that such reactions are intensified if the death is sudden or unexpected. Probably the most comprehensive evidence of this comes from Dr. Parkes, who carefully followed the course of bereavement among sixty-eight Boston widows forty-nine years old or less. Parkes had already determined that these women were three times as likely to enter a hospital as their nonwidowed counterparts in the area. Next he wanted to find out if this frequency—and other symptoms of ill-health—could be related to the length of time a widow had had to prepare for the death of her husband.

To do this, he divided his sample into two groups. For the "short preparation" women, death had come to their husbands violently, by accident, through a sudden heart attack or by an acute illness that ran its course in a few days. The "long preparation" group, in contrast, had some reason to believe that death might be inevitable. Many of these wives had nursed their husbands through a lingering illness. Even though the end came as a shock, they had, in a sense, anticipated their own grief.

It is not surprising that members of this latter group made a noticeably better adjustment to their loss. Only 42 percent of these women showed signs of depression thirteen months later, compared with over 75 percent of the others. They were less likely to be emotionally disturbed, or feel guilty and resentful. And they were more likely to remarry, to be sociable and to visit their late husbands' graves. Parkes explains these disparities by pointing out that a slower death allows the survivor more time to come to terms with reality. For the suddenly bereaved, death is a blow that has given them no chance to tidy up the loose ends of marriage; something has happened not only to the deceased, but to them. Often they are caught in a web of guilt and self-reproach. "Grieving," Parkes adds, "becomes a way of life."

Accepting the Inevitable

These investigations would mean little if they did nothing more than satisfy our curiosity. In fact, they have taught physicians much about how to deal with grief as a treatable illness. Freud coined the term the "work of mourning" for this process of coming to terms with loss; for, although time itself is a powerful healer, it is helped by certain positive steps we can take to shorten the often drawn-out reaction, and mitigate the more painful aspects of grief. One can, indeed, work at it.

The Rev. Edgar Jackson, a Methodist minister who has written extensively on grief therapy, outlines three ways in which mourning can be made more effective. In brief, he recommends talking out, feeling out, and acting out one's grief. By talking out, Jackson means dealing with death as a problem that differs from other problems in its irrevocability, but not in its capacity for being tempered. Anyone who has ever lost a parent or a spouse knows how difficult it is to express one's state of mind during the first week or two of bereavement, when the shock of the event makes itself felt most acutely. For it is during this period that we are least willing to accept the truth; the commiserations, "He's gone to a better world," or "At last she is out of her misery," ring hollow and trivial. Even if we agree, it often seems inappropriate to be talking about the dead so openly. This reluctance is reinforced by a death-denying and death-defying culture. After a lifetime of avoiding the subject, it is difficult for us to grapple with it at a time when we are deeply and personally involved.

Yet for most people this is probably the best time to talk out their grief. The deceased himself need not be the central topic of discussion; rather, it is the feelings of the bereaved, the symptoms of grief, that lend themselves to rational discourse. If we understand that acute reactions are commonplace, that it is normal to be "all shook up" and that the manifestations of grief often take bizarre forms, bereavement is less frightening. Moments of panic, dizziness and hysteria; shortness of breath; nausea; loss of appetite—all these fall within an expectable range of symptoms over the short term. It is remarkable what a little curbstone psychotherapy by a minister or a friend can do to restore one's equilibrium. Even discussing the manifestations of grief with others has a positive value. According to Dr. Jerome Steiner, of Columbia University, this helps convert the "I" experience into a "we" experience "wherein unfamiliar physiological reactions are shared and thus are less frightening. A feeling perceived as 'unique' becomes perceived as 'general' and human." Yet such an approach is often regarded as an invasion of privacy; it is assumed that the bereaved wants to be left alone.

If talking helps put our grief in perspective, feeling out acts as a cathartic, restoring some of the emotional balance to our lives. This was the function of the wailing wall in ancient times (and still is among some inhabitants of Jerusalem). One could uninhibitedly weep and tear one's hair. Today, weeping is done in private, if at all; society expects us to be decorous in our grief, and public display of deep feeling, if not wholly frowned upon, is often a source of embarrassment. As a result, feelings that should be expressed openly are suppressed—held inside where they add to the confused and fragile web of moods that is woven by the bereaved. More than the loss itself, it is this holding back that probably brings on depression. Unable to sort out his feelings, to vent his rage or express his helplessness, he is driven back into himself. Crying or even screaming can be an effective defense against the immediate blow that assails us and, unlike responses to other crisis situations, is an acceptable response to death. One is not being childish on such occasions, but rather more adult than many of us dare to be.

Acting out, the third side of Edgar Jackson's grief triangle, is a natural extension of feeling. "Actions speak louder than words." In mourning, the message is really directed at ourselves to make it easier to live with an unbearable truth. Sheer physical activity gives us some control over grief; we are no longer passive victims of a catastrophe, but combatants in the struggle.

Dr. Samuel Klagsbrun, of St. Luke's Hospital in New York, believes that physical action mobilizes the emotions and provides a channel equal in outlet to the feelings that are blocked. One of his patients, following the death of her husband, was unable to work through her acute grief and had to be hospitalized. When sedative drugs and conventional psychotherapy proved inadequate, Dr. Klagsbrun encouraged her to tear the bedsheet in anger, and he even helped her to get started! Centuries ago, this primitive reaction was observed in the practice of rending one's clothes.

Few people carry grief to this extreme; in ordinary circumstances it is seldom necessary. What does seem to be required, however—although it is not always practiced—is some type of mourning ritual. This sort of acting out mitigates grief by enabling one to share it with close friends and others. Funerals can serve this function by telling the bereaved that death is not only a family's loss, but a community's loss as well. Grief that is ritualized, even when it is not shared, is easier to bear.

Is it possible to have effective mourning rituals that are not backed by a religious faith? Studies of bereaved people indicate that better adjustments are made by those who do have a well-defined church affiliation. Interviewing widowers in Cleveland, John W. Bedell reported this to be particularly true among Catholics. Probably the most stringently observed rites occur among Orthodox Jews, for whom the period of *shiva* (the first seven days after burial) becomes a crucial act of psychological withdrawal and self-sacrifice. Sexual relations are proscribed, washing up and the wearing of shoes are forbidden, social pleasantries are omitted. The mourner must not do any work, not even read the Bible except for such books as *Job* and *Lamentations*. Couches and beds are given up for the ground or hard benches. Rabbi Steven Moss of New York remarks that the bereaved "is forced to face the fact of the other's death directly and realistically . . . head-on and alone." Only after *shiva* does he gradually resume his life with the living.

Modern life makes it difficult to carry out prescribed rituals. The tightly knit community that enforced them is a thing of the past; personal independence is prized; mourning clothes are thought too lugubrious; and displays of grief are likely to be regarded as a sign of poor adjustment. One result, as has been noted, is that grief, suppressed on its own terms, reemerges as an illness to be tranquilized or treated according to the whim of the physician. The act of mourning, which once left people secure in their grief, gives way to inaction and confusion.

This seems to be particularly true of white people. The psychologist Richard Kalish, comparing blacks, Japanese-Americans, Mexican-Americans and whites in the Los Angeles area, notes that the latter "are least likely to participate in rituals for the dead." Yet, except for the Mexican-Americans, all the groups agreed that they would try very hard to control their emotions in public. The natural release of feelings so typical of many ethnic groups is blocked, Kalish thinks, by white decision-makers who project "their own view of the human condition."

Anticipating Grief

One reason why survivors of those who died slow deaths do better than those who are suddenly bereaved is simply that they begin their grieving early. But sometimes it is too early. Dr. Glen W. Davison, of the Southern Illinois University School of Medicine, has coined the term waiting vulture syndrome for relatives who "have processed their initial sense of loss after realizing that a patient will die, but before the patient's demise." The drooped head with shoulders falling forward and the general exhaustion that come from long vigils at the bedside testify to their discomfort and announce, in effect, "we're ready too soon." In these instances, Dr. Davison writes, the relatives may need more attention than the patient. One head nurse told him, "I believe we are doing everything possible to make them comfortable."

During World War II, Dr. Erich Lindemann saw servicemen's wives who, having prepared themselves for the possible loss of their husbands, were unable to cope with the reunion when the men came back. Not infrequently, the wife demanded an immediate divorce—she had done her grief work too well.

Most relatives of the dying are not waiting vultures, for if anything, one's presence at a fatal illness is more likely to be falsely cheerful, as part of the effort not to let on that one knows. Therapists agree that this unrealistically cheerful attitude is harmful both to the patient and his relatives. In fact, the dying person himself may sense this false jollity and take the initiative in preparing his survivors for the loss. In my community, a young city councilman dying of cancer openly discussed his imminent death with his wife and young children, even to the details of his funeral. Because they were able to grieve together, the family was prepared to deal with its loss realistically when death came, and the widow found she could take over and manage her husband's successful grocery business.

In preparing for the death of a loved one, says Dr. Kübler-Ross, one should try to understand the patient's own mood and share it with him; help him finish his unfinished business; help him grieve. Pinching his cheeks and asking him to be sociable mocks his true feelings. The patient may want you simply to sit silently and hold his hand. "Don't go in and say, 'Don't cry, it's not so bad.' Say, 'It takes a man to cry, if that's the way you feel,'" Dr. Kübler-Ross advises. Grief is caring; much of the guilt feeling that follows death is our conscience telling us that we did not show the dying that we cared while there was still time.

The Long Road Back

Today, doctors perform crisis intervention among the bereaved much as they do in other traumatic illnesses. When abnormal grief, characterized by despair, worry, depression and self-neglect, can be spotted in time, much can be done to restore the person to health.

St. Christopher's Hospice in London is an institution for the terminally ill. From long experience, doctors there know that mourning begins before the patient dies. Thus, nurses at St. Christopher's are asked to observe relatives closely and, based on their assessment, to predict which among them will probably take it hardest and require help later on. Their predictions are remarkably accurate, and St. Christopher's family support service follows up all cases referred to it by the staff.

The hospice also finds that the need for such intervention is usually reduced if families become part of the treatment group. Relatives are encouraged to take their meals with patients, to participate in social activities with them—a wheelchair race across the grounds is one such event—and to make the hospice a kind of second home. Visiting hours are liberal, and children are always welcome. All of this, the staff believes, helps turn anticipatory grief toward constructive channels. A police sergeant dying there summed it up when he spoke of his experience as a "bringing together" illness.

At Tufts Medical Center in Boston, social workers begin

working with the families of cancer patients three months before the expected death and continue for six months afterwards —the critical period when family disorganization, brought about by the illness, is most likely to occur. Dr. Melvin Krant, who supervises this project, believes that when death is certain the close relatives need as much help as the patient. He tells his staff, "Try to arrange a final good-bye between the patient and his family. Try to treat the survivors medically if they need help. Try to arrange for permissions for autopsies or organ transplants, if this seems feasible. Go to the wake. And finally, attend the funeral." Many problems of the bereaved, he thinks, are caused by the abrupt desertion of the hospital personnel, who are most intimately involved in the patient's illness. In most institutions, he says, "The message to the family is 'go home.'"

Dr. Kübler-Ross advocates "screaming rooms" in hospitals for those so overwhelmed by grief that conventional outlets are insufficient. One woman, whose child was dying of cancer, was advised to go to the chapel, where she could grieve and pray. "Who needs a chapel?" she retorted. "I need just the opposite. I need to scream and rage and curse." Sometimes, Dr. Kübler-Ross thinks, this can be "good grief." And drugs, she adds, keep people calm when they should express their feelings.

Six years ago, at Montefiore Hospital in the Bronx, New York, staff psychologists began keeping track of close relatives of patients who had died in the hospital, comparing them with a nonbereaved group from among 25,000 clients of a prepaid medical health plan. The chief problem, they found, was that mourners did little or nothing about their grief during the first six months, after which there was a noticeable increase in visits to the doctor. People who were already sick got sicker. And, for some reason, Jewish subjects were more likely than others to resist being helped. Dr. Irwin Gerber, who heads this project, thinks that, in an urban setting, grief becomes too private. There is not enough community involvement to share the burden.

Going on the assumption that many bereaved people are too

proud to ask for help, Montefiore has initiated a form of telephone therapy. Psychologists call up the survivor, much as they might pay a friendly visit; from these conversations it is often possible to determine the bereaved's state of mind and, if necessary, to discuss his problems in subsequent calls. Face-to-face therapy follows when this seems desirable.

Some of the surviving relatives who did come in for help exhibited a curious, yet not uncommon, symptom: they acted as though their parent or spouse still lived. Doctors attributed this to unresolved conflicts between the mourner and the deceased which persisted after death. To resolve the problem, doctors hit upon the notion of letting the survivor go on believing in this postmortem presence. Such people might be persuaded that if a relative had been hostile and ungenerous in life, he might well change his attitude and become more understanding and forgiving now that he was "on the other side." And if the deceased, in this sense, was alive, it was often easier for the survivor to talk about him and express his true feelings.

This need on the part of some people to deny death accounts for the considerable interest in spiritualism in this country, a subject which will be discussed in Chapter Nine. In England, many widows interviewed by Dr. C. Murray Parkes described visits to seances or Spiritualist churches.

Clearly, most of us are not so inclined. Nor do most of us seek out, or even need, psychiatric help. Probably the most effective therapy for the average person is contact with others who have experienced a similar loss. Some few years, at the Laboratory for Community Psychiatry in Boston, Dr. Phyllis Silverman started a widow-to-widow program in which women whose husbands had died earlier pay regular visits to newly bereaved widows, offering them help and understanding at this critical time. From this idea has grown more elaborate programs aimed at bringing survivors back into community life. In Westchester County, New York, the Family Service has organized a Widowers and Widows Club, staffed by volunteers who have been through the ordeal of bereavement. An active schedule includes regular membership meetings, workshops, theater and opera parties, bridge lessons, trips, a monthly newsletter and training in home visits to families who have lost a close relative. The club has not, as some predicted, turned into a marriage bureau; there are simply too many women members for the number of men!

Bereavement specialization is a new profession in our society. Be it represented by store-front mediums or newspaper columnists, ministers or psychologists, the art of grieving is undergoing a modest revival. Yet in spite of these efforts, most people today are left to work out their grief alone. Dr. Robert Fulton, of the University of Minnesota, in a survey of largely rural inhabitants of that area, found that less than 15 percent of the people he talked with were contacted by a doctor, social worker or clergyman during the period immediately following the death of a loved one. Fulton speaks of the abandoned widow and says she is most likely to be called on by the funeral director trying to collect his bill.

Curiously, it is the funeral director who has emerged as the most accessible of these bereavement specialists. By coming to collect his bill—or perhaps to prove that he has earned it—he is sometimes the most helpful person around. And this, more than anything, helps explain the new look in funerals.

CHAPTER VIII

Bury the Dead?

RESIDENTS OF SCOTTSDALE, ARIZONA, a conservative, well-heeled community not far from Phoenix, are as accustomed to funeral processions as people anywhere. The cortege leaves Hansen's Funeral Home, or one of the town's churches, and wends its way to the cemetery a few miles away. People don't take much notice unless the deceased was especially prominent; in that case, the line of cars might stretch for two or three blocks, tying up traffic at intersections. By and large, however, funerals in Scottsdale are a routine affair for everyone except the mourners.

But on one particular occasion about three years ago residents blinked at a strange procession indeed. The familiar gray hearse was followed by a single limousine and twenty-five motorcycles. Even at its funeral pace, the cortege was unusually noisy; to many spectators, it was an unseemly way to pay one's respects to the dead. The helmeted riders—some with their girlfriends perched on the pillions—were wearing blue jeans and leather jackets.

Three days before, a member of their motorcycle club had been killed in an accident. At first the funeral director had resisted the idea of letting the young people ride to the cemetery on cycles; it just wasn't done. But the club leader convinced him, and the boy's family, too, that the deceased would have wanted it that way. The members were paying their respects out of deep feeling, rather than convention. For in a sense, they were his true family.

At the graveside, once the committal service was over, each young man stepped forward in turn, ripped the club insignia from his sleeve and flung it on the coffin. Then six members grabbed spades and filled the grave. What most impressed the boy's parents, however, was that many of these usually swaggering, high-spirited youths were in tears.

This incident is not as unusual as it may seem. All over the country, funerals are being adapted to the lifestyle of the deceased, often at the behest of young people who see traditional funeral practices as empty and meaningless. In Maine, a teen-age girl whose brother had just died called a funeral home and asked the director if she could come over and do some "painting." The puzzled undertaker, thinking that she simply wanted to assuage her grief by doing something creative, invited her to come. But the painting, he discovered, was on the casket itself! The girl decorated it with psychedelic designs and colors that expressed her own feelings toward her brother.

In Louisville, Kentucky, a sixteen-year-old girl was kidnapped, tortured, raped and murdered. Five weeks later, her decomposed body was found in a roadside grave. At the funeral home, a few hours after the girl's parents made arrangements for a traditional Baptist service, her four brothers arrived to countermand the orders. The two oldest—bearded college students—explained that they had persuaded their parents to let them arrange the service. They had even been to see the minister and he, too, had agreed. What followed at the church, two days later, was a Christian burial interspersed with folk-rock music by a guitar-playing vocalist and readings from American Indian lore and Oriental literature. To those who had known this young girl, it was a wholly appropriate act of remembrance.

Like dying itself, the American funeral is being challenged on the ground that it frequently does not symbolize what the deceased stood for in life and thus no longer serves the true needs of his survivors. Traditional rites, whatever their cohesive social value—their message to others that life goes on—are in the process of breaking up; they are being replaced by a multitude of groping and tentative efforts to instill authenticity into a ceremony that has become all too often barren and, in sociological parlance, dysfunctional.

Whether we call it adaptive or authentic, this type of funeral produces both moving and bizarre results. At his own request, Charles A. Lindbergh was buried, unembalmed and uneulogized, less than eight hours after he died, in a tiny church cemetery in Hawaii; the only mourners present were his widow and one son. The burial was entirely in keeping with the world-famous man, who cherished privacy and had lived the latter years of his life outside the limelight.

Committals that attempt to preserve the spirit of the deceased are not always as simple as Lindbergh's. A few years ago, the captain of a yacht owned by the daughter of a multimillionaire real estate and railroad tycoon, died after forty years in her service. Knowing that the yacht was his whole life, she decided to give him the burial at sea that he had always wanted. Fortunately, she was able to do it in a style grander than most deceased sailors are accustomed to. Surrounded by his charts and books, the captain's body was propped in his cabin; and, in what was certainly one of the most expensive burials in history, the yacht was towed several miles off the coast of Florida and sunk—all $60,000 of it!

Are Funerals Really Necessary?

Every society, in every age, has arranged some kind of parting ceremony for its dead. Like birth, religious confirmation and marriage, death is a rite of passage that deserves recognition by one's family and immediate community. To die unacknowledged is to not have lived. The question, then, is not whether a funeral, but what kind?

Centuries ago, when theological considerations predominated, funerals were primarily for the benefit of the dead. The passage led to heaven; the service itself was a launching pad to immortality. The common practice among the ancients of burying food and personal possessions with the corpse illustrates how literal was their conception of the journey.

Today, immortality is less persuasive. Funerals are arranged in memory of the dead but for the benefit of the living. For many families, this is the ultimate challenge in the game of status-seeking. The deceased achieves an ex post facto glory that was denied him in life, while the survivors assuage both their vanity and their guilt. Much can be done with a bronze casket, a lead vault, a complement of lodge brothers or sisters, a wake or visitation, a suitable eulogy and a desirable lakeview gravesite with perpetual care and a headstone towering over other corpses less fortunate. If it is too late to reassure the person in whose name all this is done, it is timely indeed for a family conscious of its position in the community.

All this is a doubtful business; it is also expensive. One investigator claims that "the American public spends more money on funerals and accessories each year than is spent on all hospitals and sanitoria." This may be an exaggeration, but the cost is undeniably huge—about $2 billion annually, and, among ceremonial expenditures, second only to the amount invested in weddings.

It is hardly necessary to repeat in detail the long catalogue of complaints directed at the funeral industry. Jessica Mitford, in her bestseller, The American Way of Death, drew attention to the excesses of a custom, once simple and functional, that has become elaborate and hollow. In Mitford's view, this represents largely a conspiracy on the part of undertakers to take advantage of grief-stricken relatives. The full-service funeral can be described as a smorgasbord of goodies designed to convince the client that what has happened has really not happened at all. Princeton University professor of theology Paul Ramsey has described these funeral preparations as "the American way of not dying."

Most of us can only guess what goes on in the embalming room, but in the slumber, or reposing, parlor, one sees the miracles that have been wrought. Viewing the body is a way of being assured that death is not so terrible, and that it may not even be final. The casket, with its inner-spring mattress and pleated satin lining, is a model of comfort. A pseudonaturalism is the object, and, in the case of children, this is sometimes carried to grotesque extremes. The Rev. Fr. Vincent Fish, an Episcopal minister in Illinois, tells of the time he went to the funeral home with the parents of a young child who had died and "found that the child was in a playpen in a sitting position, holding a doll." The undertaker insisted that mothers found this idea comforting.

Economically speaking, there is no doubt that viewing the corpse is one of the fundamentals of the economy of the funeral industry. One can add that the florists don't come off so badly, either. Extravagant floral offerings announce the time of death (a simulated clock in a wreath of flowers) or its tentativeness (the vacant chair waiting for its occupant to return). Music bridges the gap to eternity ("Tell Mother I'll Be There") while the tears flow.

Above all, the rite assumes a sacred tone, even for the most unredeemed sinner. Every funeral home has its chapel, for with the decline in church funerals—a study in Philadelphia indicates that 90 percent of all burials today are conducted out of funeral homes—the undertaker preempts the supernatural symbols of religion, just as he performs the work of impresario and stage manager once entrusted to the minister. Writing of a typical New England industrial community which he calls Yankee City, the sociologist W. Lloyd Warner describes the funeral director's role as "the producer who fashions the whole enterprise so that other performers, including the minister, the eulogist, the organist, the vocalist, family, and mourners can act becomingly and get the approval and praise for the funeral's success and receive the sensuous satisfaction that the funeral's symbolism evokes." No wonder many ministers look upon the funeral director with considerable hostility.

According to Dr. Robert Fulton, the emerging prestige of the undertaker threatens many clergymen with a loss of status. He has not only taken over many of the functions formerly carried out by the church, but he does so at a considerable profit to himself. ". . . clergymen discover that the cabinet maker who assisted him yesterday in the conduct of the funeral, today not only offers to take complete charge of the funeral, but also is prepared to hold the service in his own 'chapel.' To many clergymen this is not only galling personally, but is also contrary to the tenets of their faith."

But the role of the funeral director does not stop with the interment of the body, or the collection of his fee. He is now a "crisis intervenor" and a "bereavement specialist." Grief therapy, in fact, is the newest addition to the funeral director's already extensive line of goods and services. One mortician speaks of himself as a doctor of grief. At a recent symposium in New York, funeral directors were described by one of their spokesmen as the caretakers and caregivers of the community. The minister can hardly be blamed for resenting the intrusion of an outsider who is motivated, not by a sense of calling, but by the more dubious belief that good grief is good business.

Or can he be blamed? If funerals have in large part been lost to the church, it is possible that satisfactions of the market-place, as well as the slackening of religious belief, account for the shift. In numerous surveys (some sponsored by the funeral industry itself), bereaved survivors overwhelmingly report that the funeral director is often more helpful than the clergyman. By the very nature of his profession, he is the last person to lavish care on the body of the deceased and the first to pay attention to the needs of the survivors. In short, he does the dirty work.

When Robert Fulton analyzed questionnaires from 1,248 respondents in several midwestern cities and followed up with 315 personal interviews, he garnered some surprising results. Fulton's purpose was to uncover the attitudes of the American public toward death, funerals and funeral directors in the wake of prevalent criticism of contemporary funeral customs. Although he himself believes that burial ceremonies have become meaningless and dysfunctional, the public apparently does not share this view. A majority of his respondents approved of traditional funerals, and thought, too, that one of the most useful functions of the funeral director was the comforting of the bereaved. In Boston, Dr. Phyllis Silverman reports that the widows she worked with indicated "that the funeral director was more helpful" than either the family physician or clergyman. In the opinion of Dr. Otto Margolis, dean of the American Academy McAllister Institute, this may be simply because it is the funeral director who is there to bear the brunt of the immediate grief.

Some undertakers now list their establishments as bereavement counseling centers. Postdeath encounter sessions for the family are held on the premises for several weeks following the funeral; and, to their credit, these morticians invite clergymen and psychologists to join in the meetings. Less to their credit is the fact that they are probably ill equipped, on a theoretical basis, for handling emotional problems that may require professional attention.

Several years ago, the psychologist Robert Kastenbaum studied a cross section of students enrolled in a college of mortuary sciences. "It was found," he wrote, "that many people who plan a career in this field . . . have a fairly low level of intellectual interest and output. There was little indication that intellectual challenges were welcome. The typical student expected to absorb certain necessary facts of know-how from his course work, but showed no zest for further knowledge or inquiry."

The most pronounced shortcoming among these future funeral directors, however, was their ambivalent attitude toward death itself. Anxiety was common. Writes Kastenbaum:

> The typical student in this sample had a pained and brittle attitude toward death. Discomfort became evident as soon as the first death question was raised in the classroom. Instantly the room was filled with cigarettes that looked like so many emergency flares burning for help; the young men and women began to twitch as though their chairs had just been electrified, and there was a scattering of giggles and obscene remarks. This was by far the strongest reaction either of the researchers had ever encountered when introducing the topic of death in a classroom situation—and the students were tomorrow's funeral directors!
>
> In general [Kastenbaum sums up] there was no evidence to indicate that the career choice had been based upon a particular commitment to the problems of bereavement, or an exploration and resolution of the meaning of death in their own lives.

Perhaps the lack of intellectual interests and commitment to the psychological requirements of their profession can be explained by the generally limited education of funeral directors. Half the states require only a high school diploma for licensing, the others either one or two years of college at most. Prof. Charles H. Nichols, a trustee of the National Foundation of Funeral Service, reports that the median education for undertakers entering the profession in 1970 was 12.2 years (high school) for whites and 10.1 years (tenth grade) for blacks. In sum, a majority of funeral directors have no more than a secondary school education. These are the men and women who advertise themselves as bereavement counselors.

To their credit, however, a few morticians employ professionals for this work. A Denver, Colorado, mortuary has supplied a postfuneral counseling service for the past fifteen years; the present counselor, Dr. Carl M. Davidson, a retired Methodist minister, makes house calls within ten days after the service to see if there is any way he can be of help. Basically, he thinks, the value of the service is to let the survivor know that he hasn't been forgotten. At such a time, almost everyone seeks an outlet for his grief and if the caller is a stranger, especially a symbolic stranger in the person of a minister or priest, "people tend to reveal more about their true feelings." Dr. Davidson's prescription for this one-time visit is simple: "Let the person cry and don't try to give advice."

Sensitive to criticism—and no other American business has been so criticized on so many grounds—the American funeral director has begun to fight back. The industry's trade association, the National Funeral Director's Association, maintains well-financed lobbies in the state capitals and in Washington. Laws supported by them, for example, make it unnecessarily expensive to cremate a body. In some states, this must be done in a casket which is burned up with the corpse! And in all but a few states, the funeral director's lobby has successfully blocked legislation that would compel the undertaker to itemize his services. The present system of buying a funeral is based on the price of the casket; that the family may not want the full range of services makes no difference.

But the major effort of the Association is directed at convincing the public that the full-service funeral, with all its ceremonial trappings, is psychologically important to the survivors. Although critics see this argument as a subtle form of brainwashing motivated primarily by economic interests, a surprising number of behavioral scientists concur with the undertaker. Funerals, they say, are good for you.

To View or Not to View

Some psychologists believe that the most important time for the bereaved is the moment of truth when he stands in front of the open casket and looks at the dead body. Such an experience, painful as it may be, brings home the finality of death. In Robert Fulton's words, "viewing the body is part of the rite of separation." Something deep within us demands a confrontation with death, a last look that assures us that the person we loved or admired is, indeed, gone forever. Far from being barbaric, viewing is seen as an important psychological adjunct to grieving. It is easier to give up the deceased if the body is visible and, equally important, if it is laid to rest in our presence.

Two researchers, Jeanette R. Folta and Edith S. Deck, have confirmed the importance of this practice in several empirical investigations. "Our studies have shown," they write, "that among both families and friends lack of viewing prevents the development of the level of awareness and leads to feelings of disbelief for months and even years after death. . . ." Quite the opposite assumption is drawn by Rabbi Maurice Lamm and Naftali Eskreis, who note that "there is no mask of death in the Jewish ritual." Their article in the *Journal of Religion and Health*, "Viewing the Remains: a New American Custom," claims that this invasion of the deceased's privacy is anything but therapeutic for the survivors. "By making a display of the flesh minus the mind we are in fact demonstrating our lifelong emphasis on appearance over value. The person is manipulated as one would a piece of merchandise and reduced to a mere object. . . . The tendency of those attending funerals is to note that 'he looks good' rather than 'he was good,' and conversations tend to dwell on the person as a man of means rather than a man of ends."

Despite the assertions of Lamm and Eskreis, however, the custom is not especially new. It dates from the time the embalming process was perfected, thus enabling the body to be preserved for long periods of time. (Lenin has been on view in the Kremlin Wall for over fifty years, and hundreds of Russians have lined up to see him. Interestingly, the effect of this pilgrimage is to prove not so much that he is dead, but that his influence still lives.) Viewing became more common in the United States during the Civil War, when the returned bodies of soldiers were proudly displayed in their military splendor to admiring townspeople. With the growth of the funeral home as a distinct business enterprise during the latter part of the nineteenth century, a custom that had formerly been limited chiefly to soldiers, dignitaries and heads of state became available to the ordinary man. And today, what was once a patriotic tribute to the dead has become an act of social obligation. Moreover, it is an obligation that can be stunningly expensive.

Neither the Jewish nor the Roman Catholic religion allows the funeral service to be conducted with the coffin open, and in most Protestant churches the practice is discouraged. Whatever viewing takes place, therefore, is usually arranged in the church or funeral home prior to the service.

What *is* new about the custom is the cosmetology—the restoration of the corpse to make it appear as lifelike as possible. The face is rouged to a healthy pallor, disfigurations are removed, the mouth straightened, sunken cheeks filled out, and the hair dressed and groomed with a final permanent or trim. Morticians have little to learn from the artists at Madame Tussaud's waxworks. They argue, reasonably enough, that no family wants its departed laid out as though ravaged by a terminal illness. And psychologists tend to agree that the memory image of the deceased is an important factor in the survivor's adjustment to loss.

To find out just how true this might be, a funeral director in Florissant, Missouri, Gene S. Hutchens, sent questionnaires to 100 people he had served over a nine-month period, all of whom had bought traditional funerals. Sixty-three replied. A majority were Catholic. Although the survey was hardly scientific (a sampling of those who had opted for nontraditional services would have been necessary to make a fair comparison), it did indicate that residents of this midwestern community were satisfied with the kind of funeral they had selected. Viewing was especially important. To the question, "Did the open casket help you realize and accept the fact that he or she was dead?" fifty-two respondents replied yes and nine said no. (Two did not answer this question.) Fifty-five of the sixty-three persons queried thought that the physical appearance of the corpse left "a pleasant memory picture." By a large majority (fifty-one), these people agreed that the traditional-type funeral had been of value in bereavement, although a somewhat smaller number (forty-four) said the memory of such a funeral had been helpful in easing grief later on. Only seven of the sixty-three respondents said they would do it differently in the future.

How important the beautified appearance of the body may be in these circumstances is open to question, for the fact is that the cosmetic, lifelike approach may actually make it harder to accept the reality of death. The Amish, for example, insist on viewing the body without any restoration, regardless of how it looks. Critics of the funeral industry say that, although viewing may be psychologically helpful, the costly cosmetology that is usually included adds little to the final impression. What is remembered, in the long run, is not the body but the person.

Burial versus Cremation

Another and broader study tends to confirm the reactions gathered by Gene Hutchens. Dr. Robert Fulton surveyed 565 Minnesota residents, both rural and urban. Seventy-five percent of these people had lost their husbands, the remainder were widowers. A majority attended church or had a nominal religious affiliation. Only 10 percent of the sample had not used a traditional funeral service. Most of this group came from the professional, upper-income, nonreligious segment of the population.

Fulton emphasizes that the findings of this recent study are still preliminary, but if they "prove out" upon further analysis, many of the arguments for elaborate and emotional funerals will be convincingly reinforced. For example, when people participated in these types of funerals, which included viewing the body of their spouses, they reported fewer adjustment problems afterwards. They had a warmer and more positive recall of the deceased. Important, too, was the fact that they experienced better relations with other family members after the death.

In striking contrast, those who did not have a traditional funeral suffered a greater range of problems in their postbereavement lives. There was an increased use of alcohol, sedatives and tranquilizers; recalling the deceased in positive terms was less likely to occur; feelings of hostility toward others was common; and, in general, adjustment to death was poor. Significantly, members of this group were much more likely to cremate (this occurred in one-third of the cases), or to substitute a "disposal" service for a regular funeral. Even among these professionals, however, women tended to treat the man's body more traditionally. They rarely cremated their husbands, whereas the men frequently cremated their wives, although not their children. Moreover, Fulton found that when a family pet died, it was almost always buried, often with a little service at the graveside.

Perhaps a child is, in fact, closer to one's heart than a spouse—more deeply loved and harder to relinquish at death. Perhaps it represents the expression of an emotional need which upper-middle-class people tend to deny when they are dealing with adults. Sentiment, rather than reason, predominates. Whatever the explanation, 80 percent of these cremators and nontraditionalists said they "would do it differently next time." This included all of the men.

Surveys as complex as Fulton's should be approached with caution. Many factors other than funerals enter into the problems that follow bereavement. It is quite possible, for example, that some men cremate their wives because they lack a warm and positive image of them before death. Adjustment problems, moreover, may reflect the fact that better educated, more successful people are not as used to coping with an irrecoverable loss. Less fortunate families tend to stick together during a crisis, and they usually have more experience with the unpleasant side of life. They are inclined to deal with these things emotionally rather than rationally, and this, in fact, may mitigate the effects of bereavement.

Society has always employed some kind of ceremony that does more than simply dispose of the body; a custom so universal can hardly be without meaning. Yet it is a custom that is gradually declining as more and more people turn to substitute rituals. Although not more than 4 percent of the general population in this country are cremated, among professional groups the proportion is much higher (about one-third in Fulton's sample), and in England cremation is increasing among all classes. Even in the United States, the trend is away from elaborate funerals and open casket visitations.

I became personally aware of this while I was doing research for this chapter. Ted P., a friend of twenty years, died suddenly from a heart attack. As a member of a local memorial society which arranges simple, preplanned services, he had specified that there was to be no funeral at his death, nor was his body to be embalmed and put on view. There was, however, a memorial service a few days later at which Ted was honored *in absentia*. The minister stood in the empty chancel of a Unitarian church and spoke glowingly of his achievements as a father, a husband and a man of social conscience. It was an effective eulogy, as far as it went, and not a few tears were shed in the course of it. The church was crowded, but something was missing. A man I talked with afterwards put it well. "Everybody was here," he said, "but Ted."

If simpler services, or none at all, are becoming more and more prevalent, the funeral director himself may be largely to blame. Added to the extraordinary expense of a lingering terminal illness, the full-service funeral is a luxury that puts many families in debt. Writes sociologist Ruth Mulvey Harmer, who made an extensive study of funeral costs, "I know of some instances in which widows were forced to sell their homes to pay funeral bills. In many cases, families have been forced to seek welfare because the insurance money had to be turned over to the undertaker."

To many critics, the $2 billion a year spent for funerals is simply tribute exacted by outmoded social custom and the undertaker's keen willingness to take advantage of a family crisis. (Some years ago, a survey by the Catholic magazine *Jubilee* found that 41 percent of Catholic and 51 percent of Protestant clergymen felt that bereaved families were exploited, at least some of the time, in arranging funerals.) In a 1974 study of all funeral homes in the Washington, D.C., area, the Federal Trade Commission came up with a typical total bill of $1,886, including cemetery charges, but not including the cost of the grave plot. Depending on the funeral home patronized, the buyer of the least expensive funeral offered may pay anywhere from $210 to $900. And some funeral directors are notorious for making the prospective client ashamed of buying a "cheap" casket, for it is the price of the casket that determines the total cost of the funeral. When the Senate antitrust committee investigated this situation in Ohio, they found that a $234 casket, for example, added up to a $1,080 funeral. If the buyer was willing to settle for a $90 casket—and could find an undertaker who would sell him one at that price—his final bill came to less than $500. In both cases, the services performed by the funeral home were essentially the same.

But with few exceptions, the simple, inexpensive funeral is virtually nonexistent. In New York City, a Ralph Nader public interest group made such a request, anonymously, of sixty funeral homes. Half of the quoted prices were above $750 and some ranged as high as $1,200. And this was only a beginning! As much as $700 more might be required to purchase, open and close a grave. If the buyer can be convinced that the deceased is better off in a lead vault, add another $200.

Other accusations have been leveled at the undertaker. A

twenty-dollar pine coffin is not, as he may insist, against health regulations. Nor is embalming a legal necessity unless the body is to be shipped some distance for burial. Moreover, it has no value for sanitation and public health, says Dr. Elix Ives, professor of genetics and pediatrics at the University of Saskatchewan. Refrigeration is just as good, and cheaper. Yet the family may find itself saddled with the expense of embalming and many other items, before it gives its consent or is even asked. Habeas corpus undoubtedly works to the undertaker's advantage, for once he is in possession of the body it is impractical for the family to seek out another funeral director.

In many states, should cremation be decided upon—and it will rarely, if ever, be suggested by the undertaker—the body must still be delivered to the crematorium in a casket by a licensed mortician. All of this costs money, and, although cremation itself is relatively inexpensive—generally well under $100—the extras add up. One documented example illustrates how the widow of a man who left instructions not to "spend one penny you don't have to" ended up with a $798.75 bill, even though there was no funeral! The undertaker's services, in this case, included the following: transfer of the body, $70; burial permit, $15; preparation room, $25; sanitary care, $45; arrangements and supervision, $245; casket, $215; hearse, $72; fifteen copies of the death certificate, $33.75; crematory charge, $72; and certification of certificates, $6. The $215-casket, incidentally, went up in flames.

The person who might want to shop around for a sensibly priced funeral before he dies may discover that this is impossible; in some states the law prohibits funeral contracts and the quoting of prices in advance of death. Spokesmen for the industry argue that this is to protect the unwary from signing up for funerals that may later prove to be beyond their means, but it is equally effective in preventing the prospective customer from finding out what the service is going to cost his family until it is too late. Justified or not, laws such as these testify to the existence of the influential funeral lobbies in our various state capitols.

District 65, Retail, Wholesale, and Department Store Workers Union, which has long paid $2,000 in death benefits to the family of a deceased member, now finds that well over half of this sum is eaten up in funeral bills—the average in 1971 was $1,339. Seeking ways to reduce burial costs, this progressive union at one point considered opening its own mortuary, only to find that the law of the state in which is was to be located forbade anyone but a funeral director from owning a mortuary. District 65 in New York City, however, has figured out one way to save on death expenses; it bought several tracts in a local cemetery, "block booking" its membership in advance, at an average cost of thirty dollars a gravesite. (Comparable private sites in the New York metropolitan area range from $200 to $473.) The union also has arrangements with several funeral homes to provide a simple but dignified funeral service at a full cost of $175. A somewhat more elaborate production can be had for $315, still about one-third the price of self-arranged funerals.

Probably the most interesting fact to emerge from the union's experience in this field is that a great many of its members don't want an inexpensive burial even when it is available. As a result, a $600- to $700-plan has been set up, using an oak or mahogany casket in place of the pine casket. There is much evidence, in fact, that many blue-collar people, especially those with strong ethnic ties, want and expect "the works" when they die.

Frank R. Galante, a New Jersey funeral director who serves a largely Italian clientele, reports that the funeral procession itself is a source of great importance—and some expense—to the survivors. "Most of the families I serve want the procession to go by the home of the deceased and often by his or her place of business," he adds. Simple, inexpensive funerals, let alone memorial services, are almost unknown among the poorer classes, especially in the case of blacks, for whom "death is often the only time when there is a real luxury," as writer Michael Harrington puts it. "Dying is a moment of style and status, at least in the impoverished world of the racial ghetto." The black funeral, with its "dress-up" mourners, its uninhibited weeping and glorious hymn-singing, and, above all, its sense of mourner participation, provides a deeply moving experience and a cathartic release that few white people are privileged to know. Who is to say that the price of such an experience is too high? "Fabulous funerals of black people yield much attention for the living," announced a headline in the black magazine *Ebony*.

Perhaps the question, then, comes down to this: Is the high cost of dying worth it in terms of later memories and grief therapy? Are the poor and the blacks, those who frequently spend a disproportionate amount of their savings, or go into debt, for full-service funerals being exploited or are they buying something of intangible, but no less measurable, value? Who is to put a price tag on a ceremony that may help restore the family and communal links that death ruptures?

Sociologist Vanderlyn Pine, who comes from a three-generation family of funeral directors, thinks that paying for funerals "represents a secular and economic ritual formerly performed by more religious customs and ceremonies." Because many of the traditional rites that once helped people cope with death have broken down, "monetary expenditures have taken on an added importance." What may seem like exploitation to an outsider, he believes, is really a professional service that society once performed but has now relinquished. Pine adds that his father stocked inexpensive, rough box coffins as a regular part of his line. He sold only eight in fifteen years.

Reforming the Funeral

Funeral directors are sensitive to the barrage of criticism that has been leveled against them in recent years. The adaptive funeral is becoming more common, and the undertaker himself is undergoing a humanizing face-lift. He is less likely to live some distance from his mortuary and tell his neighbors that he is in the furniture business. High-school and even grade-school classes now visit funeral homes much as they do police stations and museums. No longer does the undertaker smuggle the remains of the deceased out of retirement colonies in the dead of night. I know one small-town funeral director who encourages the family to accompany him to pick up the body at the hospital and even help him dress it, if they wish. Rather than personifying the minister of death, the modern funeral director seeks a reputation for being a regular downtown American, a joiner of civic organizations and a wearer of sports jackets and plaid slacks. A recent convention of the American Funeral Directors Association was held in Las Vegas. The undertaker has, in effect, come out of the closet.

No doubt this new image is good for business, but one questions how far it should be carried. At an embalming school in Farmingdale, New York, students visit nearby institutions for the indigent to get to know inmates whose cadavers they will someday be practicing on. They say they want to be able to look upon the cadaver as a person.

The funeral director's grief counseling has already been mentioned, and modern funeral homes are now called by some of their owners "crisis intervention centers." What all this seems to point to is a sharpening tug-of-war for the body, and even the soul, of the deceased among clergymen, social workers, psychiatrists and undertakers. "Let's Get Rid of Funeral Homes" is the title of a recent article in the magazine *U.S. Catholic.*

The movement to simple funerals poses an economic threat to the country's 43,000 funeral directors, and it is gaining momentum. In its *Manual for the Funeral*, the Commission on Worship of the Methodist Church complains that too many funerals are being conducted in funeral homes and recommends that they "be held in the house of worship when this is possible." The casket should remain closed during the service and should not be a status symbol. The use of flowers within the chancel should be avoided, the commission adds, and organists should be discouraged from "overuse of organ stops which suggest ultrasentimentality."

Unitarians recommend burial without embalming within the quickest possible time, to be followed by a memorial service a week or so later. Cremation is preferred, but they warn against buying an expensive casket to burn. Prearranging the details, "giving the funeral director the necessary directions, written out," is also suggested. Quakers are predictably in favor of funeral simplicity, which may take the form of a candlelight service, some music and the testimony of the family "and of such friends as may be moved to speak." A few Friends meetings have gone further by eliminating the funeral director entirely. According to Ernest Morgan, author of *A Manual of Death Education and Simple Burial*, these groups have formed burial committees which handle all funeral arrangements themselves. A supply of plywood boxes is kept on hand, and the body is transported to the cemetery by station wagon. Friends dig the grave and conduct a burial service. Although Quakerism is far from Roman Catholicism in doctrine, the practice Morgan describes follows closely in all respects but the funeral mass that which still obtains in that most Catholic of regions, rural Ireland. The funeral home is a recent introduction to Ireland and is found only in the larger cities. In the countryside it is still common for the grave to be dug by friends of the deceased, and the coffin is frequently carried to the site strapped on top of the family car. The Irish wake, however, is something for which the Friends have no equivalent.

Paradoxically, the Humanists, who deny the existence of a God or an afterlife, are close to the more traditional churches in at least one respect: They are not afraid of showing their feelings. Corliss Lamont, a leading Humanist spokesman, argues that the funeral should *not* "try to avoid stirring up the emotions." In his *Humanist Funeral Service*, Lamont emphasizes three major themes that have value for survivors: "man's kinship with Nature, the naturalness of death and the far-reaching social interactions and ideals of human living." This service, which lasts about twenty minutes, includes music, readings from the Bible, meditations, brief personal remarks about the deceased, poetry selections (John Masefield is one of those recommended) and a committal service at the grave or crematorium.

The most active challenge to accepted funeral practices comes from the nonprofit funeral and memorial societies which have sprung up in 120 cities in the United States and Canada. Although total membership is relatively small—about 500,000—these societies augur a rapidly growing consumer consciousness about death. One group, the People's Memorial Association, claims that in a single year, 1971, it saved its 766 members some $850,000. Working with local funeral directors, it was instrumental in helping families get the kind of funeral they could afford, often on a preplanned basis.

A breakaway group of funeral directors, the National Selected Morticians, has already drawn up a Code of Good Funeral Practices which aims at correcting most of the practices objected to by the reformers. The code includes not overpricing, itemizing bills, respecting the personal choice of the family, and a particular responsiveness to the needs of the poor. A directory of establishments that subscribe to the code is furnished by the Washington, District of Columbia, based Continental Association of Funeral and Memorial Societies.

Preplanning can undoubtedly save money; for a fifteen dollar fee one can sign up with another Washington organization, the American International Funeral Registry, Ltd. Registrants file instructions as to what kind of funeral, if any, they prefer and how they want their body disposed of. Included in the options are cremation and donation to medical science. This right of self-disposition, already a law in some states, is intended to supersede the family's right to make arrangements. Not surprisingly, funeral directors don't like it. Every corpse given to medical science, generally speaking, is one less funeral. When I asked one of our local undertakers what he thought of the idea, he snorted, "It's a gimmick. I have a file this thick downstairs of arrangements people have made for themselves, and I don't charge fifteen dollars."

But preplanned arrangements, if they are made without consultation with close survivors, can sometimes have disastrous consequences. Dick H., a one-time neighbor of mine who moved to London several years ago, got word that his father had died suddenly in New York's Columbia-Presbyterian Hospital. He flew back to find that the elder Mr. H. had left instructions for no funeral; moreover, his body had been willed to the hospital. By the time his son arrived it had already been cannibalized for medical science. "There was no one to bury," Dick said bitterly when I saw him. "I came back to nothing." Dick's relationship with his father had been extremely close, and he deeply regretted that he would never be able to visit his grave. And in his anguish, Dick, who is Jewish, made the only gesture that seemed appropriate: he flew to Jerusalem and pinned a note in his father's memory on the Wailing Wall of the Old City.

Dick's visit occurred soon after the local councilman referred to earlier died of lung cancer. Marty B., in his early forties, had been ill for two years. One thing he wanted was to be remembered. He did not deny the fact that he was dying, nor was this finality concealed from his four young children. One of them wrote a poem that was read at the funeral service. Marty himself selected the hymns to be sung and chose his pallbearers. He would have enjoyed, I think, the wake that preceded the funeral—the last look that his many friends found to be a fitting farewell. Barbaric? Not in this case. Marty's funeral reflected not only his own lifestyle, which was a bit flamboyant, but a sense that the pain of death can be at least partly assuaged through ceremony.

The Deep Freeze

The human tendency to deny the reality of death has been one of the themes of this book. The biological extension of life, organ transplants and heroic medicine all point to man's refusal to accept the physical cessation of life. It is no longer the Fountain of Youth that men seek to counter the mutability of human existence; it is a foolproof means of defying disease and the process of wearing out. And because enormous strides have been made in this direction, what better hope is there for physical immortality than the suspension of biological life, when it begins to fail, until definitive cures are available? If frog sperm can be successfully frozen and thawed, why not the human organism? Why not thaw out the cancer patient, for example, when a cure for cancer has been found?

This is the theory behind Richard C. W. Ettinger's book, *The Prospect of Immortality*, and the subsequent formation of the cryonics movement. Cryonics—more properly, cryogenics—aims to halt the dissolution of the body at death. By storing a person at a supercool temperature, it is theoretically possible to preserve him indefinitely.

This is not, however, a simple process. Blood is drained from the veins; arteries and lungs are perfused with a glycerol fluid to retard cellular damage; and the patient is then wrapped in aluminum foil and stored, like frozen food, at a temperature of −79° C. The process, however, does not end there. A sealed capsule becomes what is hoped the temporary home of the "deceased." Temperature is further reduced to −196° C. through the use of liquid nitrogen; this ensures that no further cellular deterioration takes place. And here, in cryonic suspension, the patient awaits ultimate resurrection. All this costs about $10,000, plus $1,200 a year in storage costs. To cover these initial expenses, individuals who contemplate going the cryonic route are encouraged to take out an insurance policy naming the Cryonic Suspension Society as beneficiary.

At present, about fifteen persons are in cryonic suspension in various parts of the country, including the pioneer "cryonaut," James H. Bedford, a seventy-three-year-old retired psychology professor who died in 1967. As the first man in a cryo-capsule, Bedford experienced some nitrogen "boil-off" problems, and it was feared for a time that he had thawed out. Apprehensions were put to rest when members of the Cryonics Youth Association investigated. Bedford, they reported, was "frozen and well in Southern California."

Other candidates for suspension have not been so fortunate. Andrew D. Mihak, who died of a heart attack in 1968, was given the initial fast-freeze treatment by the New York Cryonics Society at the request of his wife. Enthusiasm waned, however, when, two days later, it developed that the widow was broke and would not be able to pay for end-stage freezing and storage. Mihak was defrosted and given a military burial on Long Island.

Eventually, if the movement stays alive, hundreds, if not thousands, of men and women may elect to defy death via the deep freeze. Members of the Cryonics Society have already contracted for suspension, and many have set aside money to pay for it. Their motto is, "Never say die." An analysis of the membership made by sociologists Clifton D. Bryant and William E. Snizek indicates that a majority are atheists and an unusually high number are devotees of science fiction. For many, cryonics is a substitute religion. "Unwilling to accept the promises of organized religions regarding a spiritual afterlife," Bryant and Snizek write, "cryonics members opt for a type of materialistic, active mastery over their own destinies."

Meanwhile, as they wait for immortality, cryonics enthusiasts make the most of this world. Conventions, fund-raising dinners and proselytizing occupy much of their spare time; members have married one another; they edit newsletters and write books. The movement has become a sodality in which the here-and-now seems to have taken precedence over the hereafter. But as a movement it does not seem to have much of a future, even in cryonic suspension, and might best be described as a bad idea whose time has not come. Membership has declined in the past few years and the number of persons who actually take the glacial plunge seems to have peaked at fifteen or so, despite a reputed waiting list that promised many more. Financial problems have beset the freezing-interment end of the business, insurance companies have refused to honor the Cryonics Society as a beneficiary of some policies, heirs have contested the wishes of the deceased and, in general, the novelty of cryonics has begun to wear off.

But probably the most serious obstacle to the movement's growth is simply the doubt, on the part of many people, that cryonic suspension works. Ideally, a person who is dying should be deep-frozen *before* he is dead. Few, if any, however, want to take this gamble. And although it is scientifically possible to preserve a corpse in cold storage indefinitely, there is no evidence that once thawed out such a person can be revived, even with the antifreeze removed and fresh blood pumped in. Even assuming that this were possible, there is no assurance that the disease that killed him would not be replaced by another for which medicine has not yet found a cure. The resurrected individual would have no choice but to die all over again.

The Decline of Necropolis

In one sense, cryonics is an extreme example of man's reluctance to accept the dissolution of the human body after death. There are other less extreme practices that have been tested by time. In ancient Egypt the mummifying of bodies ensured long life for the corpse, and, indeed, mummies on exhibit in the British Museum are in an excellent state of preservation 3,000 years after the person's death. Lenin's lifelike countenance stares up at hundreds of thousands of visitors to his tomb in the Kremlin wall.

In our own country, the preservation of the dead has received another impetus with the introduction of mausoleums—some of skyscraper dimensions—and concrete burial vaults. Both defy nature to do its worst (futilely, one might add, since decay takes place in any case). No dust-to-dust here, and no return to the source of one's origins—the earth itself. Some critics add that the burial vault is just one more way of exploiting the guilt feelings of survivors. Unfortunately—or fortunately, depending upon one's point of view—this newest appurtenance to funerals has run into an unforeseen snag. Many grave plots in older cemeteries are simply too narrow to hold a burial vault. One reason for this is that Americans eat more and better than they used to, and so they are larger at death than formerly. This necessitates a bigger coffin which, in turn, requires a larger vault. An item in a funeral directors' magazine, *The Casket and Sunnyside*, notes that "this creates a serious problem in various cemeteries which have narrow plots that cannot accommodate the larger burial vaults . . . these vaults cannot be put into the graves." The writer of the article adds that, in some instances, this has created a highly embarrassing situation for the funeral director, who is forced to remove the casket from its vault while grieving survivors look on.

The cemetery has always reflected society's class structure: paupers are buried unceremoniously in potter's fields; the well-to-do are entombed in spacious plots beneath imposing monuments, well insulated from their poorer neighbors. Almost everyone there gets "perpetual care,"—once he is admitted to the club; Indians and blacks are frequently excluded from cemetery associations. Status is maintained in death as in life and the posthumous American will pay more for a site overlooking the river than an inner location or one that fronts the highway. Plastic flowers guarantee that someone cares, although with a minimum of inconvenience. Death may be the great leveler, but this inevitable misfortune is quickly corrected at the burial site.

As a social environment, however, necropoles typify our psychological ambivalence toward death and dying. If the dead rest in peace, the living carry on as though nothing had changed. Forest Lawn Memorial Park in Los Angeles, celebrated in Evelyn Waugh's *The Loved One*, is, indeed, the land of the living, with its concert halls, wedding chapels, movies, museums and gift shops—"God's Own Million Dollar Little Acre." A profit-making enterprise, Forest Lawn is so popular that it is included in the Gray Line tour of greater Los Angeles, along with Disneyland and Knott's Berry Farm.

More typical of large city cemeteries is Greenwood, occupying 478 acres of the Gowanus Hills section of Brooklyn, overlooking New York harbor. Chartered in 1838, Greenwood has remained an oasis of rural seclusion in the midst of urban development. Thousands of trees shelter its tombstones; flowering shrubs, combined with floral pieces on the graves, give it the appearance of a vast garden. Some twenty-two miles of roadway and thirty miles of winding paths, with names such as Landscape Avenue, Strawberry Hill and Primrose Path, provide the aura and nomenclature of suburbia. And like suburbia, it is well guarded against urban intrusion. Spiked iron fences surround the entire cemetery and visitors are requested to check in with the guard. Indeed, this necropolis has been able to do for the dead what no city has been able to achieve for the living, protection against urban blight and crime. Despite some vandalism, Greenwood may well be the safest place in Brooklyn.

But Greenwood, like most urban cemeteries, is running out of space. With a present census of more than half a million bodies, it is already more heavily populated than many good-sized cities. And with 1,800 new interments each year, the remaining space will be occupied within five years. One solution, already adopted by some cemeteries, is to employ the double-depth burial (euphemistically called companion spaces). A California cemetery has added a "babyland," where three infants are buried in a space normally occupied by one adult. Yet even if Greenwood were to choose this method, it would still reach total occupancy in less than eight years.

An even more urgent problem is that our cities are running out of space for cemeteries. Some 2 million acres of choice land in the United States is already given over to graveyards; in many urban areas they represent the last open space left. Roger Starr, commissioner of Housing and Urban Development for New York City, estimates that 4,000 acres now utilized for cemeteries in the city could ultimately provide housing for 200,000 families. Proposals to relocate some of these cemeteries, however, have met with overwhelming resistance, and, because the law recognizes the sanctity of burial grounds, cemeteries are generally immune from land-use legislation.

Nevertheless, the pressure for relief is building up. According to the American Society of Planning Officials, "If the idea of 'perpetual care' were pursued far enough we should eventually use all our land for the interment of the dead and have no land left for the living." Although this statement is patently an exaggeration, the problem cannot be ignored. Cemeteries have already been relocated to make room for new highways and airports; as long ago as the 1920s San Francisco began moving all its burial grounds out of town. Most ended up in Colma, a small community which is known as Cemetery City; today, a majority of its citizens are engaged in funeral-related enterprises.

Worried about their survival, city cemetery associations have turned to a more radical, if less costly, solution: why not make these areas available for recreational purposes? Three years ago, the Roman Catholic Archdiocese of Chicago directed that its thirty-seven cemeteries, covering some 5,000 acres, be opened to outsiders who might want to fish in the lakes or picnic in the groves. Youngsters are permitted to play baseball and football in the undeveloped sections, and bicycling is allowed on the paths.

A suburban Pittsburgh cemetery has given the green light

to cross-country racing, and Woodlawn Cemetery in the Bronx is a favorite spot for joggers. Boston's fifty cemeteries have become recognized as nature preserves and bird sanctuaries. Writing in *Natural History* magazine, Jack Ward Thomas and Ronald A. Dixon report that ninety-five species of birds and fifty species of animals, including red foxes, opposums and muskrats, had taken up residence in these city and suburban burying places which, because they are protected, enjoy their own wildlife ecology. The authors suggest that these open spaces, with their picnicking, bird-watching and strolling facilities, provide an outlet for the activities of the living that may outweigh their value as a resting place for the dead. And almost all cemeteries which have gone multipurpose report that much less—rather than more—vandalism has resulted. Accessibility has seemingly brought a new respect for gravestones and monuments.

To date, however, relatively few cemeteries have deliberately converted to recreational use. "This is a memorial park, not an amusement park," says A. W. Crompton, manager of Woodlawn Cemetery, near San Francisco. "Would you want to find somebody with a lunch spread out on your mother's grave?"

In any case, turning burial grounds into part-time playgrounds does not solve the shortage of space. In most metropolitan areas, there is simply no room for expansion as housing developers covetously eye suburban land that once might have been turned over to crypts and tombstones. The dead, like the living, have become victims of escalating real estate values.

And like the living, they may have to settle for a new kind of upward mobility: the high-rise mausoleum. Down in Nashville, Tennessee, seventy-two year old H. Raymond Ligon, the city's busiest funeral director, is building a twenty-story structure, five stories of which are completed and in use. Designed in the shape of a cross, Woodlawn Mausoleum will have an eventual capacity of 129,000 bodies, recruited by a staff of fifteen salesmen and served by ten repose rooms and open-all-night funerals. It has been called "The Death Hilton" and "The

Poor Man's Taj Mahal." But Woodlawn will soon be superceded by a $14-million, thirty-nine-story glass and reinforced concrete mausoleum planned for Rio de Jáneiro. Because this city of 4.5 million is cramped into a narrow strip of land between mountains and sea, conventional burial space is at a premium and plots have risen to $5,000. Vaults in the mausoleum are priced at about $1,000. This facility is already known as "The Big Condominium in the Sky."

Like cremation, these "cubbyhole" burials make death anonymous. And this, some psychologists think, is precisely their drawback for surviving relatives, who need to territorialize their dead for the sake of human continuity. Rightly or wrongly —and there is little evidence that widespread cremation in Japan (75 percent of all deceased) and England (60 percent) has seriously disrupted the social fabric of the survivors' lives— new disposal methods have accomplished what the cemetery never succeeded in doing: they make death democratic. In the urn or the mausoleum, all men are equal.

We simply don't know the effect of this on survivors of cremations and stacked burials. Dr. Robert Fulton's Minnesota studies of disrupted emotional lives among those who cremate their dead are hardly definitive, as he himself points out. But if they are even partially indicative of human response to the way a body is disposed of, we may be in trouble. For many survivors a grave is an entombment of memories and a vital link to the past. I know a young woman who traveled from New York to Nevada to visit the grave of her father, who had died when she was a small child. The experience was worth months of psychotherapy in resolving her conflicting feelings about a man she had hardly known and barely remembered. A grave was proof, somehow, that he had existed.

Vance Packard has called us a nation of strangers; constantly on the move, changing jobs, localities—and wives—we have lost our roots. In a mobile society, only the dead stay put and they, too, are losing out to the forces of change.

CHAPTER IX

The Question of Survival

ONE EVENING in September 1967, Episcopal Bishop James
Pike appeared on a network television program sponsored by the
Canadian Broadcasting Company. This in itself would not have
made news, but Pike had come to Toronto for a special reason:
he wanted to communicate with his dead son, who had committed suicide two years before.

The seance had been arranged by Allen Spraggett, the religion
editor of a Toronto newspaper who had persuaded Arthur Ford,
America's best-known medium, to meet Pike and do what he
could to contact the departed spirit of James, Jr. The two men
had never met before and they chatted amiably in the studio
for half an hour before the seance was taped. What happened
then made headlines all over the world. To many viewers, it
cast doubt on the bishop's sanity, if not his credulity. To others
it confirmed Ford's well-publicized psychic powers. For Pike
came away from the seance convinced that the information he
received from the "other side" was so private that it could have
come to Ford's attention only by direct contact with his deceased son.

Pike was a troubled man at that time. A naval officer in

World War II, and a former attorney with the Securities and Exchange Commission, this stimulating thinker had entered the ministry in mid-life, rising in the Church hierarchy with unaccustomed swiftness to the rank of bishop, only to be removed from his post in Northern California for certain doctrinal heresies. Then came a period of study in Cambridge, England, where he roomed with his son, who was going to school there. During one of the young man's visits to the United States, he killed himself, and for this the bishop understandably felt guilty. Had he, in some way, betrayed him as a father?

When Pike resumed his residence in Cambridge, living in the same apartment, strange things began to happen: clocks stopped repeatedly at 8:19 (the time of Jim, Jr.'s death); fresh milk turned unaccountably sour; postcards from the boy were found on tables and chairs, somehow removed from the desk drawer in which Pike had put them. Later, he was to admit that these manifestations might have been illusory, brought about by his own acute grief. (And from what we know about the psychology of grief reaction, this was very possibly the case.) But at the time Pike was convinced that his son was struggling to communicate with him.

When Pike met Arthur Ford in 1967, he had already had sittings with two other mediums, a Mrs. Ena Twigg, in London, who had been recommended to him by the canon of Southwark Cathedral; and the Rev. George Daisley, in Santa Barbara, California. Neither seance was entirely satisfactory, although during the Twigg sitting Pike was pleasantly surprised to hear from his old friend, the theologian Paul Tillich. Still seeking more conclusive evidence of his son's afterlife, he turned, at Spraggett's suggestion, to Arthur Ford. What could he lose? Ford, after all, had a worldwide reputation for uncannily prying into the most recondite secrets of his sitters' pasts, a gift that he attributed to his mediumistic powers.

But Arthur Ford was also, in his own way, a troubled man. Suffering from a severe heart condition, he had only a few years to live and was far from the height of his powers. He was also afflicted with recurrent bouts of alcoholism. Still, his reputation was formidable. He was a "society medium," at onetime president of the National Association of Spiritualists whose sitters had included Queen Maud of Norway, Upton Sinclair, Aldous Huxley, the psychologist William MacDougall and thousands of ordinary people who came away from his seances convinced that they had, indeed, been in touch with some deceased relative. In Bishop Pike's case, one of the most convincing bits of evidence came when Ford's control, Fletcher, revealed several small and trivial details about the bishop's predecessor in California, the Rt. Rev. Karl Morgan Block, which Pike believed had never been public knowledge. There were also intimate communications from his son and a message from the former chaplain at Columbia University, who referred to things that only Pike would know about.

Even so, Pike was not completely satisfied with the sitting and three months later arranged for a private sitting in Ford's Philadelphia apartment. On this occasion, he was accompanied by his secretary (later his wife), Diane Kennedy, and another woman member of his staff. Miss Kennedy transcribed Fletcher's messages verbatim. "Pike hoped for information which would shed light on his dead son's last hours," writes Allen Spraggett in his biography *Arthur Ford: The Man Who Talked with the Dead*. "The sitting completely fulfilled its purpose of satisfying Bishop Pike that, through Arthur Ford, genuinely supernormal processes were at work."

Ford went on to become a spiritualist intermediary for Edgar Mitchell, the astronaut, and Senator Mendel Rivers of South Carolina. And Pike wrote a book about his experiences called *The Other Side*. "From being accused of not believing enough," he quipped (a reference to his doctrinal troubles with the Church), "I am now accused of believing too much." How enduring this new faith in spiritualism might have been we will never know; Pike died in the Sinai desert, his body undiscovered for several days. Some speculated that he sought out death, hoping to be reunited with his son.

But the mediums had not heard the last of Bishop Pike. Diane Kennedy Pike, who had been with him shortly before he disappeared, rushed to London for a sitting with Mrs. Twigg, Pike's first contact with professional spiritualism. "I have carefully evaluated the tape record of a session held with Mrs. Ena Twigg of London during the search for Jim before his whereabouts were known or his death confirmed," she later wrote in a magazine article. "In that session there were sufficient references that corresponded to the circumstances of our ordeal . . . to affirm that Jim communicated through Mrs. Twigg." Five months later, she arranged to have sittings with two other mediums, but received only one further communiqué "that I felt certain was from Jim."

Then, a few years later, came revelations of a quite different kind. They came not to Diane Pike, but to Spraggett, Ford's biographer. Moreover, the messages he got were far from supernormal. Working with the Rev. William Rauscher, a friend of Ford's and the literary executor of his estate, Spraggett was sifting through the medium's papers when he came across an obituary from the New York Times on the Rt. Rev. Karl Morgan Block, the "spirit" whose bits of information from the other world had so convinced Bishop Pike of Ford's extraordinary gifts. "Every one of these supposedly unresearchable items was mentioned," Spraggett writes. For example, Block's epithet, "ecclesiastical panhandler," which Pike believed was known to only one other person, was referred to in the obituary. Ford had apparently researched the Pike seance in advance. And that was not all. Ford also had a file on Bishop Pike that went back several years. He kept a notebook about prominent people who had died and, in Spraggett's words, "had a marked propensity for clipping obituaries." A private secretary of Ford's later declared that "Arthur Ford never went to a thing like the Pike sitting without untold research," including a perusal of Who's

Who and even early school records. Even so, some information that came through in the sittings could never be traced to research and, despite proof that Ford cheated at times, Spraggett believes that "evidence supports the hypothesis that Arthur Ford was a genuinely gifted psychic." Certainly, he convinced hundreds that this was so.

The Arthur Ford story did not end with his death in 1971. The publisher of his book, *The Life Beyond Death*, claims that the communication that ends the book was "dictated" by Ford from the other world. Not to be outdone, the psychic popularizer Ruth Montgomery asserted that she had received an entire book-length communication from the "spirit," via automatic writing on her typewriter. Her book, *A World Beyond*, purports to be an intimate glimpse into the spirit world, as experienced by Arthur Ford. There, the souls of the dead are recycled into the bodies of babies about to be born. Old friends from the earth-world are also reported on: the good Bishop Pike, for instance, has found peace at last, studying philosophy with his son as the prelude to another life on earth.

Tricks or Treats?

One need not take Mrs. Montgomery's book seriously (although thousands apparently do) to appreciate the insatiable hunger that people experience for evidence that the dead, once they have left us, are not, in a literal sense, beyond all recall. This is the ultimate expression of faith in man's immortality: if the dead can talk to us, is this not proof that we, too, will never die?

The most remarkable aspect of this will to believe is that it is by no means confined to the uneducated, the simple and the gullible. Bishop Pike, for example, was a man of considerable intellectual attainment. Although, as a priest in the Episcopal Church, he could be expected to believe in some kind of immortality, even hard-headed scientists who ordinarily demand evidence for their beliefs frequently share this faith. Many years ago, professor of psychology J. H. Leuba sampled a number of physicists in teaching posts. He found that more than half of them believed in immortality in spite of their scientific approach to knowledge.*

One of the best-kept secrets of men in public life was the long-standing practice of Canadian Prime Minister W. L. Mackenzie King of visiting mediums, especially when he went to London. A bachelor who was deeply devoted to the memory of his dead mother, King "talked" with her for decades—or so he was convinced. (King was also supposed to have communicated with Franklin D. Roosevelt, after the latter's death, and to have received valuable advice of a political nature.) The brilliant Aldous Huxley was no stranger to spiritualism, and after his first wife, Maria, died, he received several messages through the medium Eileen Garrett, although these did not come at sittings.

Communications from the dead are by no means limited to family members. Forty-three years after the Battle of Britain, Lord Dowding, who was air chief marshal at the time, told an audience in London, "There is a great organization of Air Force men on the other side, and I receive frequent messages from them." Thomas Edison, a firm believer in clairvoyance and telepathy, once planned to invent a machine to contact the dead, but, unhappily, he died before he got around to it.

Although hardly the force it was three or four generations ago, spiritualism is undergoing a modest revival on the crest of the current fascination with the occult. Taken under the wing of parapsychology—the scientific study of extrasensory perception, clairvoyance, telepathy and similar unexplainable psychological states—it is achieving a new respectability. Perhaps much of this can be explained as a reaction to the cut-and-dried,

---

* Forty-four percent of the physicists surveyed said they believed in God and 51 percent affirmed a belief in immortality. For psychologists the figures were 24 percent and 20 percent, respectively.

mechanistic model of the world that science presents to us. But as we have seen from the two previous chapters, no small part of man's susceptibility to deceit—if this is what it is—comes from his highly ambivalent attitude toward death and the unsuspecting way in which the human psyche tricks itself when confronted with death's reality.

Acute grief can produce hallucinations that are sometimes mistaken for phantasms of the deceased—"I know it's John; he comes to my room every night." Dr. C. Murray Parkes has noted the frequency of these hallucinations among the widowed. Then, too, the rational approach toward death which characterizes the modern trend in funeral practices leaves little or no room for its mystery; the irrational may reassert itself later in an effort to deny the loss. It is easier to believe in—or at least hope for—a life after death when death is deritualized.

Visions of the dead are less likely to occur in plain daylight and to people who have no need to experience them. In 1960, A. D. Cornell, a member of the British Society for Psychical Research, performed an experiment demonstrating how important the setting is to a belief in apparitions. Donning a Halloween-type ghost costume, he paraded around in a churchyard that abutted a heavily traveled street. Although passers-by stopped to stare, no one mistook him for an apparition. Similarly dressed, Cornell also walked across the screen of a crowded movie theater during a performance. Thirty-two percent of the audience did not notice him at all and, of those who did, a great many confused him with a polar bear. Not expecting an apparition, they did not see one.

Many American adherents to spiritualism belong to the National Spiritualist Association of Churches, an organization dating back to 1892. Individual congregations are called by such names as the Temple of Metaphysical Science or the Chapel of Spiritual Truth, and their services—at least those that I have attended—combine hymn singing, some traditional prayers, a sermon (often emphasizing reincarnation) and a good deal of what can only be called fortune-telling. Most Spiritualist churches include a resident medium, who may perform at the regular service and is also available for private sittings. As part of their creed, members recite the following: "We affirm that communication with the so-called dead is a fact scientifically proven by the phenomena of spiritualism."

A Spiritualist publication, *The Psychic Observer and Chimes*, lists some ninety churches and psychic centers, including a Certified Mediums Society, authorized by the New York State legislature to "license mediums throughout the country." Fulfillment centers in Los Angeles also offer courses in "Development of Medium Ability." George Chapman, for example, claims to be in communication with Dr. William Lang, a surgeon who died in 1937. In his trance states, Chapman "loans" himself to the kindly old surgeon and continues to treat the sick today, using the seance as a consulting room.

Among the high points of the Spiritualist experience are the summer encampments that draw thousands of members to such places as Surprise Lake, Washington, Petoskey, Michigan, Lilly Dale, New York, and Chesterfield, Indiana. Reminiscent of nineteenth-century chatauquas, these camps offer an intensive two- to four-week combination of summer vacation and Spiritualist renewal, with faith healing and seances as part of the package. One of the largest camps is at Chesterfield, between Indianapolis and Fort Wayne; it has been in business for eighty-eight years and attracts upwards of 50,000 persons in a good season. Three hotels (free to visitors), spacious grounds, an art gallery, museum and an impressive stone cathedral testify to Chesterfield's financial success, if to nothing else. Chapel services and lectures are held daily in the cathedral, and for the more occult-minded there are clairvoyances, billet readings, seances—even an ESP workshop. A private sitting with a medium costs as little as three dollars.

But there seems little doubt that Spiritualist camps have

become a happy hunting ground for unscrupulous mediums. Arthur Ford, at one time a star attraction at Camp Lilly Dale, ended his appearances there when he became convinced that most of the other mediums were fakes. In May 1960, two researchers found what they considered conclusive proof of fraud at Camp Chesterfield. The late Tom O'Neill, editor of *Psychic Observer*, and Dr. Andrija Puharich were given permission to photograph materialization seances using infrared film. When developed, the photographs showed the "spirits" to be the camp mediums dressed in cheesecloth and muslin. And in 1965, Allen Spraggett was similarly disillusioned. ". . . certain phony facts that I fed to the first medium with whom we sat—including exact names, all bogus—turned up in every subsequent sitting we had there."

The fact is that anyone with the right equipment and enough chutzpah can become a medium and go into business for himself. And getting the equipment is not difficult. A firm in Columbus, Ohio, carries on a worldwide business supplying life-size manifestations, astral bodies, ectoplasm, swaying and talking trumpets and similar ghostly paraphernalia guaranteed to fool the gullible, if not necessarily the skeptical. The late Prof. C. J. Ducasse, of Brown University, once conducted a seance using these mail-order props with unintended results. "A number [of sitters] were so terror-stricken," he writes, "that their hair literally rose upon their heads—and we had to quickly turn on the lights and turn off the spirits. . . ."

The Mediums and Their Message

For true Spiritualists, belief in the living dead is a faith no less strange than the faith many Christians have in the existence of miracles, the soul, and the reality of God. The difference is that the Spiritualist points to evidence to confirm his belief.

This evidence has been the subject of intensive research ever since the Fox sisters, fifteen-year-old Maggie and eleven-year-old

Kate, heard mysterious table rappings in their home near Hydesville, New York, in 1848. The rappings were alleged to be caused by the ghost of a man who had been murdered years before, and whose skeleton was later found in the house. Whatever the real reason, the weird rapping phenomenon at Hydesville caught the nation's fancy and "rappomania" (as one newspaper called it) spread like wildfire. Others found that they, too, could make physical objects perform unlikely feats and, as competition grew, added even more bizarre exploits to their repertoire. Table-turning became a parlor game in thousands of homes, and, for the more sophisticated medium, trance-speaking purported to bring messages from the dead. Mysterious and untouched trumpets played celestial music, and sometimes the dead person himself appeared briefly as an ectoplasmic manifestation. It is hardly necessary to add that these seances took place in dark or dimly lit rooms, and the sitters were not always certain what they had really seen or heard. Nevertheless, the craze went unabated, and by 1854 it was estimated that some 30,000 mediums practiced their trade in the United States—often in the lobbies of hotels and the lounge cars of railway trains.

Looking back on this era, it is difficult to appreciate the mass gullibility that infected so large a segment of the American people. As today, this phenomenon was by no means confined to the uneducated. Harriet Beecher Stowe regularly visited mediums to contact her dead son, and during Lincoln's first presidency his wife, Mary Todd, arranged for seances at the White House. Lincoln himself attended some of these, although there is no evidence that he believed in the medium's powers. More likely, he wanted to comfort Mrs. Lincoln—their son, Willie, had recently died—and to protect her from unscrupulous Spiritualists. "Their talk and advice sounds very much like the talk of my cabinet," he remarked once.

There is no doubt that most of the mediumistic phenomena was fraudulent: conjuring tricks that were exposed, even at the height of the movement. Nevertheless, out of this passion for communicating with the dead grew a sizable Spiritualist Church, with membership rising in the 1850s to 2 million believers, and sympathizers numbering many more. Among these latter were such prominent Americans as Horace Greeley, William Lloyd Garrison, James Fenimore Cooper and William Cullen Bryant. Social historians explain the movement's growth in terms of the emotionally unsettling effect of the pre–Civil War and wartime upheavals, which provided fertile soil for a new and simplistic faith in life after death. This was especially the case for those who lacked, or had given up, a more conventional Christianity. Strictly speaking, the "supernatural" does not exist for Spiritualists. The universe consists of an Infinite Intelligence; the biologically dead continue their existence on a higher plane while remaining aware of earthly phenomena. Some of these deceased become spirit guides for the living, and it is they who come to us through the medium.

Spiritualism made even more vigorous headway in England, where it appeared soon after its onset in America, although its vogue there might be attributed to quite different reasons. Nineteenth-century England was fascinated with almost everything romantic and inexplicable: swooning maidens, ghosts, mesmerism, phrenology, thought transference and other strange phenomena which suggested some occult force at work in a society that had begun to find its eighteenth-century rationalist legacy altogether too tidy and lacking in excitement. And to this reaction was added a new trauma of deep psychological import: Darwin's theory that man was not divinely created, but the product of evolutionary adaptation and natural selection. Many people who could no longer accept a fundamentalist Christian explanation of Godly purpose and human immortality found in spiritualism both a solace and a rational explanation for human survival that fit Darwin's concept of evolution. In short, life did not end at death, but evolved into disembodied thought and personality; and even these human attributes were capable of "materializing" themselves in palpable form.

Probably few Victorians consciously thought about spiritualism in Darwinian terms. But the stage had been psychologically set, and the movement spread so rapidly, and produced such seemingly spectacular results, that American mediums flocked to England to offer their services, the Fox sisters, now grown up, among them. The most sought after of the psychic emigrés was a young man named D. D. Home, who was soon to entrance both England and the continent with his good looks, charm, social graces and an undisputable gift for convincing his sitters that he embodied psychic powers hitherto unheard of. Home not only offered a direct-dial hookup with the dead, he proved it (seemingly) with what today would be called extraordinary psychokinetic evidence. He made chairs and tables dance about the seance room with alacrity, caused untouched musical instruments to play tunes and, on one occasion, levitated himself to the ceiling, floated out a window and returned, still floating, through an opposite door. Another of his "gifts" was the ability to handle hot coals, presumably by interposing a layer of cold air between the coal and his hand. Home operated only in the best houses, where he often stayed as a social guest, and numbered among his most devoted followers Elizabeth Barrett Browning, who was thoroughly convinced of his genuineness. Her husband, Robert, was not; as a result, Home has been immortalized for us in Browning's long, iconoclastic poem, "Mr. Sludge, the Medium."

Long before the century was out, most of the physical phenomena attributed to the other-worldly powers was exposed as a hoax. (One of the Fox sisters, late in life, admitted that her table rapping was simply a unique ability to crack her toe joints.) But a residue of doubt remained. Too many mediums predicted events that later took place; images and thoughts could, apparently, be conveyed from the mind of one person to another. Perhaps the dead did not really speak to the living, but when all the claptrap was stripped from the seance room evidence still pointed to something beyond the realm of trickery, mysteries that might be unlocked within the human psyche itself. If people have widely varying mental abilities in the conventional sense, why should they not also enjoy different degrees of sensitivity to the paranormal? Such a hypothesis would explain the gift that some mediums purportedly had for reading minds and producing apparitions.

Spiritualism might have died a natural death in England had it not been for the nagging doubt that the world that we see and sense is not necessarily the world that exists in its more recondite manifestations. In brief, the movement was made at least partly respectable by a new, skeptical and somewhat scientific interest on the part of those completely outside it who were, on the whole, nonbelievers. The result was a conviction that, if spiritualism could be studied and tested by university professors and hard-headed scientists, there must be something to it.

All this came about when a brilliant young poet and teacher, F. W. H. Myers, took up the subject in the early 1880s. And he took it up with a dispassionate, empirical attitude. Myers had had 367 sittings with mediums and, although he remained unconvinced of survival after death, too many of his experiences at these seances were unexplained to be written off as the product of trickery or illusion. He became convinced that, if he had not communicated with the dead at such times, he had been, at least, in touch with living persons of supernormal powers—those today we would call psychics.

With the help of a number of Cambridge colleagues, Henry Sidgwick, Edmund Gurney and an Australian law student, Richard Hodgson, Myers founded the Society for Psychical Research in 1882. During the next twenty years, their ranks were bolstered by such prominent Britons as William Gladstone, Arthur Balfour, and a number of scientists, including Alfred Russell Wallace who, with Darwin, developed the theory of evolution. Both Tennyson and Ruskin became members, and Freud was to join later. One of the most active members of the American branch of the society was William James. By 1900,

membership had climbed to 946 and included an impressive
cross section of the British intellectual community.

The purpose of the S.P.R. (as it came to be known) was to
investigate every psychic phenomenon that came to its attention. As new mediums with reputed paranormal powers cropped
up, one or more of the S.P.R.'s investigating committee would
be despatched to test them. Voluminous reports were written,
and the society published a journal that conceded nothing to
the scholarly standards of the age. With the exception of Sir
Oliver Lodge, the Myers group decided that evidence of survival after death was unconvincing. What the investigators did
agree on, however, was the existence, not of occult forces, but
of human powers that defied empirical explanation. Myers
coined the term telepathy to account for many of the mediumistic phenomena. His hypothesis held that material in the
sitter's subconscious mind (or subliminal self, as Myers preferred) "told" the medium, who was usually in a trance and
therefore highly susceptible to telepathic messages, information
purporting to come from the dead.

A knottier question, which Edmund Gurney tackled, was that
of phantasms or apparitions of the dead. Gurney interviewed
hundreds of people who had seen these phantasms—sometimes
collectively—under everyday circumstances. The seemingly
spontaneous and widespread appearance of phantasms in England in the latter half of the nineteenth century was the subject of much debate, and the fact that most people who saw
them had nothing to gain by deception lent credence to their
reality. Today, of course, psychologists do not find apparitions
particularly strange, and they are certainly not considered proof
of survival of the dead. The ability of people to hallucinate,
especially the image of a dead spouse or child, is considered
well within the range of explainable behavior.

Physical phenomena in the seance room were more easily
disproved, or at least disbelieved. The Myers group found little
to persuade them that discarnate beings could lift heavy tables

six inches off the floor or write out the answers to questions on locked slates. After 1900, when professional magicians began to take an interest in the society's work, it was easily shown how much of this phenomena was conjuring. (In the United States, Harry Houdini, who was also to wage war against mediums, asserted that there was no physical side effect of the seance that he could not duplicate.) But even before the magicians' secrets had been revealed, the S.P.R. had devised its own method of detecting fraud. Investigators simply held the medium's feet and hands while he performed. The picture of two dignified, bearded Cambridge professors, stretched full-length on the floor, each clasping a woman's ankle, hardly conforms with our notion of Victorian decorum, but it was through just such commonsense methods that the S.P.R. went about exposing its subjects.

The most baffling challenge came from an illiterate Italian girl, Eusapia Palladino, who was brought to Cambridge from her native Naples after having astounded skeptical researchers in Italy and France. Eusapia's repertoire included all the conventional table tilting acts and then some. Chairs walked across the carpet, curtains billowed wildly, an untouched accordian provided musical interludes. At the Cambridge sittings, Myers found himself being buffeted about the head and back. That all this should be taking place in an English drawing room, which the medium had never been in before, and under the scrutiny of decidedly skeptical sitters, was more than the investigators could explain. In their bafflement, they sent for Richard Hodgson, who was then in Boston. Eusapia, meanwhile, was housed, fed and taken on sightseeing and shopping trips.

Hodgson, who prided himself on a hard-headed approach to all psychic claims, very quickly unraveled the mystery. The key to Eusapia's "gifts," he told his colleagues, lay in the fact that her sitters kept her under *too much* control. They were so busy with their own strategy that they could not detect the cunning by which she deceived them. Posing as an "amiable imbecile," in the words of Alan Gauld, professor of psychology at the University of Nottingham in England, and a member of the Council of the S.P.R., Hodgson disarmed her with his apparent naiveté. "Hodgson . . . found that Eusapia was working her hands close together, and then by a deft move inducing both controllers to accept the same hand, thus freeing the other hand for mischief. She would also free a foot in a similar way. Practically all the phenomena at the last sitting were undoubtedly fraudulent, and all the regular sitters were able to observe the fraud in action. . . ."

The Case of Mrs. Piper

Eusapia's exposure was a setback to those among the Myers group—Oliver Lodge, in particular—who had come to believe that some mediums could, in fact, communicate with departed spirits. Eusapia was apparently not one of them. Their hopes were revived when no less distinguished a person than William James, the Harvard psychologist, reported to the S.P.R. that he and his wife had had a number of sittings with a Boston medium, Mrs. Leonore Piper, who had conveyed uncannily accurate information about deceased and little-known members of their families. James was sufficiently impressed by her gifts to send some twenty-five other persons to her under various pseudonyms.

Hodgson, now back in the United States, was delegated to make his own investigation, and he began a series of anonymous sittings with Mrs. Piper. Since he was originally from Australia, her "messages" from early friends, now deceased and struggling ardently to get in touch with him, seemed especially convincing. The Cambridge group, having been burned more than once, remained skeptical; it was suggested that Mrs. Piper be brought to England.

In 1889, accompanied by her two children, the now-famous Boston medium arrived in Liverpool, where she stayed briefly with Sir Oliver Lodge. From there she went to Cambridge and finally to London, living in rooms chosen by "a special committee set up to investigate her powers." Her movements were observed wherever she went, and numerous strangers were brought in for sittings. Since the spirits summoned by Mrs. Piper performed no apports, levitations or other physical hocus-pocus, it was not necessary for her to divert attention by forcing her witnesses to control her. The medium was the message, and for the next several months the message came through loud and clear. Myers himself found particularly convincing a message from Edmund Gurney, who had recently died.

True, there were certain problems with Mrs. Piper. Her control, a French Dr. Phinuit, was constantly fishing for information from his sitters, but on a good day he might dispense with this tactic and come right to the point, although there was no evidence that he could either speak or comprehend French. Phinuit, the committee concluded, was "a secondary personality of Mrs. Piper's." Such caution, however, hardly explained the evidentiary character of her communiqués from the dead. Lodge, a confirmed Spiritualist to begin with, had no doubt that he had heard from the hereafter and it existed.

Mrs. Piper returned to America where, for the next fifteen years, her sittings were under the control of Hodgson, whose doubts waned as the medium waxed. All sittings were recorded by a secretary and the information conveyed in them checked for verification. The proof, Hodgson came to believe, was unassailable. This once-skeptical researcher died a committed believer in spiritualism.

At the deaths of Sidgwick, in 1900, and Myers in 1901, the S.P.R. had accomplished its task. They had made psychic research respectable and had laid the foundations for the exploratory and investigative approach that continues today. Sidgwick was never fully convinced that the living can talk with the dead, but Myers, who had no less than 150 sittings with a Mrs. Thompson in the year and a half preceding his death, came to accept the possibility without question. "I do not feel the smallest doubt that we survive death," he wrote to J. A. Symons. Myers's book, *Human Personality and its Survival of Bodily Death*, published posthumously in 1903, is his testament to this belief and the most ambitious documentation (1,360 pages) ever attempted on the subject of personal immortality.

But the drama was not quite over. Before he died, Myers placed in a sealed envelope a message that he hoped would verify his survival through mediumistic contact. The message was deliberately cryptic, and its contents would only be meaningful to those who had known him well. After several attempts, a Mrs. Holland succeeded in "getting through" to Myers, who told her, "I appear to be standing behind a sheet of frosted glass . . . which blurs sight and deadens sound—dictating feebly—to a reluctant and somewhat obtuse secretary." This was followed by several literary and classical references which, it was hoped, could be verified by the message in the sealed envelope. When it was opened, however, the message was as cloudy as Myers's "sheet of frosted glass," and only by the most tortured of interpretations could it be construed as evidence that he was, in fact, communicating with those left behind.

This did not discourage the Society for Psychical Research which, thanks to the dominance of Oliver Lodge, became increasingly less interested in investigating spiritualism than in espousing it. Even Eusapia, who was then operating on the continent, was reinvestigated and given a clean bill of health! Agnostics like Sir Arthur Conan Doyle, who wanted a rational explanation for believing in immortality, became ardent—and uncritical—publicizers for spiritualism, and in London the British College of Psychic Science was founded to train mediums. To a degree, psychic research became coopted by the very people it was supposed to be investigating. This might have ended any further efforts at research had it not been for a new interest from an unexpected source: orthodox psychologists who, ordinarily, would not be "caught dead" exploring the possibility of life after death.

Enter the Scientists

William James, of course, had been an early member of the society and one-time president of the American branch (later to become independent). As much philosopher as scientist, he had been entranced by the redoubtable Mrs. Piper. More interested in the speculative aspects of immortality, he never applied to mediumistic claims rigorous scientific tests beyond the powers of his own observations. These observations, however, were not uncritical, and James never became a full-fledged convert to spiritualism. Mrs. Piper, he believed, was simply "in possession of a power as yet unexplained."

James persuaded his colleagues at Harvard to take a more open-minded view toward behavior that could not always be interpreted along strict empirical lines. Psychology, it should be remembered, was at this time a relatively new field, organized around the physiological processes of the body. Depth psychology, as Freud conceived it, was only beginning to take hold in certain quarters, and a mechanistic model of man prevailed among most scientists. This made James' interest in psychic events all the more daring, a stance that was justified only by his towering reputation.

James' most notable convert was the young British-born psychologist William MacDougall, who had come to Harvard from Oxford. MacDougall became attracted to psychical research through James' work with Mrs. Piper, and, although he doubted that she provided a bridge to the dead, he was mystified by what he saw. (Moreso, in fact, than the psychologist G. Stanley Hall, of Clark University, who invented a fictitious niece, fed her questions through Mrs. Piper and received, of course, fictitious answers.) A maverick on the Harvard faculty, MacDougall continued his investigations after James' death and in the 1920s found a colorful subject in the person of Margery, a Boston medium who, in her private life, was the wife of a well-known surgeon, Dr. LeRoi G. Crandon.

Margery did everything that Mrs. Piper claimed to do, and

quite a bit more. Sitters were grouped closely together, and there was a good deal of physical contact between them and the medium, who appeared for these occasions in a dressing gown with nothing underneath. Among her more spectacular effects was the ability to materialize spare parts—an extra hand, for instance—which seemed to protrude from between her legs. Other parts were more nebulous, suggesting ethereal rather than corporeal qualities, although the dim lighting made identification difficult. One male sitter felt sure his hand had touched a woman's breast.

All this intrigued the experts. Whately Carington, a British psychologist, had several sittings with Margery and before he returned to England reputedly had a love affair with her, and borrowed money from Dr. Crandon as well! His investigations could hardly have been unbiased. MacDougall, although he couldn't explain the ectoplasms, was doubtful of what he saw. At one seance, an extra hand "resembling an inspired jelly fish flopping about the table" seemed to have come through parturition from Margery's thighs.

In 1925, when she stepped forward to claim $5,000 offered by *Scientific American* to any medium whose authenticity could be verified, MacDougall served on the committee to investigate her claims. Another member—there were five in all—was Harry Houdini. The committee split four to one against Margery, and it was MacDougall's opinion that she was a fraud. Later evidence would tend to bear him out, for when Dr. Crandon's files were secretly examined it was found that he had surgically enlarged Margery's vagina, making room for the extra hand—in Mac-Dougall's opinion, an animal lung—which so impressed the sitters. The medium continued in business nevertheless, and William Butler Yeats had a sitting with her in 1932. MacDougall explained her appeal on the psychological grounds that she satisfied needs that upper-class Boston society generally ignored. In effect, her seances were the forerunner of what today might be called a sensitivity group.

Back in England, Whately Carington was later to try another type of experiment. A single spirit communicator, he reasoned, would be likely to employ a consistent, characteristic style even though speaking through different mediums. But this did not turn out to be the case. Carington concluded that it was the medium, not the spirit, who was communicating.

By this time MacDougall had realized that the whole approach toward psychic investigation was much too unscientific. Rather than meet the psychics on their own ground, which provided numerous opportunities for deception, he suggested that research take place in the laboratory, with the medium replaced by ordinary subjects who might or might not have psychic powers. Few universities, however—and certainly not Harvard—were willing to become involved in such dubious experiments, and only after he transferred to Duke University in 1927 did MacDougall get the support he needed. Working with a young assistant, J. B. Rhine, he set up the country's first parapsychology laboratory and, in effect, launched a new academic discipline, however suspect it might remain in the eyes of traditional psychologists.

MacDougall did not live long enough to participate in the exciting developments that began to come out of the Duke laboratories in the 1930s. But there is no doubt that he had fathered a more empirical approach to psychic research. Rhine's primary interest was in extrasensory perception, and for a good many years his work was concentrated in this field. Subjects were tested for their ability to identify geometric shapes on cards they could not see, scores were kept and statistical analyses made to determine to what extent the results were based on chance. After thousands of such tests, Rhine was able to demonstrate, statistically at least, that some people's power to perceive objects concealed from them far exceeds the laws of probability. Such people have come to be known as sensitives.

Modern survival research is an outgrowth of these early formulations of the Duke laboratories. (Now retired, Rhine carries on his work at the privately endowed Foundation for Research into the Nature of Man in Durham, North Carolina.) Such variants of psychic power as precognition, clairvoyance, out-of-body experiences, and even poltergeists have all come under examination, although not always as strictly as critics of the movement would like. Nevertheless, MacDougall's insistence on a laboratory setting has become an accepted procedure, and he would be delighted to learn that psychologists no longer visit mediums; rather the mediums—a few, at any rate—come to them.

One such was Eileen Garrett, an Irish-born medium who had studied at the British College of Psychic Science. Mrs. Garrett numbered among her friends Sir Arthur Conan Doyle, an indefatigable proponent of spiritualism whose own communications from the "other side" she was to receive three months after his death in 1930. Her control at the time was Uvani, an Arab soldier who had lived in the fourteenth century and who spoke in broken English. "Here I am, Arthur Conan Doyle," the voice announced. "I am in a nebulous belt lying outside the earth's surface and having life and being because it is of the same structure and matter of the earth itself." Doyle (or rather, Uvani) went on to explain that this new existence was "neither heaven nor hell," but "a combination of both."

Mrs. Garrett had acquired a considerable reputation as a lecturer and psychic before she moved to the United States in 1939. What set her apart from most mediums was a willingness to subject herself to scientific scrutiny (unlike Arthur Ford, for instance, who never made himself available to testing in Dr. Rhine's laboratory.) Convinced that Uvani was "a split-off of my subconscious mind," she sought a rational explanation of her powers, which were exhibited not in an atmosphere of dim lights, incense and physical conjuring, but on an empty stage, sometimes before thousands of people. And although Mrs. Garrett gave up seances in 1931, at age thirty-eight, she went right on getting communications from the dead. Their evidentiary information, moreover, impressed a good many observers.

During several visits to this country, she submitted to a number of different test procedures, with mixed results. The Phipps Psychiatric Clinic at Johns Hopkins University found no positive indication of supernormality. A New York City psychologist, Hereward Carrington, tested her response to a word list in both waking and trance states to see if Uvani would respond differently from the "real" Mrs. Garrett. He concluded that with certain key words—those which were emotionally laden—Uvani did, indeed, react quite differently from Eileen Garrett. (The responses were measured by a galvonometer.) A doctor at Roosevelt Hospital in New York, after six months of tests, discerned a marked variation in blood pressure, EEG readings and other measures of bodily function between Mrs. Garrett when she was awake and when she was in her Uvani trances. He concluded, for instance, that Uvani had diabetes, for when he was present the medium's blood sugar was extremely high. A subsequent examination by five doctors in London, however, failed to confirm the conclusiveness of these changes which, it was thought, fell well within a range that could be explained by normal activities.

Mrs. Garrett was nothing if not cooperative; it was almost as though she suffered from an undiagnosed illness and was seeking the help of the doctors. And it was in this spirit that she traveled to Duke University in April 1934, for an exhaustive series of trials with Dr. Rhine. Rhine approached the question of Uvani's existence indirectly. If he were a spirit entity, he might not possess possible telepathic powers attributed to his medium; and conversely, if Mrs. Garrett did not exhibit these powers and Uvani did, one might infer that he was an independent being. Sixteen thousand trials were held altogether: 14,425 waking and 1,575 in trance. The results seemed to disprove Uvani's separate existence, for although Uvani-Garrett together achieved a score considerably higher than could be accounted for by chance, it was not weighted in Uvani's favor. Rhine concluded that Mrs. Garrett had ESP powers, shared equally by both personality states.

Mrs. Garrett submitted to a variety of other tests, none of which produced any clear evidence of communicating spirits. Probably her most valuable contribution to psychic research was to establish the Parapsychology Foundation in 1951 to support additional research in the field. No aspect of parapsychology— ghosts, reincarnation, clairvoyance, psychokinesis—was to be excluded. The only requirement was that all research was to be conducted by approved scientific methods. Mediums would be investigated and poltergeists run to earth. If there was an afterlife, it could surely be discovered by the sophisticated tools of modern science.

The New Quest for Immortality

Supported by grants from the foundation, and armed with the newest methodology, parapsychologists stepped up their efforts to explore psychic experiences that had always resisted explanation. The old terminology of the seance gave way as the trance came to be called an altered state of consciousness; precognition replaced prophecy; ESP dethroned telepathy; and psi came to stand for the seemingly transcendental experiences of clairvoyants and mystics. In the hands of experimenters, spiritualism was deprived of its religious ideology and given an up-to-date language. In short, it was hoped that, if the professional scientist could not provide a reliable map to the world beyond the senses, he could at least demystify some inherently mysterious phenomena.

The possibility of reincarnation, for example, is being investigated by Dr. Ian Stevenson, professor of psychiatry at the University of Virginia Medical School. Dr. Stevenson has studied more than 1,000 cases of reported reincarnation and concludes that at least twenty of these appear to be genuine. (His book, *Twenty Cases Suggestive of Reincarnation*, has recently been reissued by the University of Virginia Press.) Discarnate beings, Stevenson believes, can appear in new bodies—residual personalities, so to speak, that remember their lives under a previous existence.

Reincarnation, of course, has long been a tenet of Theosophy, but it is only recently that the Bridey Murphy phenomenon has come under scientific investigation. Stevenson is not alone in this research. Anyone who suspects that he has had a former life is invited to write to a West Palm Beach, Florida, group of psychologists who placed a classified ad in *The New York Times* ("Seeking Evidence of Pre-existent recollection. . . .") which suggests that "regression through hypnosis" may bring out the latent person you were before birth.

Another researcher, Dr. Karil Osis, of the American Society for Psychical Research, explores survival of the human personality through observations of dying patients. In 1961, Dr. Osis undertook a study of deathbed visions on the premise that such visions might be real rather than hallucinatory. Osis based his survey on the knowledge that many dying people report seeing close relatives in their final moments and interpret the experience as a sign that they are being "called for" by those who have predeceased them.

A lengthy questionnaire was mailed to 5,000 physicians and 5,000 nurses throughout the country. Emphasis was on hallucinatory behavior, either as reported by the patient or observed by others. Six hundred and forty questionnaires were returned by respondents who claimed to have made 35,540 observations of dying patients. Of this total, 1,370 had, in fact, hallucinated at the end. To ascertain the nature of these hallucinations in detail, Osis followed up the respondents by telephone.

The information he gathered provides some fascinating clues to the terminal stage of life, amplifying many of the experiences we reported in Chapter Six. One major finding of this survey is that less than 10 percent of the 35,540 patients retained consciousness during the last hour of their lives. A physician explained this low ratio largely by the fact that "man dies doped." For those who were conscious, however, fear did not seem to be the dominant emotion (although pain and discomfort were common); rather, a substantial proportion of patients were elated, and of these more than 1,300 experienced deathbed hallucinations, 746 such experiences being described to nurses or doctors by patients themselves.

Could such phenomena, however, also be typical of people in good health? Osis compared his figures with two British surveys of hallucinatory behavior among the general population and found that deathbed visions in his sample were ten times as frequent as those reported in the British survey. An even more interesting trend emerged when the kinds of visions were compared: in an overwhelming majority of cases, people in normal health hallucinate living persons; the dying, however, hallucinate mainly the dead.

Osis next set out to discover if these deathbed visions were induced by drugs or other physiological conditions. On the contrary, he found that the patients most likely to hallucinate were those who, far from being delirious or "high," suffered the least impairment in their "psychological and physiological equilibrium." Moreover, the frequency of these apparitions increased with the educational level of those who saw them, ruling out the possibility that they might be traced to a belief in superstition.

But what about the cultural expectations (as Osis terms them) of the modern, and educated, patient? One need not be superstitious to have acquired a whole set of somewhat unconscious beliefs about death and the possibility of another world. When a Gallup Poll taken in 1960 asked the question, "Do you believe there is, or is not, a life after death?" almost three-fourths of those queried said there is such life. Psychologists have long known that what they call an expectancy set facilitates perception. People see what they want, or expect, to see; the patients Osis reports on might well have had visions of what they expect will happen at death. This hypothesis would also account for the tenfold increase in hallucinations among the dying over those in normal health. On balance, the survey supports a subjective, rather than a survival, explanation of the phenomena. Many people do, indeed, experience visions at the time of death, but this may simply represent an inner psychological need rooted in expectation and hope.

Contemporary Survival Research

Traditionally, the question of immortality has been left to theologians and philosophers. Their arguments are necessarily inductive, and belief in immortality is largely a matter of faith. Spiritualism attempts to offer proof of survival by producing both manifestations of the dead and messages from them. But even in its heyday, its proofs were not very convincing and there were certain logical difficulties besides. Why, for example, did the spirits wait until the middle of the nineteenth century to begin communicating with the living? Why did certain departed French notables speak in English or, for that matter, at German seances, in German? And why, in the final analysis, were their messages to the loved ones on earth usually so trivial and unimportant?

Survival research today utilizes an up-to-date laboratory approach. Julius Weinberger, an electronics engineer from Huntington, Long Island, is conducting experiments with "direct voice" mediums to test their claims that it is the voice of the departed, and not their own, that is heard at the seance. Weinberger makes voice prints of these messages and compares them, when possible, with recordings of the deceased's voice made while he was alive, possibly on a home tape recorder. Weinberger also compares the "spirit's" voice with that of the medium.

At the Stanford Research Institute, teams of investigators run tests for clairvoyance and precognition which may indicate a psi factor that defies bodily death. Elsewhere, computer experts have been called in, information theory has been borrowed from the social sciences, and electronic wizardry tracks voices from outer space. The conclusion of these experiments: the messages from beyond are still coming through.

The medium, however, may be quite different. For several years, Konstantin Raudive, a Latvian who worked in Germany and Switzerland, "tuned into" the spirit world by means of sensitive tape recorders and shortwave radios. Raudive's experiments began when he picked up unexplained human voices during the taping of an ordinary conversation among several friends. Largely unintelligible at first, these extraneous sounds could not be explained electronically. Moreover, an analysis of their content suggested that they were too human sounding to be accounted for by sunspots or random high-frequency radio waves. Intrigued, Raudive set about to systematically "capture" these voices in subsequent trials.

Raudive's book, *Breakthrough*, describes his three years' work in identifying some 72,000 voice interventions. In effect, he ran seances in which the recorder or radio was the medium and questions were directed to the "spirits" through a microphone. Sometimes the recorder was connected to a radio and the wavelength changed to get continual static. Strange voices would break through the static and often, Raudive believed, they answered questions that had been beamed into space.

From a scientific point of view, these experiments meet one important test: because the proceedings are recorded, the voices can be studied and analyzed when the session is over. There are, however, two difficulties that should not be minimized. The spirits, Raudive pointed out, don't speak plain English (or any other language) but have their own unique vocabulary and syntax. Words are grammatically altered, and sentences come in telegram style. The messages cannot be deciphered until someone breaks the code. The deciphered messages may be well worth waiting for, since Raudive claimed to have heard from Hitler, Churchill and Goethe, among others. One sitter, Dr. Andrija Puharich, relates that it took him about twelve hours to train himself to hear the voices; he became "totally convinced that the effect was genuine." The other problem is simply that Raudive himself had to be present for the extraneous sounds to register on the tape. This suggests that Raudive, rather than the recorder, was the real medium, somehow transferring the messages to the tape. But whatever the explanation, his seances produced some uncanny results.

In 1969, two electronic experts in London challenged Raudive to submit his experiment to an outside panel. All equipment used was factory-fresh, so it could not have been tampered with. The two requirements insisted upon were that the voices should identify someone present by name, and that they should answer a question. After sorting out a number of ethereal communications, it was possible to interpret one message as "Raudive is there." More impressive was the question period during which a Catholic bishop asked to hear from a deceased Russian friend. He got messages in both German and Russian—or so those present were convinced.

Do the voices really come from outer space? It may well turn out that Raudive picked up telepathic messages from the sitters rather than the spirits and beamed them through some form of psychic energy onto the tape. Such energy, it is postulated, might register in the form of electromagnetic waves of very high frequency. In this view, Raudive was the mediator between the sitters' thoughts and the sensitive recording device.

Another explanation has been put forward by the British biochemist, Prof. E. Lester Smith. It may well be, Smith speculates, that the messages are recorded by "subliminal ventriloquism. . . . Raudive and the other mediums may go into a light trance and whisper the messages through nearly-closed lips . . . quite unaware of what [they] are doing." And listening to the tapes, Professor Smith adds, may actually be an exercise in "audible tea leaf" reading. Just as tea leaves suggest definite patterns if stared at long enough, so might cryptic noises under prolonged study be interpreted as words. The effect, Smith thinks, is subjective. Following Raudive's death in September 1974, little has been done to verify his work. Nor has Raudive's "spirit," at this writing, reported in to the earthlings.

The tantalizing possibility exists that, if people do have a psi ability that operates independently of the physical senses while they are living, it goes right on operating after life has ended. William G. Roll, a parapsychologist at the Psychical Research Foundation in Durham, North Carolina, posits three possible means by which this hypothesis might be tested: (1) there must be an actual awareness that the self extends beyond the body while a person is still alive; (2) it must be possible to verify this objectively; and (3) this "out-of-body" self must be capable of existing independently of the physical organism—of acting on others and being detected by them. Roll writes:

> The indications are ... that what we call personality continues to exist after death of the body as a kind of field or system of associations around the objects with which the person was in physical contact when he was alive. ... In the same way as the gravitational field of a material object is part of the gravitational field of the earth, the consciousness of a person seems to be part of wider consciousness of which he may or may not be aware. ... [Thus] it would be illogical to expect consciousness to disappear with the death of the individual.

Dr. Robert Morris, a former researcher at the foundation, puts it somewhat differently. "Survivable aspects of personality," Morris calls them theta aspects or TA, "may be due exclusively to psi abilities of the living ... any form of TA which is postulated to survive death would naturally exist before death and therefore can be studied in experiences of living beings. ..."

In practical terms, this might show up in the form of hauntings or poltergeists. The enormous popular literature on this subject, however, is no indication that any poltergeist has been run to earth. The most that can be said is that some strange cases remain unexplained. Swaying chandeliers, mysterious knocking, falling dishes, gyrating furniture—these are the familiar signs of a visiting poltergeist. The Psychical Research Foundation's investigators have looked into dozens of these reported occurrences without much success. They conclude that most such hauntings appear to be caused by a living person, frequently a mischievous child. Other cases appear to be explained by psychokinetic energy of which the agents are unaware. The poltergeist activity, William Roll believes, is an involuntary outlet for aggression. This might explain why "haunted houses" cease to be haunted when the occupants move out. The S.P.R. in England not long ago explored an especially baffling case by simply renting the house in question for three weeks and moving a team of investigators in. During their residency, however, absolutely nothing unusual happened. Nevertheless, the Spiritualist Association of Great Britain advertises a twenty-four-hour service for people who are bothered by ghosts. (Its task force gets about thirty calls for help a month.)

More fruitful are the Psychic Research Foundation's controlled experiments with OBEs, or out-of-body experiences. Using a laboratory setup, investigators employ two types of psi tests to explore both OBE and field consciousness states. In one test, an attempt is made to detect the person in areas "occupied" by his consciousness. In short, is his presence felt by others (including animals) and can it be measured by heat-sensitive instruments? The other test asks the OBE subject to obtain verifiable information about the place he is "visiting."

This super ESP is not possessed by everyone, but the Durham researchers have located certain individuals who seem to be able to bring about an OBE at will. One of them, Stuart K. ("Blue") Harary, a Duke University student, has proved especially successful. Harary projects himself into one of several detection labs from a "launch site" about half a mile away. Assistants who monitor these experiments are not told when the OBEs are to occur (there are usually two a night when the experiment is being run) or which lab Harary's free-floating "self" will visit. Harary himself is not given instructions until a few minutes before the launch, at which time he is briefed on what he is to do during the visit. Lying on a bed, he prepares himself by filtering out all outside stimuli and concentrating on the forthcoming separation of consciousness from self. Under such conditions, Harary claims, he is usually able to "leave" his body and "travel" to the designated target.

The results of several extended trials are, if inconclusive, nonetheless promising enough to justify further research. With human detectors, for instance, Harary's "presence" was felt more often than would be accounted for by chance, although not unusually so. Heat-sensitive instruments have shown no response to these visits, nor have gerbils and snakes, but kittens that he has handled previously prove to be especially good detectors; one in particular, who is observed to be active and meowing when thrust into the target laboratory, regularly settles down, stops crying and seems quite contented when Harary is having an OBE.

The foundation is working with other OBE subjects, one of whom, George Kokoris, is attempting "visits" from his home in New York to the Durham facility. At this point, Dr. Roll's hypothesis is far from demonstrated, and critics point out that, even if such paranormal transactions among the living could be proved, they would not necessarily indicate the survival of psi capacity beyond death. For instance, George Zorab, a biologist who writes on parapsychology, thinks that research points to a physical, rather than mental, explanation of psi phenomenon. And since there is some evidence that animals also have this ability, it would not appear to represent a "soul" or higher consciousness that might continue after death.

Dr. Gardner Murphy, one-time director of the Menninger Clinic and a lifelong student of parapsychology, has written, ". . . there is, so far as [I] know, no survival evidence which is completely unambiguous, complete in itself, and free of all competing or alternative explanations." There may be, he believes, a dualism "between normal and paranormal processes," but the paranormal phenomena, like the normal, might best be regarded as an expression of certain conscious or unconscious needs of the individual.

One such need is for immortality. Ironically, those who have done most to question belief in human survival, the scientists, are now being called back to rediscover it. Evidence accumulates that there is in fact something outside sensory perception as we normally experience it. The psi that seems to link communication among the living through ESP may also prove to be a soul that binds human beings in an ethereal and dematerialized afterlife of pure energy and disembodied consciousness. This, at any rate, is the direction of modern survival research. But one suspects that wherever this quest may lead, its influence will be most vividly felt in this world, rather than in the next.

CHAPTER X

A Natural Death

On the face of it, the modern world, with its fetish for biological immortality, has made spiritual immortality seem superfluous. Yet it is difficult to separate the idea of death from the notion of survival. Perhaps in talking with the dead we are really trying to communicate with the loss in ourselves. Deprived of faith, without a good reason for dying or a humane way of going about it, modern man finds very little left to die for.

Is it possible to put on the boxing gloves again and have it out with ourselves in the middle of the night? One asks this question hopefully, but the answer is unclear. The boxing ring that our fathers knew is no longer there, the referee is gone, and the seconds have been replaced by respirators and intravenous tubes. The Valley of Death has given way to intensive care, and the shadows of eternity have rolled back to reveal the antiseptic Now. As the crisis approaches, Dr. Melvin Krant has noted, the minister is pushed out of the sickroom and the EEG machine is wheeled in. Often it does no more than perform the last rites.

It is along these lines that the wrenching necessity of dying into the world—of relinquishing belief in a future life for a

humanistic present—will have to be mitigated. For this, thanatology—the study of death and dying—has become the new
theology, albeit a largely secular one. As a movement, it has
created dilemmas no less painful than those arising from
technology. In the backlash of lingering old age, of chronic
disease, of machine dying, there lurks the notion that if death
is somehow made more dignified it becomes more acceptable.
It is no longer to be denied and, above all, it is not to be
fought off. I call this the new fatalism; for although death is
inevitable, it is not so inevitably evil that it must be speeded
up. In any case, death with dignity is meaningful only if we
know of what dignity consists in a terminal life. And what it is
not necessarily is an easy death.

A not-so-obvious role for thanatology, therefore, is to remain skeptical of those who would protect the dying by hastening their end. The fallacy of euthanasia is that it makes death
unnatural; for, although the euthanasist protests machines that
prolong life, he uses them—in some variant—to end it. Worse,
he encourages the acquiescence of those whom he presumes to
help.

Much of this paradox lies in a confusion of terms. The good
death is not necessarily an easy death; it is one which permits
a person to die in character: Socrates drinking the hemlock,
Father Damien with leprosy, the average man with a sense of
life-fulfillment. Yet today, the easy death is seen as inherently
good. Modern man is no longer thought brave enough to die a
painful death. Hence the right to die has become not a last
resort but a first, and the living will an insurance policy that
indemnifies us against an untidy end. One pays but a single
premium for this protection: life itself.

Medical technology has, indeed, created ethical dilemmas,
and no machine ever gave tender loving care. Yet there is no
reason to reject the marvels of medicine simply because they
are sometimes abused. People have always died with some
kind of help, whether it be from opiates, oxygen tents or other
means. Removing these adjuncts hardly provides a dignified

death. Ideally, we die when we are ready to die, and in this respect modern medicine gives people a chance to prepare themselves.

In her book, A Very Easy Death—the title is ironic—Simone de Beauvoir describes the last painful days her mother spent in a Paris hospital. Against what she terms her better judgment, the daughter consented to an operation that prolonged this elderly woman's life a mere thirty days. Yet in this brief period they came to know each other with a poignance and wisdom that a whole lifetime had denied them. For Maman, the pain of dying (the fact is, she thought she was convalescing) confirmed a world that still possessed her in the devotion of others. For Simone, the anguish of watching her mother die tapped a well of unsuspected feelings about the value of her own life. In this context, no death is easy, certainly not for the survivors.

"There is no such thing as a natural death," de Beauvoir has written, "nothing that happens to a man is ever natural since his presence calls the world into question. All men must die; but for every man his death is an accident and, even if he knows it and consents to it, an unjustifiable violation." Dying at one's own pace and in one's own style, de Beauvoir reminds us, gives one a chance to pull the loose ends of life together; to forgive old hurts and to be forgiven; to mourn and be loved; to cherish what is precious in the moment and to know that pain can be rewarded by fortitude. None of this need be without dignity, and all of it takes time.

It is often said that death is a greater problem for the living than for those who die. This is why we see a movement to encourage quick dying. The sudden heart attack or stroke victim, the automobile fatality, the gunshot target who is dead on arrival—these people are appreciated for having died instantly, saving the rest of us the messy problem of watching them die gradually, in less convenient circumstances, at some later date. They are supposed not to have suffered, and we are thought to have been immunized against suffering (but we know that it usually goes underground, to torment us later). What we avoid

are social responsibilities: the geriatric programs, the problems
of a costly and lingering convalescence, the burdensome challenge of making a place for the old in a society that worships
youth. This society is "programming its members to die
quickly," the psychologist Stanley Keleman has written.

But the problem is not eliminated by quick death; it is compounded. How quick is quick? How old is old? At what point
should the leukemia patient be allowed to die naturally; that is,
in pain? When does life cease to have quality and meaning?
Sudden death does not answer these questions. The great
danger of induced dying is that it sanctions an equivalent cal-
lousness toward the living, of which there is enough already. In
the name of mercy, it diminishes our humanity, which exists
to be shared not least with those who are most helpless. It
argues against the value of hope and the necessity for change.
Our society is very ambivalent on this question, and the day
may come when the suicide prevention center operates next
door to the euthanasia lab.

If we believe that life is precious, that it has meaning to the
end, we need not shorten the process to satisfy someone else's
ideal. The revolt against the use of extraordinary measures to
prolong the lives of the hopelessly ill is not surprising. The
danger in this is that the extreme case tends to become the
norm for those who are less hopeless. Yet we need not justify
the harshness and pain of dying on an abstract or moral level
to satisfy still another ideal. What we can do is add a new
social environment to dying and, coincident with this, develop
humanistic attitudes to ensure that technology does not become self-defeating. Living *while* dying becomes the central
concern. Is such a revolutionary approach possible?

Community of the Dying

In the early 1960s, a young doctor, then on the staff of St.
Joseph's Hospital in London, conceived the idea for an environment that would provide this kind of terminal care. A nun and

former nurse, Dr. Cicely Saunders persuaded Britain's National-Health Service to underwrite the operating expenses. The physical structure was built with private contributions. It is not be called a hospital—and certainly not a home for incurables—but St. Christopher's Hospice, named for the patron saint of travelers. In the Middle Ages, hospice meant a community of people whose common goal was to care for travelers who had no other place to stay. St. Christopher's was conceived as a way station for people nearing the end of their journey in life.

The hospice opened in 1966 and, in its few years of existence, has become a model for care of the dying the world over. Some 2,000 visitors a year—doctors, nurses, medical students, ministers—come to St. Christopher's to study its system. Perhaps lack of system is a better term, for the hospice is unique in its lack of regulations, its almost total liberation from conventional hospital practices.

St. Christopher's Hospice is in the London suburb of Sydenham, a fifteen-minute train ride from the city proper. A visitor is surprised to find it on a street of upper-middle-class homes, set apart only by the spaciousness of its grounds. The dying, in short, have not been zoned to some other part of town.

More surprising is the presence of children; these belong to members of the staff and they are seen everywhere. In the garden, a few elderly residents tend the flowers; and, although many patients are in wheelchairs, none is calling for help. One is impressed by St. Christopher's matter-of-factness; it does not seem to be administered so much as shared. (Where else are rooms set aside for younger persons who want to visit in private with their fiancés or spouses and, quite frankly, to make love?)

Some of the ward patients have brought their own furniture: a favorite chair, a bookcase, a table. There are no signs to persuade the visitor that the residents are in good hands—none are needed.

It is apparent that Dr. Saunders's approach to terminal care is a radical one. Here are some other features that impressed me:

Patients who can walk are permitted to eat their meals in the cafeteria, along with doctors and nurses. There is little patient-staff protocol.

If a patient is able to sit up, he is brought to the hospice by car (rather than ambulance), addressed by name and welcomed as though he were entering a social club. (Quite possibly, he already belongs to the Pilgrim Club, a group of seriously ill persons living at home for whom future hospitalization may be necessary. The group meets in one of the lounges of the hospice to discuss the illnesses of its members, to give people a "taste" of the hospice and to reassure them that it is not a frightening place. A snack bar serves drinks and refreshments.)

If the patient arrives by ambulance, he is met at the door, not with a stretcher, but with the bed that he will occupy. Six-bed wards are large enough to provide everyone with his own personal space, a room within a room.

Visiting hours run from eight in the morning until eight at night, and there are no restrictions on children. Even pets are permitted to visit their master or mistress—accompanied, of course.

There are no nurses' stations. As a result, nurses spend their spare time visiting with patients rather than each other.

The patient's folder includes a sheet on his feelings and mental attitude, as well as the usual medical data.

Garden parties are held in good weather and everyone's birthday is celebrated on the appropriate day. Among the games: wheelchair races for patients who feel up to them, with a prize going to the winner.

Under the National Health Service, no patient is required to pay, although families sometimes contribute to the hospice's fund for new equipment.

Drugs are given on demand, although such requests are seldom necessary. Medication is so finely titrated with the patients' symptoms that pain is rarely a problem. As a consequence, less, not more, narcotics are used than in many hospitals where the suffering patient must beg for relief. Liquor, too, is acceptable. "We encourage relatives to bring in alcohol if they know the patient would enjoy it," Dr. Saunders says. "I mean quite honestly that a bottle of whiskey may be more valuable than a whole great basket of oranges."

Stranger things than whiskey have come into the wards. During my visit to St. Christopher's one very old man with etymological interests had suspended a chrysalis over his bed. The whole ward waited expectantly for the moth to break through and fly away, as it eventually did.

Prayers are said on the ward twice a day, although the patient is under no obligation to take part. At noon, the *angelus* is beamed through television earphones that include a "house" channel, but it is easily tuned out. Although nonsectarian, St. Christopher's is staffed largely by Catholic nuns and physicians, many of whom were foreign missionaries before returning to London. Recently, two patients decided they wanted to make the trip to Lourdes. The hospice, which does not discourage this sort of thing, made arrangements for the journey. Dr. Saunders holds out no prospects of a cure for these people, but reasons that they may benefit psychologically.

There is no denying the fact, she says, that bodily pain is real. Out of this has come the celebrated "Saunders cocktail" of diamorphine, cocaine, alcohol, syrup and chloroform water. Given at four-hour intervals, it acts *before* chronic pain begins and, in Dr. Saunders's words, "erases the memory and fear of pain" that is often as destructive as pain itself. The mixture is not a sedative, and patients remain alert and functioning. Because it contains heroin, the Saunders cocktail cannot be prescribed in the United States.

Those who enter St. Christopher's have been diagnosed as beyond recovery. Yet, for some, the quality of care is so powerful that the course of their illness is arrested; from 8 to 10 percent of all patients are sent home, not as cured, but with months and sometimes years to live. The truly terminal have no desire to leave, and death by suicide is unknown. "A very small number of patients have wanted to discuss euthanasia with us," Dr. Saunders has written. "No one has come back to make a considered request to carry it out. Once the feeling of pain and isolation have been relieved they never asked again."

The hospice may sound too good to be true. My own observations convinced me that not many of its residents would change places with those in the most expensively endowed medical center. St. Christopher's problem is having to turn away applicants. (To make it easier for friends and family to visit, patients are generally limited to those who live within a six-mile radius.) As a result, a domiciliary program has been developed for those who can be cared for at home under the supervision of the hospice staff. The patient, or his doctor, can telephone for advice or help on a twenty-four-hour-a-day basis. Many of these people are waiting for a place to open up for them in the hospice. "Who would think," a staff doctor said to me, "that people would be clamoring to enter a hospital for the dying?"

What can a place like St. Christopher's teach us? On a practical level, it makes terminal care about 30 percent less expensive when compared with conventional hospitals. The dying are not paying for a costly overhead designed to benefit the living. At present, some thirty hospitals in Great Britain follow St. Christopher's lead in some degree. There are none in the United States, although Hospice, Inc., a New Haven, Connecticut, group, has received a state charter and is planning its physical facilities.

Many people question whether dying should be made yet another subspecialty in an already fragmented profession. Says Dr. Kübler-Ross, "We should not institutionalize people. We can give the families much more help with home care, visiting nurses . . . and financial help in order to facilitate the final care at home." But with the prohibitive cost of dying it is actually cheaper for most patients to die in a hospital. The majority of private insurance plans pay nothing for home care. For those who are sixty-five and over, Medicaid pays the doctors' bills, but most doctors don't make house calls. And those who do are no longer certain that in this technologically enraptured age the little black bag provides an adequate symbol of competence. The poor in particular find it advantageous to be admitted for institutional care—paradoxically, it is mainly the well-to-do who can afford to die at home.

The hospice idea is one way of reconciling this dilemma. Unfortunately, bricks and mortar alone don't make a hospice. The strength of St. Christopher's is the dedication of its staff and its radical break with hospital conventions. Our own bureaucratic society worships the institutional niche. Once in it, we are virtually prisoners programmed by forces outside our control. What is unnatural about dying in America is not so much the medical apparatus that defies death, but a social environment in which it makes little sense to go on living. Intensive care has failed, and intensive caring is absent. "In our hospital," a nurse told me once, "patients who are dying are supposed to get on with it. They shouldn't take too long."

A young male nurse described an encounter with a seventeen-year old girl dying of cancer. She rang the call button, and when he asked what he could do for her, she begged him, "Please, hold me in your arms." He is not supposed to do this, but he lifted her off the pillow and clasped her to his breast, rocking her gently while she wept. He was almost ashamed as he described this incident. It is out of character, and against regulations. "I had to be sure that none of the staff was watching," he added.

In Boston, Project Equinox, at Tufts Medical Center, is trying to break down some of the barriers that separate the dying from the living. One way to do this, believes Dr. Melvin Krant, the director, is by involving the patient in as many decisions as possible. Conferences are held at which the hospital staff, doctors, the patient and his or her family discuss the illness, not simply as a medical case, but as a profoundly disruptive human event. Nothing is done behind the patient's back, and, insofar as he is capable of it, he is put in charge of his own life. Not the least benefit of this approach is the preservation of self-respect.

Project Equinox sees about 600 new patients a year. The decision may be to operate, to use cobalt or whole-body radiation, to go for broke—if this is what the patient wants. No one is encouraged to die quickly, but neither are they allowed to die neglected. Most patients are treated at home, their families assisted in managing the illness and in handling their feelings about the impending loss. If death comes, it is not unusual for members of the staff to attend the wake or visitation.

Not far away, at Massachusetts General Hospital, Dr. Avery Weisman continues the psychological autopsy he began at Cushing Hospital. This is called Project Omega. Unlike the physical autopsy, it deals with the person while he is still alive, endeavoring to uncover the psychosocial factors that contribute to a fatal illness. These are often more instrumental to the outcome than the physical disease.

"Illness is far too important," Dr. Weisman writes, "to be left to physicians." Treatment teams include ministers, psychologists, social workers, even members of the family, and their aim is to focus on emotional problems that are destructive to patient morale. Project Omega wants to know about the intact person —his individual feelings· and values, his responsibilities and relationships. How do they affect the course of treatment and the quality of his terminal life? If we can discover this, Weisman thinks, the patient need no longer be "a specimen and a statistic'" but a human being. He might even be allowed to die in peace.

Of an estimated 7,000 private hospitals in the United States, only 1 percent now have active counseling programs for dying patients. At Billings, in Chicago, a staff of twenty-eight chaplain-interns—many with training in psychotherapy—roam the wards for the benefit of any patient who wants someone to talk with. "Our job usually begins when the person has been written off medically," said one young chaplain. "We try to do what his physician can't or won't do."

The Clock Without Hands

Freud believed that the individual could never consciously imagine his own death because it was something he had not previously experienced. More likely, we conceive of dying in intellectual terms while emotionally denying the fact that it applies to us. We employ, in other words, an "as if" approach: death will come, but we go on as if it might not. Few people, indeed, lay down and die when told that they have an incurable disease. On the contrary, in some cases they "come to life" in an effort to make better use of what time remains to them.

A young college chaplain I once met had been ill for two years with leukemia. "I have chosen not to ignore it," he says. "Time has become a precious commodity, a clock without hands." Illness has freed him to control his time and relationships better. He now walks out of meetings that don't interest him. He is more capable of making decisions. He feels less guilt about traveling and enjoying himself. Approaching death has given him an awareness he never had before, it has become a form of consciousness-raising about his own life values.

Not everyone is as mature in the face of death as this man, but psychiatrists think that almost everyone can achieve a threshold of acceptance with some help. At St. Luke's Hospital in New York City, Dr. Samuel Klagsbrun works with patients who have chronic or degenerative diseases that are rapidly worsening. By openly discussing their feelings with him, they are better able, he thinks, to come to terms with their situation.

I watched him interview a twenty-four-year-old girl who has lupus, a fatal kidney disease from which her twin sister has already died. Because her sister had an adverse reaction to the medication, and died anyway, she refused all treatment except periodic dialysis. Offered a kidney transplant, she again refused, resorting instead to special diets and a blind faith that she will live. For six years she has fought off death, even improved, but now her condition is deteriorating.

"I'm not afraid to die," she said.

"Do you have a timetable?"

"No. I want to push it as far as I can . . . I don't want to cover up what's wrong with me. I want to feel the pain as well as the pleasures."

"Even if that means a shorter life?"

"Exactly."

"It sounds to me like you're committing suicide."

"It's my life."

The purpose of psychotherapy is to get her to consider the options. As an adult, she has a legal right to refuse treatment. But as a patient, she should know the implications of her decision, and it is not at all unlikely that she has chosen the right course. If she dies she will die as herself, with more dignity than would perhaps be possible otherwise.

A more aggressive stance is employed by Dr. Lawrence LeShan, who encourages patients to maintain what he calls an open encounter with death. Since there is seldom a strict timetable, even among the hopelessly ill, the time remaining to one can be used constructively. For Dr. LeShan, dying provides an opportunity not for a peak experience, but a creative one. He seeks to help the patient remain in vital contact with things that are important to him.

Such an approach, he believes, may actually prolong life. One of his patients, a doctor, was told that he had three months to live. Each of LeShan's therapeutic sessions with this man lasted up to four hours, until both were exhausted. But out of this came the admission that the patient had really wanted to be a sculptor, for which he had shown some talent as a young man. Although terminal, he made two trips to Italy, created several statues and lived not three months but two years.

"I tell my patients, 'Your life is worth fighting for,'" LeShan says. "Sell it at the highest price you can get." Typical is the sixty-eight-year-old woman dying of cancer who decided to write a history of ballet. Filling her hospital room with books, playbills and newspaper clippings, she worked until the very end. "The book was not completed but her life was," LeShan concludes, adding that "the object of therapy is not to get the patient to accept death, but to build his strength to face the crisis." The fear of death, he says, drops off when one fights for life.

For several years, Dr. Ned Cassem, a Jesuit psychiatrist at Cambridge, Massachusett's Youville Hospital, has been doing research into the emotional lives of the dying. He concluded that Christian preparedness for death—the Church's traditional objective—could best be achieved if patients were encouraged to talk about themselves. From this stemmed another helpful discovery: where there is an effort to share the dying person's fears, considerably less pain medication is necessary.

Dr. Edwin S. Shneidman notes that many people are willing to accept the fact that they are dying, but don't want to know how soon. "A dying person will not permit himself to hear more than he is prepared to digest at that moment. He very rarely 'knows' more about his condition than is good for him." Thus, encouraging a person to talk about his death is not as blunt as it seems. At Billings, for example, if a patient denies that he is dying, this denial is supported, to the very end if necessary. In the view of Dr. Samuel Klagsbrun, it is important to respect a patient's fantasies, no matter how unrealistic they may be. At the same time, the patient will often enter into the world of the therapist, identifying with him as a form of support. Kurt Eissler thought that sharing the psychological burden of an illness with another person "mobilizes the archaic trust in the world and reawakens the primordial feelings of being protected by a mother. . . ." In this way, the suffering of the dying can be reduced to a minimum, "even in cases of extreme physical pain."

Learning to Play the Piccolo

Margaret L. McClure, the director of nursing at Maimonides Medical Center, in Brooklyn, New York, uses a unique expression for sharing this psychological burden. She calls it "playing the piccolo." Figuratively speaking, the caregiver accompanies the dying person step by step to the end of his journey. Playing the piccolo, McClure says, means supporting the patient's dignity through expert care, being there when needed, respecting him as a person.

Sometimes this accompaniment is unexpectedly literal. Dr. James S. Eaton, Jr., once cared for a man who, in his youth, had been a street-corner tap dancer in the French Quarter of New Orleans. As death approached, his meager family and colleagues were summoned from the floor lounge to pay their final respects. Doctors and nurses began to drift away. "Don't you all leave yet," one of the sons called out. "He came to the foot of his father's bed," Dr. Eaton recalls, "along with the old man's dancing partner, his protégée. Then, in the middle of this twelve-bed ward, with nurses and doctors standing around a bit embarrassed and impatient, the two mourners began a slow tap dance with tears streaming down their faces, in tribute to the old man. Only a few dry eyes were left when they finished a few minutes later."

The piccolo player might also encourage aggression, even anger. This can be a healthy response to dying, as Dr. Kübler-Ross has pointed out. In Dr. Morton A. Lieberman's study of institutionalized elderly patients in Chicago, it was found that aggressive people were more likely to survive the shock of an illness than people who passively accept it. Die they do, sooner or later, but in the meantime they have kept an image of themselves that is rewarding in its own right. These "difficult patients" simply refuse to be rushed into dying.

Next comes the most heroic act of all: giving the dying permission to die. He must know that every person and possession he holds dear can be voluntarily surrendered; that the most important people he will leave behind are willing to be let go. It is his last request and their final gift. In all probability the dialogue will be conducted silently, in gestures, in the speech of the eye and the language of the touch. Dying puts words to silence, and it is these words we remember longest. Only then do we turn off the machines and draw the curtain, not in triumph but in sadness.

Because more than one person is needed in order for someone to die, all of us who are still strong, who believe that life is too short as it is, must learn to play the piccolo. In this sense, what is taken from us is given back not in the heaven of our imagination, but in the hell—and humanity—of our everyday lives. Death's ultimate bequest is to show us a world in which we recognize ourselves.

NOTES

Chapter I, The God from the Machine

Pages 6–7 Patricia Grosso's comments on hospital care are from "Death Is Not the Enemy," a paper written for a Foundation of Thanatology conference, New York, November 1–2, 1974. Dr. Feifel's statement on death as a public event appears in the *Encyclopedia of Mental Health*, vol. 2 (New York: Franklin Watts, 1963), p. 434. The Montemarano case was widely reported in the daily press. A good summary of the issues and outcome was in David A. Andelman, "Doctor Charged with Murder in Long Island 'Mercy Killing.'" *The New York Times* (January 21, 1974), pp. 1, 53. The comment, "It is morphine, not cancer, that kills them," was made in a personal communication to the author.

Pages 9–10 The story about London's Neasden Hospital is reported by Louis Lasagna in "Physician Behavior Toward the Patient," in Orville G. Brim et al., eds., *The Dying Patient* (New York: Russell Sage Foundation, 1970), pp. 87–88. The survey of Swedish attitudes toward death is discussed by Gunnar Biörck in "How Do You Want to Die?" *Archives of Internal Medicine* 132, no. 4 (October 1973), pp. 605–606.

Page 11 Life-or-death decisions as seen by public health officials appear in Andie L. Knutson, "Cultural Beliefs on Life and Death," in Brim et al., eds., *Dying Patient*, pp. 52–53. The novel *They* by Marya Mannes (New York: Doubleday, 1968).

Page 13 Avery Weisman's comment that "isolation and neglect" is more dreaded than physical distress appears in his "The Patient with a Fatal Illness—to Tell or Not to Tell," *Journal of the American Medical Association* 201, no. 8 (August 21, 1967), p. 154. The abandonment of the dying patient is from Richard A. Kalish, "Social Distance and the Dying," *Community Mental Health Journal* 2, no. 2 (Summer 1966), pp. 152–155. See also Richard A. Kalish, "Life and Death: Dividing the Indivisible," *Social Science and Medicine* 2 (1968), pp. 249–259.

Pages 14–15 Personal information given here about Dr. Kübler-Ross was obtained through interviews with the author. "Society has interdicted death . . ." is one theme developed by Philip Aries in *Western Attitudes Toward Death from the Middle Ages to the Present* (Baltimore: Johns Hopkins University Press, 1974). The skull-and-crossbones traffic sign is mentioned in R. Sterba, "On Halloween," *American Imago*, 5, no. 3 (November 1948), p. 224.

Page 16 The concept of megadeath is discussed by Edwin S. Schneidman in *Deaths of Man* (New York: Quadrangle, 1973), pp. 180, 182. For a discussion of some of the reasons we deny death, see Robert Kastenbaum and Ruth Aisenberg, *The Psychology of Death* (New York: Springer, 1972), pp. 205–208.

Chapter II, Violent Death—and the Gift of Life

Pages 19–20 The Curtin material is from a personal interview with the author. Information about the cost of kidney transplantation and the number of transplant candidates was supplied by the Institute of Allergy and Infectious Diseases, National Institutes of Health, Bethesda, Maryland. Comment on the California State Highway Patrol was made by Dr. Benjamin Burton of the Institute of Allergy and Infectious Diseases in a personal interview with the author. Dr. Warwick's article on body-rescue teams was excerpted from *Medical Opinion and Review* by the *Wall Street Journal* (June 24, 1968), p. 12.

Page 21 The story of Lev Davidovitch Landau is in Lasagna, "Physician Behavior Toward the Patient," in Brim et al., eds., *Dying Patient*, pp. 88–89.

Pages 22–23 Material on the Harvard Ad Hoc Committee and the death of Robert Kennedy is discussed in Newton J. Townshend, "Death: Is a New Definition Needed?" *Medical Economics* 45, no. 25 (December 9, 1968), pp. 25–32. See also *Journal of the American Medical Association* 205, no. 6 (August 5, 1968), p. 5, for a full account of the Committee's report. The Bruce Tucker case was reported in "First Details Are Disclosed on Virginia Heart Transfer," *The New York Times* (May 31, 1968), p. 44. A more complete discussion of this case can be found in Robert M. Veatch, "The Virginia 'Brain Death' Case," *Hastings Center Report* 2, no. 5 (November 1972), pp. 9–13. The Arkansas decision on the accidental death of a husband and wife is described in David Hendin, *Death as a Fact of Life* (New York: Norton, 1973), pp. 42–43.

Page 24 The Oklahoma incident is discussed in Townshend, "Death," p. 25. Death—or life—by decapitation is in Hendin, *Death as a Fact of Life*, p. 44.

Page 25 The Oakland, California, homicide case and its implications for transplant medicine was reported in "Heart Operation Key Issue in Trial," *The New York Times* (October 29, 1973), p. 5. Robert Kastenbaum's description of death by feigning is in his "Psychological Death," in Leonard Pearson, ed., *Death and Dying* (Cleveland, Ohio: Case Western Reserve University Press, 1969), pp. 3–8.

Pages 26–27 Anecdotes concerning premature burials are included in John D. Arnold et al., "Public Attitudes and Diagnosis of Death," *Journal of the American Medical Association* 206, no. 9 (November 25, 1968), pp. 1949–1954. Precaution against premature burial is described in Kastenbaum, "Psychological Death," in Pearson, ed., *Death and Dying*, p. 5. The case of the elderly London woman prematurely consigned to a mortuary was reported in the [London] *Daily Telegraph* (May 30, 1974), p. 1: "Until recently, very little attention was paid to diagnosing death in medical schools." The survey is in Arnold et al., "Public Attitudes and the Diagnosis of Death."

Page 28 Dr. Henry K. Beecher's warning against updating death is in his "Ethical Problems Created by the Hopelessly Unconscious Patient," *New England Journal of Medicine* 278, no. 26 (June 27, 1968), pp. 1425–1430. Figures on the number of kidney transplants performed annually in the United States are furnished by the Institute of Allergy and Infectious Diseases.

Page 29 Dr. Charles K. Hofling's suggestion on "death boards" is in his "Terminal Decisions," *Medical Opinion and Review* 2, no. 10 (October 1966), pp. 43–44. The Seattle committee on transplantation is noted in Henry K. Beecher, "Scarce Resources and Medical Advancement," in Paul Freund et al., eds., *Experimentation with Human Subjects* (New York: Braziller, 1969), p. 79. "In some cases, while the committee deliberated, the patient died . . ." The full discussion is in Jesse Dukeminier, Jr. and David Sanders, "Legal Problems of Scarce Medical Resources: The Artificial Kidney," *Archives of Internal Medicine* 127, no. 6 (June 1971), pp. 1133–1137.

Page 30 The survey of dialysis centers by Katz and Proctor is reported in Roberta G. and Richard L. Simmons, "Organ Transplantation: A Societal Problem," *Social Problems* 19, no. 1 (Summer 1971), p. 45. The Detroit man who wanted to buy a kidney was reported in "$3,000 Offered for a Kidney," *The New York Times* (September 12, 1974), p. 36.

Pages 30–31 Survival rates for heart transplant recipients are regularly compiled by Sandra L. Kamisar, National Heart and Lung Institute, Bethesda, Maryland.

Pages 31–32 The material about Dr. Norman Shumway and his patient, Richard Cope, is in "Heart Transplantation: Alive and Well at Stanford," *Medical World News* 15, no. 31 (August 13, 1974), pp. 25–44.

Page 32 The cost of heart transplants is discussed in Robert J. Glaser, "Innovations and Heroic Acts in Prolonging Life," in Brim et al., eds., *Dying Patient*, pp. 118–120. See also Irving Ladimer, *The Challenge of Transplantation* (New York: Public Affairs Pamphlet no. 451, 1970), p. 17.

Page 33 The observation that life can be difficult for transplant survivors is made in Francis D. Moore, *Transplant* (New York: Simon and Schuster, 1972), pp. 156–161. The suicide rate of dialysis patients is cited in F. Patrick McKegney and Paul Lange, "The Decision to No Longer Live on Dialysis," *American Journal of Psychiatry* 128, no. 3 (September 1971), pp. 267–274.

Pages 33–34 A nontechnical survey of recent advances of immunology can be found in *Immunology Research* (Washington, D.C.: Public Health Service, National Institutes of Health, D.H.E.W. publication no. [N.I.H.] 73-529. 1973).

Pages 34–35 Donor cards—not many carry them. This opinion was furnished by Irving Ladimer, Director, National Transplant Information Center, New York, in a personal communication to the author. Comments on the "medical right of eminent domain" by Blair Sadler were also made in a conversation with the author.

Pages 35–36 The anecdote about Dr. Belzer's trip to Holland was made in a tape recording by Samuel L. Kountz. Dr. Terasaki's description of a national transplant communications network is in "National Utilization of Cadaver Kidneys for Transplantation," *Journal of the American Medical Association* 228, no. 10 (June 3, 1974), pp. 1260–1265.

Page 36 Dr. Willard Gaylin's "Harvesting the Dead," *Harper's* 249, no. 1492 (September 1974), p. 26.

Pages 36–37 Dr. Reemtsma's experiments in cross-species grafting were described in an interview with the author. ". . . baboons . . . fight like hell to keep their kidneys" was a personal comment by Dr. Donald Kehoe to the author. The problem of transplanting a ram's heart is in Thomas Thompson, "The Year They Changed Hearts," *Life* 71, no. 12 (September 17, 1971), pp. 68–69. See also Moore, *Transplant*, p. 236.

Pages 37–39 Development of an artificial heart is described in *The Totally Implantable Artificial Heart. A Report of the Assessment Panel of the National Heart and Lung Institute.* (Washington, D.C.: DHEW publication no. [N.I.H.] 74–191, 1973.)

Page 39 ". . . modern medicine is depriving man of a natural vision of death . . ." Ivan Illich's remarks on this subject were summarized in his "The Political Uses of Natural Death." *Hastings Center Studies* 2, no. 1 (January 1974), pp. 3–30.

Chapter III, The Search for Longevity

Pages 40–41 For more on the life-span seminar, see Harvey Wheeler, ed., *Report on Project Life Span* (Santa Barbara, Calif.: Center for the Study of Democratic Institutions, 1972). A summary of the conference can be found in Richard A. Kalish, "Added Years: Social Issues and Consequences," in Erdman Palmore and Frances C. Jeffers, eds., *Prediction of Life Span* (Lexington, Mass.: Heath Books, 1971), pp. 273–280. A good summary of the trend in population growth among the elderly is found in Monroe Lerner, "When, Why and Where People Die," in Brim et al., eds., *Dying Patient*, pp. 5–29.

Pages 41–43 For an account of the old-age enclaves described here, see Alexander Leaf, "Getting Old," *Scientific American* 229, no. 3 (September 1973), pp. 44–52.

Pages 43–44 Alexis Carrell's experiments are described in Leonard Hayflick, "Human Cells and Aging," *Scientific American* 218, no. 3 (March 1968), pp. 32–37. Hayflick and Paul S. Moorhead's experiments are also described in the same article.

Page 45 For more on the physical symptoms of aging, see Nathan Shock, "The Physiology of Aging," *Scientific American* 206, no. 1 (January 1962), pp. 100–110. See also Nathan Shock, *Aging* (Freeport, N.Y.: Books for Libraries Press, 1968), pp. 241–260. Genetic "copying errors" are mentioned in Hayflick, "Human Cells and Aging." The notion that the body's natural immunity rejects newly formed cells in later life is discussed in Robert Kastenbaum, "Theories of Human Aging," *Journal of Social Issues* 21, no. 3 (October 1965), p. 16.

Page 46 Dr. Comfort's "space probe" analogy is in his *Process of Aging* (New York: Signet Science Library, 1964), p. 93. Dr. Sobel's stimulation theory is discussed in Kastenbaum, "Theories of Human Aging," pp. 16–17. Exercise as an anti-aging "pill" is in Rona and Lawrence Cherry, "Slowing the Clock of Age," *The New York Times Magazine* (May 12, 1974), p. 84.

Pages 47–48 Jung's thoughts on growing old are summarized in Carl Jung, "The Soul and Death," in Herman Feifel, ed., *The Meaning of Death* (New York: McGraw-Hill, 1974), pp. 3–15.

Pages 48–49 The study referred to here is in James E. Birren et al., eds., *Human Aging, a Biological and Behavioral Study,* Public Health Service publication 986 (Bethesda, Md.: National Institute of Mental Health, 1963).

Pages 49–51 Dr. Palmore's work at Duke University is described in Erdman Palmore, ed., *Normal Aging* (Durham, N.C.: Duke University Press, 1970). The material is summarized briefly in "Physical, Mental, Social Predictors of Longevity," *Geriatric Focus* 8, no. 16 (October 1, 1965), pp. 1, 3, 5.

Page 51 Material on the Institute of Gerontology in Kiev is in "Lifetime Health and Activity Levels Are Key to Long-term Survival, Soviet Study Reveals," *Geriatric Focus* 8, no. 16 (October 1, 1965), p. 2.

Pages 51–52 The Boston study by the Veterans Administration is in Charles L. Rose, "Social Correlates to Longevity," in Robert Kastenbaum, ed., *New Thoughts on Old Age* (New York: Springer, 1964), pp. 75–91.

Page 52 The study of cancer proneness among the stressed appears in Lawrence LeShan, "An Emotional Life-History Pattern Associated with Neoplastic Disease," *Annals of the New York Academy of Science* 125, art. 3, January 1966, p. 780.

Pages 53–54 David Phillips' study of anniversary deaths is in his "Birthdays and Death." Paper given at a meeting of the American Sociological Association, San Francisco, Calif. (September 1969), and discussed in Hendin, *Death as a Fact of Life,* pp. 109–110.

Pages 54–55 Reference to voodoo deaths is in Richard A. Kalish, "Non-Medical Interventions in Life and Death," *Social Science and Medicine* 4, no. 6 (December 1970), p. 657. On Curt P. Richter's experiments with rats, see his "On the Phenomenon of Sudden Death in Animals and Man," in Feifel, ed., *Meaning of Death,* pp. 302–313. This material is also summarized in Richard A. Kalish, "Life and Death: Dividing the Indivisible," *Social Science and Medicine* 2, no. 3 (September 1968), p. 255.

Page 55 The will to survive among Bergen-Belsen inmates is noted in John Hinton, *Dying* (Hammondsworth, England: Penguin Books, 1967), p. 93. Bruno Bettelheim, confined to a camp himself, made his comments on Seventh Day Adventists in an interview with the author.

Pages 56–58 On the psychological autopsy see Avery D. Weisman and Robert Kastenbaum, *The Psychological Autopsy* (New York: Community Mental Health Journal monograph no. 4, 1968). *See also* Schneidman, *Deaths of Man,* pp. 131–149.

Page 58 The geriatric cocktail hour is described in Robert Kastenbaum and Philip Slater, "Effect of Wine on the Interpersonal Behavior of Geriatric Patients," in Kastenbaum, ed., *New Thoughts on Old Age,* pp. 191–204. *See also* Robert Kastenbaum, "Wine and Fellowship," *Journal of Human Relations* 13, no. 2 (Second Quarter 1965), pp. 266–276.

Pages 58–59 Lieberman's study of deaths among Chicago's institutionalized elderly is summarized in *University of Chicago Reports. Division of Biological Sciences* (Fall–Winter 1968).

Page 59 For self-definitions of old age, see Robert Kastenbaum and Nancy Durkee, "Elderly People View Old Age," in Kastenbaum, ed., *New Thoughts on Old Age,* pp. 250–262.

Pages 59–60 Proposals for death investigation teams are made in Schneidman, *Deaths of Man*, pp. 128–130.

Page 61 The survey of retired steel workers is mentioned in D. L. Ellison, "Alienation and the Will to Live of Retired Steel Workers," in *Proceedings, 7th International Congress of Gerontology* (Vienna: Viennese Academy of Medicine, 1966). The reference to Rossle and normal death is in Arnold A. Hutschnecker, "Personality Factors in Dying Patients," in Feifel, ed., *Meaning of Death*, p. 246.

Chapter IV, "The Doctors Did Everything Possible"

Pages 62–63 The reference to the Miami institution is in "Nobody Noticed the Dead" [Port Chester, N.Y.] *Daily Item*, November 13, 1973, p. 1.

Page 63 The initial diagnosis of "dead on arrival" made by ambulance drivers is in Schneidman, *Deaths of Man*, p. 77.

Page 64 The quotation by Dr. Charles H. Goodrich is in *The Right to Die with Dignity* (New York: The Euthanasia Educational Council, 1971), p. 17. Louis Lasagna's comment on "frenzied doctoring" is in his "Physician Behavior Toward the Patient," in Brim et al., eds., *Dying Patient*, p. 78.

Pages 64–65 Elderly woman's heart restarted thirteen times is in John Dalmas, "A 'Mercy Killing' May Be No More than Letting a Patient Die" [Port Chester, N.Y.] *Daily Item* (May 30, 1972), p. 32. The letter from the *British Medical Journal* is in Lasagna, "Physician Behavior Toward the Patient," in Brim et al., eds., *Dying Patient*, p. 78. The comment by Valerie Lezoli is in Lawrence Mosher, "When There Is No Hope . . . ," *National Observer* (March 4, 1972), pp. 1, 16.

Page 66 Studies have shown ". . . almost instantaneous psychological regression . . ." is in Weisman and Kastenbaum, *Psychological Autopsy*, p. 47. The Schneidman reference is in his *Deaths of Man*, p. 83. David Sudnow's remarks are in his "Dying in a Public Hospital," in Brim et al., eds., *Dying Patient*, p. 199.

Page 67 The story of the man who wouldn't die quickly is in Barney G. Glaser and Anselm Straus, *Time for Dying* (Chicago: Aldine, 1968), pp. 11–12. Feifel's comment that "82 percent want to know" is in his "The Function of Attitudes Toward Death," in *Death and Dying: Attitudes of Patient and Doctor*, vol. 5, Symposium 11 (New York: Group for the Advancement of Psychiatry, Mental Health Materials Center, 1965), p. 635. The study referred to in the footnote is in Ann Cartwright, *Human Relations and Hospital Care* (London: Routledge and Kegan Paul, 1964).

Page 68 The notion of social death is discussed in Sudnow, "Dying in a Public Hospital," in Brim et al., eds., *Dying Patient*, pp. 191–196. His description of "winding down" a case is covered on pp. 193–208. The Kalish survey is mentioned in his "The Effects of Death on the Family," in Pearson, ed., *Death and Dying*, p. 84.

Pages 68–69 Michael Lesy, *Wisconsin Death Trip* (New York: Pantheon, 1973). How death is handled in North African villages is found in Bryant M. Wedge, discussion in *Death and Dying: Attitudes of Patient and Doctor*, p. 648.

Page 69   Kastenbaum's findings on the will to live is reported in Weisman and Kastenbaum, *Psychological Autopsy*, p. 24.

Pages 69–70   Data on malpractice suits is in "Malpractice Suits on Rise in Connecticut" [Port Chester, N.Y.] *Daily Item* (January 16, 1974), p. 4. "On the surgical ward, even a renowned scholar . . ." is in Weisman and Kastenbaum, *Psychological Autopsy*, p. 49, J. S. Bockoven's comments are in "Aspects of Geriatric Care and Treatment: Moral, Amoral and Immoral," in Kastenbaum, ed., *New Thoughts on Old Age*, pp. 220–221.

Page 72   Dr. Childs's observations on surgery are in his "Surgical Intervention," *Scientific American* 229, no. 3 (September 1973), pp. 90–98. Comments by Godfrey Hodgson are in his "The Politics of American Health Care," *The Atlantic* 232, no. 4 (October 1973), p. 56.

Page 73   "Gaining experience in techniques" is in Sudnow, "Dying in a Public Hospital," in Brim et al., eds., *Dying Patient*, p. 205. Telling the patient . . . This study, by Donald Okun, is mentioned in Hinton, *Dying*, p. 129. Dr. Feder's comments on "telling" at Mt. Sinai is in *Death and Dying: Attitudes of Patient and Doctor*, p. 616. The Noyes and Travis survey was reported in "The Care of the Terminally Ill Patient," *Archives of Internal Medicine* 132, no. 4 (October 1973), pp. 607–611.

Page 74   Patients' suspicions are discussed in Barney G. Glaser and Anselm Straus, *Awareness of Dying* (Chicago. Aldine, 1965), p. 22.

Pages 74–75   Feifel's study of death fears among doctors is cited in "Dealing with Death," *Medical World News* 12, no. 20 (May 21, 1971), pp. 30–36.

Page 75   Suicide rates for doctors is in K. D. Rose and Irving Rosow, "Physicians Who Kill Themselves," *Archives of General Psychiatry* 29, no. 6 (December 1973), pp. 800–805. See also "The Sick Physician," *Journal of the American Medical Association* 223, no. 6 (February 5, 1973), pp. 684–687. The Livingston and Zimet study is in Kastenbaum and Aisenberg, *Psychology of Death*, p. 216.

Page 76   The University of California gerontology study mentioned here is cited in "Dealing with Death," p. 53.

Page 77   The Swenson study referred to is in his "Attitudes Toward Death in an Aged Population," *Journal of Gerontology* 16, no. 1 (January 1961), pp. 49–52.

Page 76   The "Are You Afraid to Die?" survey is in Jeffers et al., "Attitudes of Older Persons Toward Death: A Preliminary Study" in the same journal, pp. 53–56. The University Hospitals survey is in Hinton, *Dying*, p. 130.

Page 77   Dr. Kübler-Ross's "Never tell the patient . . ." is from an interview with the author.

Page 78–79   The Kastenbaum survey of nurses' attitudes is in Kastenbaum and Aisenberg, *Psychology of Death*, pp. 221–222.

Page 79   The finding that some nurses would work harder to save a pet dog compared with a dying elderly patient is cited in Kalish, "The Effects of Death on the Family," in Pearson, ed., *Death and Dying*, p. 85. The comments by Jeanne Quint and Laurel A. Copp were made at a Foundation of Thanatology conference, New York, November 1–2, 1974.

Pages 79–80   Jennie O'Neill's description of dying in an Irish hospital was made in a conversation with the author.

Page 80   Dr. Hofling's reference to terminating the power flow is in his "Terminal Decisions," p. 42. The remarks by Karen Ward and Dorothy Cutler are from an interview with the author.

Page 82   The intensive care unit as "sacred space" is developed by Avery Weisman in Weisman and Kastenbaum, *Psychological Autopsy*, p. 47. The quotation by Michael Rohman is in Joan Valles, "Fears of the Dying Too Often Ignored" [Port Chester, N.Y.] *Daily Item* (February 27, 1973), p. 4.

Page 83   The reference to dying at home in England is in Hinton, *Dying*, pp. 68–69. The Sir William Osler study referred to is cited in Russell Noyes, Jr., "The Art of Dying," *Perspectives in Biology and Medicine* 14, no. 3 (Spring 1971), p. 442. The survey of British doctors is in Eric Wilkes, "Where to Die," *British Medical Journal* 1, no. 5844 (January 6, 1973), pp. 32–33. Dr. Hinton's comment on the suffering of the cancer patient is in his *Dying*, p. 69. His views on good nursing homes vs. hospitals are on p. 162. Freud's observations on avoiding those marked for death are in his "Thoughts for the Time on War and Death," *Standard Edition*, vol. 14 (London: Hogarth, 1957), p. 289.

Page 84   The quotation by Philip Slater is in his "Cross-Cultural Views," in Kastenbaum, ed., *New Thoughts on Old Age*, p. 235.

Page 86   The story of John and Bob is told in Harold Levine et al., "Partners in Dying," *American Journal of Psychiatry* 131, no. 3 (March 1974), pp. 308–310. Freud's belief in the impossibility of imagining one's own death is in his "Thoughts for the Times on War and Death," *Standard Edition*, p. 289.

Pages 87–88   The summary of the dying person's "states of awareness" is in Glaser and Straus, *Awareness of Dying*, pp. 29–115.

Page 87   The Greek patient dying of leukemia is described in Schneidman, *Deaths of Man*, p. 32.

Page 89   The material dealing with Robert E. Neale is in his *The Art of Dying* (New York: Harper & Row, 1973), p. 19. The position of the Catholic Church on "telling the patient" is in Vincent Collins, "Limits of Medical Responsibility in Prolonging Life," *Journal of the American Medical Association* 206, no. 2 (October 7, 1968), pp. 389–392.

Pages 89–90   Hinton's views on telling the patient are covered in Hinton, *Dying*, pp. 126–139.

Page 90   The use of psychotropic drugs to stimulate the elderly dying is described in Robert Kastenbaum, "The Mental Life of Dying Geriatric Patients," in *Proceedings, 7th International Congress of Gerontology*, vol. 6 (Vienna: Viennese Academy of Medicine, 1966), pp. 153–159.

Pages 91–92   The statements by Dr. Nahmias are quoted in Olive Evans, "When a Child Is Dying, the Family Must Face Life as Well as Death," *The New York Times* (September 15, 1973), p. 20. The reference to Madeline Petrillo and the Long Island couple are in this article.

Pages 92–93   The story of Barbara, Carol and Charles is in Gilbert Kliman et al., "Facilitation of Mourning During Childhood," a paper for a Foundation of Thanatology conrerence, New York, March 31–April 1, 1974.

Page 93   The reference to Dr. Fuhrman is in Hendin, *Death as a Fact of Life*, p. 151.

Pages 93–94   Gregory Rochlin's study of a child's conception of death is in his "How Younger Children View Death and Themselves," in Earl A. Grollman, ed., *Explaining Death to Children* (Boston: Beacon, 1967), pp. 51–85.

Page 94   The Omaha study referred to is in Matilda S. McIntyre et al., "The Concept of Death in Midwestern Children and Youth," *American Journal of Diseases of Children* 123, no. 6 (June 1972), pp. 527–532. The anecdote concerning Dr. Kübler-Ross is from an interview with the author.

Page 95   Rabbi Grollman's "dont's" for parents are in Grollman, ed., *Explaining Death to Children*, pp. 9–12.

Page 96   The reference to the City of Hope Medical Center is in Aubrey E. Evans, "If a Child Must Die . . . ," *New England Journal of Medicine* 278, no. 3 (January 18, 1968), pp. 138–142.

Pages 96–97   The experiment at the National Cancer Institute is reported in Joel Vernick and Myron Karon, "Who's Afraid of Death on the Leukemia Ward?" *American Journal of Diseases of Children* 109, no. 5 (May 1965), pp. 393–397.

Page 97   Dr. Patterson's views on preparing a child for a fatal outcome are expressed in Paul R. Patterson, ed., *Psychosocial Aspects of Cystic Fibrosis* (New York: Columbia University Press, 1973), pp. 3–12.

Pages 97–98   The quotation by Dr. Kliman is in "Facilitation of Mourning During Childhood."

Chapter V, *The Right to Die*

Page 100   For a discussion of the historical development of euthanasia, see Morris H. Saffron et al., *Attitudes Toward Euthanasia in Ancient Times and Today*. (New York: Euthanasia Educational Council, Inc., 1970). Information about the Euthanasia Council was supplied by the council.

Pages 101–102   The poll by the Association of Professors of Medicine is cited in Hendin, *Death as a Fact of Life*, p. 91. "Another poll of hospital doctors . . ." is also in Hendin, p. 91.

Pages 102–103   Infant "mercy deaths" at the Yale-New Haven Hospital are reported in Raymond S. Duff and A. G. M. Campbell, "Moral and Ethical Dilemmas in the Special-Care Nursery," *New England Journal of Medicine* 289, no. 17 (October 25, 1973), pp. 890–894. *See also* "Panel Told Defective Infants Are Allowed to Die," *The New York Times* (June 12, 1974), p. 18. Senator Kennedy's "Right to Survive" hearings are reported in "Doctors Divided over Euthanasia," *The New York Times* (August 8, 1972), p. 15.

Page 103   The Chicago hospital case of infant death is discussed in James M. Gustafson, "Mongolism, Parental Desires and the Right to Life," *Perspectives in Biology and Medicine* 16, no. 4 (Summer 1973), pp. 529–557.

Page 104 The estimate of six million mentally retarded is in Louis Lasagna, *Life, Death and the Doctor* (New York: Knopf, 1968), p. 189. Dr. Sackett's views have been widely publicized. A statement of his position is in his "Death with Dignity," in *Medical Opinion and Review* 5, no. 6 (June 1969), pp. 25–31.

Page 105 The study of premature babies in England is reported in Harry Nelson, "British Evaluate Care of the Newborn" [Port Chester, N.Y.] *Daily Item* (March 9, 1974), p. 8.

Page 108 The Martinez case has been discussed by a number of writers. See Ellen Graham "A Good Death," *Wall Street Journal* (January 31, 1972), pp. 1, 16. The Detroit kidney-machine decision is cited in Howard W. Brill, "Death with Dignity: A Recommendation for Statutory Change," *Florida Law Review* 22, no. 3 (Winter 1970), ref. no. 71.

Pages 108–109 The Jehovah's Witness case is in Jonas Robitscher, "The Right to Die," *Hastings Center Report* 2, no. 4 (September 1972), pp. 11–14.

Page 109 The Illinois Supreme Court decision is in Brill, "Death with Dignity," p. 5. The statement by the New York Academy of Medicine is in "Measures Employed to Prolong Life in Terminal Illness," *Bulletin of the New York Academy of Medicine* 49, no. 4 (April 1973), pp. 349–351.

Pages 109–110 The patient's "Bill of Rights" is reported in Lawrence K. Altman, "Hospital Patients' 'Bill of Rights' Backed," *The New York Times* (January 9, 1973), pp. 1, 30.

Page 110 The survey conducted by the American Nurses Association is discussed in Barbara Ellen Davis, "The Nurses Dilemma," *Dilemmas of Euthanasia* (New York: Euthanasia Educational Fund 1971), pp. 14–18. The quotation by Miss Davis is on p. 17.

Pages 110–111 The Harris poll cited here is in [Port Chester, N.Y.] *Daily Item* (April 23, 1973), p. 26.

Page 111 The allocution by Pope Pius XII is summarized in Frank Ayd, "The Hopeless Case," *Journal of the American Medical Association* 181, no. 13 (September 29, 1962), pp. 1099–1102. The Jewish view of this problem is expressed in Immanuel Jacobovits, "The Dying and Their Treatment in Jewish Law," *Hebrew Medical Journal* 2, no. 251 (1961).

Page 112 On legalizing euthanasia, see Hendin, *Death as a Fact of Life*, pp. 87–90. For a contemporary account of the Zygmaniak case, see Richard J. H. Johnson, " 'Mercy Killing' Defendant Tells of Shooting Brother," *The New York Times* (November 1, 1973), p. 47.

Page 113 A good summary of various mercy killing cases is found in Daniel C. Maguire, "Death, Legal and Illegal," *The Atlantic* 233, no. 2 (February 1974), pp. 72–85.

Page 114 Dr. Foy's comment on euthanasia is in "Doctors Divided over Euthanasia." Dr. Pincus's view is in " 'Death with Dignity' or Murder?" *The New York Times* (January 24, 1973), p. 40. The 45-year-old stroke victim is referred to in Hofling, "Terminal Decisions," p. 40. The man with irreversible brain damage is described in Lawrence Mosher, "When There Is No Hope, Why Prolong Life?" *National Observer* (March 4, 1972), pp. 1, 16.

Pages 114–115 The Robert Carter case is in Richard Restak, "A Matter of Life and Death" [Port Chester, N.Y.] *Daily Item* (December 15, 1972), p. 15.

Page 115 The account of the 87-year-old man is in Chauncey D. Leake et al., *The Changing Mores of Medical Research.* Annals of Internal Medicine 67, no. 3, part 2 (September 1967), pp. 43–50.

Page 116 The Lucy Morgan letter is in "On Drinking the Hemlock," *Hastings Center Report* 1, no. 3 (December 1971), pp. 4–5.

Page 117 Arthur Morgan's testimony is in "Doctors Divided over Euthanasia." The statement of the Council for Christian Social Action is in *Euthanasia—Good Death?* (Washington, D.C.: Council for Christian Social Action, 1972; mimeographed pamphlet). *See also* the Council's *Right to Die,* 1973. Reference to the Church Assembly Board for Christian Responsibility is in *Decisions about Life and Death* (London: Church Information Office, 1965), pp. 15–16. The Dorothy Jaeger quotation is in John Dalmas, "Medicine Can Keep Alive Some It Can't Otherwise Help" [Port Chester, N.Y.] *Daily Item* (June 1, 1972), p. 28. Information here concerning the Euthanasia Educational Council's membership is from an interview with Mrs. Elizabeth Halsey, the fund's director. HEW data on suicide rates among the elderly is cited in Dalmas, "Medicine Can Keep Alive Some It Can't Otherwise Help."

Pages 118–119 Attitudes of elderly people toward euthanasia is in Dalmas, "Medicine Can Keep Alive Some It Can't Otherwise Help."

Page 119 The statement by Chaplain Bane is in Joan Valles, "Euthanasia—Mercy or Murder?" [Port Chester, N.Y.] *Daily Item* (August 22, 1973), p. 19. Chaplain Duggan's view on euthanasia is quoted in the same newspaper in John Dalmas, "Nurses and Doctors May Be at Odds on 'Passive Euthanasia,' " (May 31, 1972), p. 48.

Page 120 Professor Means's proposal for a "committee of the person" is in his "Legal Dilemmas," in *Dilemmas of Euthanasia,* pp. 11–12.

Page 121 Dr. Zaretzki's comment on withholding treatment is in his "The Doctor's Dilemma," in *Dilemmas of Euthanasia,* pp. 5–8. Dr. Hinton's discussion of euthanasia is in his *Dying,* p. 147.

Pages 122–123 The statements by Dr. Kutscher are in Valles, "Euthanasia—Mercy or Murder?"

Page 123 Felix Deutsch's point about "dying for an idea" is in his "Euthanasia: A Clinical Study," *Psychoanalytic Quarterly* 5, no. 3 (July 1936), p. 349.

Chapter VI, The Experience of Dying

Page 124 The quotation attributed to Gen. Ethan Allen is cited in "Dealing with Death," p. 32. John Keats's deathbed statement is quoted in Noyes, Jr., "Art of Dying," p. 443. Sir William Osler's remark is in Cicely Saunders, "The Moment of Truth: Care of the Dying Patient," in Pearson, ed., *Death and Dying,* p. 52.

Pages 126–128 The interviews described at Billings Hospital occurred during a visit by the author. For the anecdote of the man who wanted a chaplain in the middle of the night, see Elisabeth Kübler-Ross, *On Death and Dying* (New York: Macmillan, 1969), p. 93.

Page 129 The remark by Dr. Nathan Scott was made in a conversation with the author.

Pages 130–131 The study by Dr. von Heim of the Swiss Alpine Club is in Russell Noyes, Jr., "The Experience of Dying from Falls," *Omega* 3, no. 1 (February 1972), pp. 45–52.

Page 132 The comments about "mystical death" are in Noyes, Jr., "Art of Dying," pp. 432–447. See also Russell Noyes, Jr., "Dying and Mystical Consciousness," *Journal of Thanatology* 1, no. 1 (January–February 1971), pp. 25–41.

Pages 132–133 Dr. Pattison's view of the final moments of life is in his "The Experience of Dying," *American Journal of Psychotherapy* 21, no. 1 (January 1967), pp. 32–43.

Page 133 Greenberger's study of hospitalized women is cited in David C. McClelland, "The Harlequin Complex," in Robert C. White, ed., *The Study of Lives* (New York: Atherton, 1963), pp. 107–119. Deutsch's remarks on guilt and death are in his "Euthanasia."

Pages 134–135 Abraham Maslow's theory of the peak experience appears in many of his writings. See his *Toward a Psychology of Being* (New York: Van Nostrand, 1968). A summary of his ideas on this subject is in Colin Wilson, *New Pathways in Psychology* (New York: Taplinger, 1972), pp. 192–195.

Pages 136–139 A description of the experimental work with LSD at the Maryland Psychiatric Research Center is in Jerry Avorn, "Beyond Dying," *Harper's* 246, no. 1747 (March 1973), pp. 56–64.

Page 139 Similar work at the Menninger hospital is reported in *Human Behavior* 2, no. 5 (May 1973), p. 38.

Page 140 Dr. Spiegel's experiments with hypnosis and the dying are described in "Hypnosis as a Therapeutic Methodology," a paper presented at a Foundation of Thanatology conference, New York, November 17–18, 1972.

Pages 140–141 Jacques Choron's typology of death fears is mentioned in Kastenbaum and Aisenberg, *Psychology of Death*, p. 44.

Pages 141–142 The desensitization procedure described here is in Elaine E. Finnberg, "Behavior Modification Techniques—a New Tool for Nurses Who Care for the Terminally Ill," a paper written for a Foundation of Thanatology conference, New York, November 1–2, 1974.

Pages 142–145 Dr. Kübler-Ross's stages of dying are explained in her *On Death and Dying*, pp. 34–121. A more concise account can be found in her "Psychotherapy for the Dying Patient," *Current Psychiatric Theories*, vol. 10 (New York: Grune and Stratton, 1970), pp. 110–117. Her views on the language of dying were given in a lecture at a conference on Death and Dying at Riverside Church, New York, May 10, 1975.

Pages 145–146 The story of Peter and Priska is in Susan Bach, *Spontaneous Paintings of Severely Ill Children*. Acta Psychosomatica, monograph no. 8 (Basle: Geigy, 1969).

Chapter VII, "We Who Now Mourn and Weep"

Page 147 The description of the Cocoanut Grove fire is in Frank S. Adams, "Boston Fire Death Toll 440 . . . ," *The New York Times* (November 30, 1942), pp. 1, 12; and "Fire Death Toll at 487 . . . ," in the same newspaper (December 1, 1942), pp. 1, 16.

Pages 147–148   Erich Lindemann's typology of grief reactions is in his "Symptomatology and Management of Acute Grief," *American Journal of Psychiatry* 101, no. 2 (September 1944), pp. 141–148. For a discussion of the Buffalo Creek floods, see Jane S. Church, "The Buffalo Creek Disaster," *Omega* 5, no. 1 (Spring 1974), pp. 61–63.

Page 149   Youngsters who regress during mourning is in I. Gregory, "Anterospective Data Following Childhood Loss of Parent," *Archives of General Psychiatry* 13 (1965), pp. 99–120. Death rates among the bereaved cited by the National Office of Vital Statistics is in B. M. McMahon and T. Pugh, "Suicide in the Widowed," *American Journal of Epidemiology* 8, no. 1 (January 1965), pp. 23–31.

Pages 149–150   The study referred to here is in W. D. Rees and Sylvia Lutkins, "Mortality of Bereavement," *British Medical Journal*, no. 5570 (October 7, 1967), pp. 13–16.

Page 150   The study by Michael Young and his colleagues is in C. Murray Parkes, *Bereavement* (London: Tavistock 1972), p. 16; see also pp. 197–198. The survey by Jane Bunch is in her "Recent Bereavement in Relation to Suicide," *Journal of Psychosomatic Research* 16 (1972), pp. 361–366.

Page 151   The reference to bereavement and ulcerative colitis is in Lindemann, "Symptomatology and Management of Acute Grief," p. 147. The study by LeShan is in "An Emotional Life-History Pattern Associated with Neoplastic Disease," p. 780. The Schmale study is noted in Parkes, *Bereavement*, pp. 18, 198. See also A. H. Schmale, Jr. and A. P. Iker, "The Affect of Hopelessness and the Development of Cancer," *Psychosomatic Medicine* 28, no. 5 (September–October 1966), pp. 714–721. Green's work on separation stress is discussed in Bernard Schoenberg and A. C. Carr, "Object Loss and Somatic Symptom Formation," in Bernard Schoenberg et al., eds., *Loss and Grief: Psychological Management in Medical Practice* (New York: Columbia University Press, 1970), p. 39.

Pages 151–152   The reference to Gyarfas and Pieper is in Jerome Frederick, "The Physiology of Grief," *Dodge Chemical Magazine*, n.d. Parkes's comments on osteoarthritis is in his *Bereavement*, p. 20.

Page 152   The quotation by Dr. Jerome Frederick is in his "Physiology of Grief," p. 8. The frequency of psychiatric care for recently bereaved widows is noted in Parkes, *Bereavement*, p. 122. The estimate of divorced parents of leukemic children by Madeline Petrillo is in Evans "When a Child is Dying, the Family Must Face Life as Well as Death."

Page 153   "Grieving for a Lost Home" is in L. Duhl, ed., *The Urban Condition* (New York: Basic Books, 1963), pp. 151–171.

Page 154   "Mourning and Melancholia" is in John Richman, ed., *A General Selection from the Works of Sigmund Freud* (New York: Liveright, 1957), pp. 124–144; see pp. 126–127 for the "work of mourning." Melanie Klein, "Mourning and its Relation to Manic-Depressive States" is in Hendrik M. Ruitenbeek, ed., *The Interpretation of Death* (New York: Aronson, 1969), pp. 237–267.

Page 155   W. D. Rees, "The Bereaved and Their Hallucinations." Paper for a Foundation of Thanatology conference, New York, November 2–3, 1973.

Pages 155–156   The "searching behavior" described here by Parkes is in his *Bereavement*, pp. 41, 47, 114–115.

Page 156 The Lindemann reference to postponement of grief is in his "Symptomatology and Management of Acute Grief."

Page 157 The quotation by Robert Blauner is in his "Death and the Social Structure," *Psychiatry* 29, no. 4 (November 1966), p. 389.

Pages 157–158 The Boston study mentioned here is in C. Murray Parkes and R. J. Brown, "Health after Bereavement: A Controlled Study of Young Boston Widows," *Psychosomatic Medicine* 34, no. 5 (September–October 1972), pp. 449–461.

Pages 158–160 Edgar Jackson's suggestions for "working out" one's grief are in his "On the Wise Management of Grief." Paper for a Foundation of Thanatology conference, New York, November 2–3, 1973. See also Edgar Jackson, *You and Your Grief* (New York: Channel, 1961). Views of Jerome Steiner are in his "Group Function Within the Mourning Process," *Archives of the Foundation of Thanatology* 2, no. 2 (Summer 1970), p. 81. The anecdote concerning Dr. Klagsbrun is from personal remarks made at a Foundation of Thanatology conference, New York, November 2–3, 1973.

Page 161 The study of widowers in Cleveland is in John W. Bedell, "Predicting Reaction to Mate Loss." Paper for a Foundation of Thanatology conference, New York, March 29–30, 1974. Rabbi Moss's explanation of Jewish bereavement customs is in his paper for the same conference, "The Grief Work Cycle in Judaism." Ethnic approaches to bereavement rituals is in Richard A. Kalish and David K. Reynolds, "Death and Bereavement in a Cross-Ethnic Context." Mimeographed report, 1973.

Page 162 Bedside problems of the family are discussed in Glen W. Davidson, "The Waiting Vulture Syndrome." Paper for a Foundation of Thanatology conference, New York, March 29–30, 1974. Wives who do their grief work too well is in Lindemann, "Symptomatology and Management of Acute Grief," p. 148.

Pages 162–163 The reference to Dr. Kübler-Ross here is from a seminar lecture on silent grief, University of Chicago, September 1971.

Page 163 The description of St. Christopher's Hospice is based on a personal visit by the author. See also Saunders, "The Moment of Truth," in Pearson, ed., *Death and Dying*, for an account of Dr. Saunders's approach to terminal care.

Pages 163–164 The project at Tufts New England Medical Center was described by Melvin Krant at a Foundation of Thanatology conference, New York, March 29–30, 1974.

Page 164 Dr. Kübler-Ross's anecdote about "screaming rooms" is from an unpublished talk at a workshop on Pastoral Care and Counseling, Christ Hospital, Cincinnati, Ohio, January 1971.

Pages 164–165 An account of the Montefiore project mentioned here is in Irwin Gerber, "Bereavement and the Acceptance of Professional Service," *Community Mental Health Journal* 5, no. 6 (December 1969), pp. 487–495. Additional grief techniques at Montefiore are described in Delia Battin, "Telephone Intervention in the Therapy of Bereaved Families" and in Arthur M. Arkin, "A Technical Device for the Psychotherapy of Pathological Bereavement." Papers for a Foundation of Thanatology conference, New York, March 29–30, 1974.

Page 165 Mutual help among bereaved widows is described in Phyllis R. Silverman, "The Widow-to-Widow Program," *Archives of the Founda-*

tion of *Thanatology* 2, no. 3 (Fall 1970), pp. 133–135. An extension of this idea is found in Jean Hall, "Self-Help Club for the Bereaved" [Port Chester, N.Y.] *Daily Item* (April 26, 1974), p. 4.

Page 166   The Minnesota survey referred to by Robert Fulton was noted in personal remarks at a Foundation of Thanatology conference, New York, March 29–30, 1974.

Chapter VIII, Bury the Dead?

Pages 167–168   The account of the Scottsdale, Arizona, motorcycle funeral was given by Vanderlyne Pine in remarks at a Foundation of Thanatology conference, New York, March 29–30, 1974.

Page 168   Painting the casket at a Maine funeral home is based on information by Raoul Pinette at a Foundation of Thanatology conference, New York, March 29–30, 1974. The Louisville incident is in William G. Hardy, Jr., "The Adaptive Funeral." Paper for a Foundation of Thanatology conference, New York, March 29–30, 1974.

Page 169   The description of Charles Lindbergh's burial is in "Lone Eagle Rests" [Port Chester, N.Y.] *Daily Item* (August 27, 1974), p. 12. For an account of Lindbergh's last days as seen by his doctor, see Milton M. Howell, "The Lone Eagle's Last Flight," *Journal of the American Medical Association* 292, no. 7 (May 19, 1975). Burial at sea in a $60,000 yacht is in "His Ship Will Go Down with the Quiet Captain" [Port Chester, N.Y.] *Daily Item* (December 22, 1971), p. 34.

Page 170   For a description of ancient funeral rites, see "Death Customs and Rites," *Colliers Encyclopedia* vol. 7, 1971, pp. 757–765. The estimate of more than $2 billion spent annually on funerals in the United States is based on the U. S. Commerce Department figures of $1.6 billion spent in 1960. To this, Jessica Mitford adds another $400 million for extras such as flowers, transportation, grave markers, etc. See Jessica Mitford, *The American Way of Death* (New York: Simon and Schuster, 1963).

Page 171   The incident of the dead child propped in a playpen is in Vincent Fish, "Acute Grief and the Funeral." Paper for a Foundation of Thanatology conference March 29–30, 1974. The Philadelphia study on the use of funeral homes is noted in Blauner, "Death and the Social Structure," p. 284. The reference to extravagant floral offerings is in Frank R. Galante, "The Italian Family and Some of Its Ways of Dealing with Acute Grief Through the Funeral." Paper for a Foundation of Thanatology conference, March 29–30, 1974.

Pages 171–172   The quotation by W. Lloyd Warner is in his *The Living and the Dead* (New Haven: Yale University Press, 1959), p. 378. Remarks by Robert Fulton on the status of undertakers and clergy are quoted in Kastenbaum and Aisenberg, *Psychology of Death*, p. 229.

Page 172   The New York symposium of funeral directors was reported in "Jewish Funeral Directors Sponsor Symposium on Grief," *The Casket and Sunnyside* 104, no. 9 (September 1974), p. 16.

Page 173   The Robert Fulton study referred to is in Kastenbaum and Aisenberg, *Psychology of Death*, p. 213. Phyllis Silverman's comment on funeral directors is in her "Another Look at the Role of the Funeral Director." Paper for a Foundation of Thanatology conference, March 29–30, 1974. The funeral director's contribution to "grief work" is in a paper for the same conference: Otto S. Margolis, "The Funeral Home as a Community Resource in Bereavement."

Pages 173–174   The study of death attitudes among mortuary students is outlined in Kastenbaum and Aisenberg, *Psychology of Death*, p. 212. The education of funeral directors is discussed in Charles H. Nichols, "Education and Mortuary Science." Paper for a Foundation of Thanatology conference, New York, March 29–30, 1974.

Pages 174–175   The Denver bereavement counselor who makes house calls is in Ann Bishop, "After Funeral Counselor Fills a Need," *Denver Post* (October 25, 1974), p. 8BB.

Page 175   Data on the funeral lobby and the laws it supports are given in Mitford, *American Way of Death*, pp. 31, 33, 34–35, 67.

Pages 175–176   Robert Fulton's statement on "viewing" as a separation rite was made in personal remarks at a Foundation of Thanatology conference, New York, March 29–30, 1974.

Page 176   The quotation by Jeanette R. Folta and Edith S. Deck is in their "Grief, the Funeral and the Friend." Paper for a Foundation of Thanatology conference, New York, March 29–30, 1974. Criticism of the open casket by Maurice Lamm and Naftali Eskreis is in their "Viewing the Remains: A New American Custom," *Journal of Religion and Health* 5, no. 2 (April 1966), pp. 137–143.

Pages 176–177   Past customs of embalming and viewing are discussed in Ruth Mulvey Harmer, "Funerals That Make Sense," *Modern Maturity* 17, no. 3 (June–July 1974), pp. 59–61. Catholic and Jewish prohibitions on viewing the body are mentioned in Lamm and Eskreis, "Viewing the Remains."

Pages 177–178   The survey of funeral users referred to here is in Gene S. Hutchens, "The Funeral Ritual." Paper for a Foundation of Thanatology conference, New York, March 29–30, 1974.

Page 178   The Amish avoidance of cosmetology on the dead was mentioned by Robert Fulton in remarks at a Foundation of Thanatology conference, New York, March 29–30, 1974.

Pages 178–179   Fulton's study of the effects of cremation on survivors was presented at a Foundation of Thanatology conference, New York, March 29–30, 1974.

Page 180   Figures on cremation are given in Hendin, *Death as a Fact of Life*, p. 227.

Pages 180–181   The quotation by Ruth Mulvey Harmer is in her "Funerals That Make Sense," p. 59.

Page 181   Variations in funeral costs in Washington, D. C. are detailed in Walter Rugaber, "F.T.C. Finds Wide Cost Spread in District of Columbia Funerals," *The New York Times* (March 1, 1974), p. 26. Reference to the Senate Antitrust Committee's investigation of Ohio funeral costs is in Sidney Margolius, "Funeral Costs and Death Benefits" (New York: Public Affairs Pamphlet no. 409, 1967), p. 11.

Page 182   The public health features of embalming, and the Ives quotation, are in William A. Neilsen and C. Gaylord Watkins, *Proposals for Legislative Reforms* (Burnsville, N. C.: Celo Press, 1973), p. 48. The legal requirements for cremation and the "documented example" were discussed in Sylvia Porter, "Cost of Cremation Low Minus Extras" [Port Chester, N.Y.] *Daily Item* (March 13, 1974), p. 46.

Page 183 Information concerning District 65's prepaid burial plan is in Margolius, "Funeral Costs and Death Benefits," p. 6. The Galante reference is in his "Italian Funeral."

Page 184 The quotation by Michael Harrington is in Glenn M. Vernon, *Sociology of Death* (New York: Ronald Press, 1970), pp. 37–38. The quotation from *Ebony* is in Morris J. McDonald, "The Management of Grief: A Study of Black Funeral Practices." *Omega* 4, no. 2 (Summer 1973), p. 141. The merits of "expensive" funerals are discussed in Vanderlyn Pine and Derek L. Phillips, "The Cost of Dying," *Social Problems* 17, no. 3 (Winter 1970), p. 416.

Page 185 P. Riordan, "Let's Get Rid of Funeral Homes," is in *U. S. Catholic* 36, no. 1 (January 1971), p. 14.

Page 186 Descriptions of Unitarian and Quaker funeral ceremonies are in Ernest Morgan, ed., *A Manual of Death Education and Simple Burial* (Burnsville, N. C.: Celo Press, 1973).

Pages 186–187 Humanist funeral practice is outlined in Corliss Lamont, *A Humanist Funeral Service* (Burnsville, N. C.: Celo Press, 1962).

Page 187 Data on memorial societies is in Morgan, ed., *Manual of Death Education and Simple Burial*. Information concerning funeral registries was obtained from the American Internation Funeral Registry, Ltd., Washington, D. C.

Page 189 C. W. Ettinger, *The Prospect of Immortality* (New York, Doubleday, 1964).

Pages 190–191 References to James H. Bedford and Andrew D. Mihak are in Clifton D. Bryant and William E. Snizek, "The Cryonics Movement and Frozen Immortality," *Society* 11, no. 1 (November–December 1973), pp. 56–61.

Page 192 The dilemma caused by too-narrow grave plots is reported in Howard Barnard, "How You Can Meet the Problems of an Oversized Casket," *The Casket and Sunnyside* 104, no. 8 (August 1974), p. 6.

Page 193 Evelyn Waugh, *The Loved One* (Boston: Little, Brown, 1948). The situation at Greenwood Cemetery in Brooklyn is discussed in Anita R. Nager, "Exploring Necropolis," unpublished manuscript written for the Environmental Psychology Program, City University of New York, 1973.

Page 194 Reference to the American Society of Planning Officials is in Hendin, *Death as a Fact of Life*, p. 210. In the same book are the observations of Roger Starr, p. 218; and the description of the moving of a San Francisco cemetery, p. 226.

Pages 194–195 Roman Catholic cemeteries in Chicago opened to outsiders is reported in Andrew Malcolm, "Cemeteries Open Gates to Recreational Pursuits," *The New York Times* (December 10, 1972) p. 76. Similar activity in Pittsburgh and the Bronx is described in Ernest Dickinson, "Cemeteries Go Public," *The New York Times* (January 27, 1974), VIII 10. The development of Boston's cemeteries as nature conservancies is discussed in Jack Ward Thomas and Ronald A. Dixon, "Cemetery Ecology," *Natural History* 82, no. 3 (March 1973), pp. 60–67. Anti-recreational attitudes in San Francisco's Woodlawn Cemetery are quoted in Dickinson, "Cemeteries Go Public."

Pages 195–196 Atlanta's "Death Hilton" is described in Paul Hemphill, "Room at the Top," *The New York Times* (December 9, 1973), pp. VI 125, 127–128.

Page 196 Rio de Janeiro's high-rise mausoleum is reported in "High Rise Cemetery Is Planned for Rio," *The New York Times* (February 13, 1972), p. 10. The reference to Vance Packard concerns his *A Nation of Strangers* (New York: McKay, 1972).

Chapter IX, The Question of Survival

Pages 197–199 Bishop Pike's television seance is described in Allen Spraggett, *Arthur Ford: The Man Who Talked with the Dead* (New York: New American Library, 1974), pp. 244, 255–262. In the same book are Pike's Cambridge experiences, p. 252; Ford's alcoholism, pp. 24, 64; his heart condition, pp. 277–278; his well-known sitters, p. 2; his control, "Fletcher," pp. 10–11, 22; Pike's death, p. 279.

Pages 199–200 Diane Kennedy's *The Other Side* (New York: Doubleday, 1968). Her sittings with Mrs. Twigg are described in Diane Pike, "Bishop Pike's Messages Beyond the Grave," *Ladies Home Journal* 87, no. 11 (November 1970), pp. 97, 148–151. The Bishop Block reference is in Spraggett, *Arthur Ford*, pp. 245–247. In the same book Ford's notebook and file of obituaries are discussed on pp. 248–251.

Page 201 The reference to posthumous dictation is in Arthur Ford, as told to Jerome Ellison, *The Life Beyond Death* (New York: Putnam, 1971), dust jacket, back cover. Ruth Montgomery's *The World Beyond* (New York: Coward, McCann & Geoghegan, 1971), was reviewed in "A Report from Heaven," *Newsweek* 79, no. 1 (January 3, 1972), p. 52.

Page 202 Material on MacKenzie King is in Martin Ebon, *They Knew the Unknown* (New York: New American Library, 1972), pp. 193–199. Remarks attributed to Lord Dowding are in Signe Toksvig, "A Pocket Guide to Heaven," *Light* 93, no. 3493 (Summer 1973), p. 77. Edison's plans for a machine to talk with the dead are discussed in Ebon, *They Knew the Unknown*, pp. 125–133. The survey of physicists noted here is in Robert Thouless, *An Introduction to the Psychology of Religion* (Cambridge: Cambridge University Press, 1971), p. 4. The Aldous Huxley reference is in Allen Angoff, *Eileen Garrett and The World Beyond the Senses* (New York: Morrow, 1974), p. 25.

Page 203 Parkes's observations on hallucinations of the dead are in his *Bereavement*, pp. 49–50. Cornell's ghostly experiment is described in Karil Osis, *Deathbed Observations by Physicians and Nurses* (New York: Parapsychology Foundation, 1961), pp. 82–83.

Page 204 The Spiritualist creed is given in Spraggett, *Arthur Ford*, pp. 122–123. Data on the National Spiritualist Association is in *Psychic Observer and Chimes* 35, no. 4 (July–September 1974), pp. 392–396. The George Chapman reference is in Bernard Hutton, *Healing Hands* (New York: McKay, 1967). The description of Camp Chesterfield is in Bill Thomas, "Spirited Sites," *Travel* 136, no. 4 (October 1971), pp. 41–43.

Page 205   Ford's disillusionment with spiritualist camps is in Spraggett, *Arthur Ford*, p. 185; the O'Neill-Puharich investigations, pp. 183–184. For Spraggett's own experiences with mediums, see pp. 194–195. The commercial availability of mediumistic paraphernalia is in Nils O. Jacobson, *Life Without Death?* (New York: Delacourt, 1974), pp. 135–136.

Pages 205–206   The story of the Fox sisters is summarized in Alan Gauld, *The Founders of Psychical Research* (London: Routledge and Kegan Paul, 1968), pp. 3–13. The spiritualist craze in America is described in the same book on pp. 13–17.

Page 206   Reference to Harriet Beecher Stowe and spiritualism is in Ebon, *They Knew the Unknown*, pp. 68–69. Mary Todd Lincoln's experiences are described in the same book on pp. 47–53.

Pages 206–209   The rise of the Spiritualist Church in the United States is in Spraggett, *Arthur Ford*, pp. 117–118. Its growth in England is discussed in Gauld, *Founders of Psychical Research*, pp. 66–87; see esp. pp. 66–70; U. S. mediums in England are noted on pp. 70–73.

Pages 209–214   The work of Myers and the Society for Psychical Research is the subject of Gauld, *Founders of Psychical Research*. See esp. p. 140 for prominent members; pp. 153–199 for Gurney and phantasms; pp. 200–210 for physical phenomena; pp. 221–245 for Eusapia Palladino; p. 322 for Myers's letter to Symons. Mrs. Piper's visit to England is told on pp. 255–258; Hodgson's sittings with her in the United States, pp. 258–266. The incident of Myers's survival message is in Robert H. Thouless, *From Anecdote to Experiment in Psychical Research* (London: Routledge and Kegan Paul, 1972), p. 157.

Page 214   Information on the British College of Psychic Research is in Angoff, *Eileen Garrett*, pp. 90–93.

Page 215   William James's relations with Mrs. Piper are noted in Ebon, *They Knew the Unknown*, p. 96. The quotation concerning G. Stanley Hall and Mrs. Piper is in Allen Spraggett, *The Case for Immortality* (New York: New American Library, 1974), p. 35.

Pages 215–216   The "Margery" story is covered in Raymond van Over et al., eds., *William MacDougal: Explorer of the Mind* (New York: Helix, 1967), pp. 180–194. The "jelly fish" quote is in the same book on p. 190. Carrington's experiment is discussed in Thouless, *From Anecdote to Experiment*, pp. 159–160.

Page 217   The Duke University experiments in ESP are described in J. G. Pratt, *Parapsychology, an Insider's View* (New York: Dutton, 1966), pp. 47–67. See also J. B. Rhine, *Extra-Sensory Perception* (Boston: Humphries, 1964).

Pages 218–220   Scientific investigations of Eileen Garrett are covered in Angoff, *Eileen Garrett*, p. 39 (for Arthur Conan Doyle); p. 166 (for the Johns Hopkins experiment); pp. 167–169 (for the Carrington test); pp. 183–186 (for the London exam); pp. 171–173 (for the Duke tests); pp. 177–181 (for the Roosevelt Hospital investigation).

Page 221   The "want ad" for reincarnates appeared in *The New York Times* (December 29, 1974), p. 39.

Pages 221–223   The deathbed material described here is the substance of Osis, *Death Observations*.

Page 223   Julius Weinberger's voiceprints of the dead are from a personal communication to the author. The work of the Stanford Research Institute is summarized in Francine du Plessix Gray, "Parapsychology and Beyond," *The New York Times Magazine* (August 11, 1974), pp. 13, 77 et seq.

Pages 224–225 Konstantin Raudive's experiments are described in Jacobson, *Life Without Death?* pp. 167–173. See also Konstantin Raudive, *Breakthrough* (New York: Taplinger, 1971). Andrija Puharich's experience with Raudive is told in his *Uri* (New York: Bantam Books, 1975), p. 38.

Page 225 E. Lester Smith's "explanation" of the voice recordings is in his "The Raudive Voices—Objective or Subjective?" *Journal of the American Society for Psychical Research* 68, no. 1 (January 1974), pp. 91–100.

Pages 226–228 William Roll's studies are described in his "Survival Research: Problems and Possibilities," *Theta*, no. 39–40 (Winter–Spring 1974), pp. 1–13. The protection against unwelcome ghosts offered by The Spiritualist Association of Great Britain is noted in "Twenty-Four Hour Ghost Service," *Parapsychology Review* 5, no. 4 (July–August 1974), p. 6. William Roll's hypothesis on poltergeist activity is in his "Poltergeist Phenomena and Interpersonal Relations," *Journal of the American Society for Psychical Research* 64, no. 1 (January 1970), pp. 66–99. See esp p. 98. See also Robert L. Morris, "What Is Our Research Telling Us about the Survival Question?" *Theta*, no. 36–37 (Summer–Fall 1972), p. 1. Experiments in out-of-body phenomena are in Robert L. Morris, "PRF Research on Out-of-Body Experiences," *Theta*, no. 41 (Summer 1974), pp. 1–3.

Page 228 The George Zorab quotation is in his "The Survival Hypothesis: An Unsupported Speculation," *Theta*, no. 11 (Fall 1965), pp. 3–4. Gardiner Murphy's comments on the ambiguity of survival evidence is in his *Challenge of Psychical Research* (New York: Harper, 1961), p. 272.

Chapter X, A Natural Death

Page 230 Melvin Krant's comment about the minister and the EEG machine was made at a Foundation of Thanatology conference, March 29–30, 1974.

Page 232 Simone de Beauvoir, *A Very Easy Death* (New York: Warner Paperback Library, 1973). For "consenting to operation" see pp. 107–108. "No such thing as a natural death" is discussed on p. 123.

Page 233 The notion of avoiding responsibility for care of the elderly, and the encouragement of quick dying, is developed in Stanley Keleman, *Living Your Dying* (New York: Random House, 1974), pp. 80–81.

Pages 233–237 Most of the description of St. Christopher's Hospice is based on a personal visit by the author. Additional information was obtained from the hospice's Annual Report, 1972–1973. For the use of alcohol by patients, see Saunders, "The Moment of Truth," in Pearson, ed., *Death and Dying*, p. 66. Attitude toward drugs is described in "Drugs Most Commonly Used at St. Christopher's" (mimeographed bulletin). The reference to euthanasia is in Cicely Saunders, *The Care of the Dying Patient and His Family* (London: Contact Supplement no. 38, n.d.), p. 7. For a general philosophy underlying St. Christopher's, see "A Therapeutic Community: St. Christopher's Hospice," *Psychosocial Aspects* (n.d.), pp. 275–289.

Page 238 The remark, "Patients who are dying are supposed to get on with it . . ." was made by Laurel Cope at a Foundation of Thanatology conference, New York, November 1–2, 1974. The account of the young male nurse and his dying patient is from the same conference.

Pages 238–239 Project Equinox was described in a paper by Melvin Krant at a Foundation of Thanatology conference, New York, November 1–2, 1974. *See also* Melvin Krant, "The Dying Patient: Medicine's Responsibility," *Journal of Thanatology* 1, no. 1 (January–February 1971), p. 19. Project Omega is reported in Avery Weisman, *The Realization of Death* (New York: Aronson, 1974), pp. 1–62.

Page 239 Avery Weisman's comment, "Illness is far too important to be left to physicians," is in his *Realization of Death*, p. 19.

Page 240 The chaplain's role at Billings Hospital was noted by John Nelson in a personal interview with the author. Freud's statement that an individual cannot consciously imagine his own death is in his "Thoughts for the Times," p. 289. The reference to the young chaplain and the "clock without hands" comes from an address at a conference on Death and Dying at Riverside Church, New York, May 10, 1974.

Pages 240–241 Dr. Samuel Klagsbrun's interview with Pat Hudson also took place at the conference on Death and Dying.

Pages 241–242 Lawrence LeShan's approach to the dying patient is from an address at the conference on Death and Dying.

Page 242 The reference to Ned Cassem is in Bill Kovach "New Hospital Practices Reflect a Need to Help Dying Patients Prepare for Death," *The New York Times* (January 21, 1973), p. 44. The quotation by Edwin Schneidman is in his *Deaths of Man*, pp. 30–31.

Pages 242–243 The Kurt Eisler quotation is cited in Janice Norton, "Treatment of the Dying Patient," in Ruitenbeek, ed., *Interpretation of Death*, p. 32.

Page 243 "Playing the piccolo" is in Margaret McClure, "The Nurse's Role Is to Play the Piccolo." Paper for a Foundation of Thanatology conference, New York, November 1–2, 1974. The anecdote about the New Orleans tap dancer is in James S. Eaton, Jr., "The Nurse, the Doctor and the Dying Patient." Paper for a Foundation of Thanatology conference, November 1–2, 1974.

Pages 243–244 Morton Lieberman's conclusion that angry patients do better is reported in "Do Not Go Gentle," *Time* 102, no. 2 (November 12, 1973), p. 88. The notion of "permission to die" is proposed in Robert E. Kavanaugh, "Helping Patients Who Are Facing Death," *Nursing* 4, no. 5 (May 1974), p. 41.

Index

Catalog

If you are interested in a list of fine Paperback
books, covering a wide range of subjects
and interests, send your name and address,
requesting your free catalog, to:

McGraw-Hill Paperbacks
1221 Avenue of Americas
New York, N.Y. 10020